Race for the Millennium

Previous books by the same author:

Go Sell: An Investigation into the Failure of the British Churches to Meet the Challenge of Investment in Apartheid (Epworth, 1975)

Agenda for Prophets: Towards a Political Theology for Britain; edited with Rex Ambler (Bowerdean, 1980)

Faith in Struggle: The Protestant Churches in Nicaragua and their Response to the Revolution (Epworth, 1987)

Mobilising the European churches, in Pauline Webb (ed.) *A Long Struggle: the Involvement of the World Council of Churches in South Africa* (WCC, 1994)

Race for the Millennium

A Challenge to Church and Society

David Haslam

Foreword by the Bishop of Liverpool

Sponsored by

The Churches' Commission for Racial Justice

Published by Church House Publishing
Church House, Great Smith Street, London SW1P 3NZ

ISBN 0 7151 6582 8

Published 1996 on behalf of the Churches' Commission for Racial Justice by Church House Publishing, Church House, Great Smith Street, London SW1P 3NZ

Back cover photograph: local churches gather for 'Unite Against Racism' rally

Printed in England by The Cromwell Press Ltd, Melksham, Wiltshire

Contents

For Sarah,
and for all those struggling for racial justice,
especially the Ogunwobi and Lawrence families,
who inspire us all; and for Jean Sindab,
fighter for racial justice, who died in January 1996.

Foreword

David Haslam has lived and worked near the heart of the events which have raised questions of racial justice with the Churches over a good many years. It is valuable that the history should be recounted, uncomfortable as some of it is.

In taking stock of where we stand today this book offers a new generation some of the raw data which tell us how we have arrived at the present situation.

Some members of the majority community, of Comfortable Britain, still like to say, 'If only you didn't make so much noise, and if only we stopped any further immigration, good community relations with equal opportunities would gradually emerge for everyone'. The history of black and Asian people's presence in this country gives the lie to such thoughts. The long established black community in Liverpool is an example of this. For generations they fitted in, kept quiet, told their children they must be at least twice as good as white people if they were to obtain jobs. That has contributed to more of a ghetto than in any other city. The violence of the 1981 Toxteth riots shocked many in this city, for whom racial disadvantage had been hidden.

A struggle is needed if there is to be racial justice and equal opportunity. For the white majority a choice needs to be made of whether to engage in that struggle. Changes will not just evolve. Perhaps the beginning of joining the struggle is to acknowledge that race is an issue in which we are all involved already.

This is a book that demands that we do something about it. For those who might feel that the 'problem' is someone else's, that 'we might have no race relations problems here in the White Highlands', David Haslam makes it clear that the problem is our problem. In setting the agenda for the turn of the century he offers clear and practical advice for those who desire to make justice happen.

Most people who read this book will never have had the experience of being on the receiving end of racial injustice. This has nothing to do with the niceties of being politically correct. Too many members of British-born minorities experience hostility and intimidation against a backdrop of low expectations and stereotyping.

Members of the Archbishop of Canterbury's Commission which produced *Faith in the City* in 1985 met black sixth formers; they were asked why teachers encouraged black pupils to pursue sport or music and discouraged them from academic subjects. A headteacher of a Primary school in South London with a high population of black children told me in the early 1970s as we went into the Assembly, 'They won't achieve much, but we try to make them happy.' It should have surprised no one that, faced with such low expectations, many children developed a poor self-picture of what they could achieve.

The racism, which we in Comfortable Britain find too often in our own minds, may be quite kindly disposed. But if it echoes the low expectations which those teachers held, it will shut the gates of opportunity on minority groups as effectively as crude hostility does. Employers who live in the 'White Highlands' may be the vital gatekeepers who open or shut the gates of opportunity. If we are to understand what exclusion feels like, we need to listen to voices which will sometimes sound bitter. A small group of Church leaders met with some young black men in south-east London. Trevor, who chaired the group, said, 'It seems to us, looking up from where we are, that there are networks where decisions are made. We should like to be part of those networks.'

The title that David Haslam has written under indicates that racial justice should be of crucial importance to Christians. We believe in God who has created us in His image. The Psalmist asks what of humanity? Why should God be interested in so frail a creature? In reply we are told that our humanity is deeply valued by God, who has made us – all of us – only a 'little less than God' (Psalm 8). So important are we that God made the choice to be born into our human experience, not as the powerful and protected, but as the weak, the vulnerable, the downtrodden, the oppressed. God has a particular concern for those who are denied a proper share of life's opportunities: those God-given opportunities that are too often protected by the powerful for the powerful.

This book will be disturbing to many people. If it were not, it would be ineffective. For it is when we are disturbed that we are open to new insights and fresh discoveries about ourselves and the world we live in.

The first stage of our transformation must be to learn respect. That is not merely toleration. To respect means to look again at someone else's experience. It is about listening carefully to what they have to tell us, even, perhaps especially, when what they have to say is hard for us to accept. Through their experiences we may discover things about ourselves we would not usually choose to face up to. We need also to learn a new framework of interpretation of our own experiences. Our own lives may equip us to understand our culture from a favoured and powerful position. The problems that disable others may not seem to affect us. We must acknowledge the disadvantages experienced by black people when they enter the market place of education, housing, health care and employment. This is not arguing for people to be given jobs for which they do not have the necessary skills. It is saying that we need affirmative action in monitoring appointments and in training which will help disadvantaged people to reach the starting gate.

We must do something positive to make justice. It is not enough to make sure that the playing field is level. Some of the players will have found that life has excluded them from entering the stadium before the game starts. When jobs are advertised through the internal mail, when opportunities for promotion or training are made through the grapevine, those already excluded are left even further outside. Time and time again the present frameworks and structures favour those already in privileged positions. For those communities who cannot obtain access to these networks the sense of exclusion and injustice is constant. The choice and ability to change the flow of opportunities lies within the established structures. A positive decision must be made to place advertisements in job centres specially used by excluded communities, or else in publications and journals which are read by black people. It must also mean including black representatives on recruitment and interviewing panels. Top management must make it clear that they will monitor the processes. These are practical decisions which are realistically attainable by most organisations.

Christians believe that all human beings are made in the image of God. That should lead us to believe that groups who are different from us will enrich the society which develops. Yet many Christians feed their minds daily with newspapers which appeal to nationalistic fears of those who are different.

Racial justice challenges each one of us to look at our own hearts. It also challenges us to look at the structures of our Church, our company and our nation. For the Gospel is about changing both human hearts and social structures.

David Sheppard

Liverpool

November 1995

Introduction

Race is going to be an even more important factor as we move towards the millennium than it has been in the past. It is extraordinary how deeply prejudice and discrimination remain rooted in British and indeed in European society. As this introduction is being written in the last weeks of 1995, the UK Government has announced a further heavy programme of measures and legislation in the fields of asylum and immigration. While some tightening of procedures may be necessary, race always seems to be the driving force in such initiatives. If it is not actually on the surface it lurks just below. Incidences of racial violence often increase when immigration and asylum changes are being propelled through Parliament.

This book endeavours to provide a context for Christians and others who seek to understand what is going on in the field of racial justice in our society, and how they should respond. It begins with a number of short case studies about what is happening to black people in Britain today. These highlight the areas of immigration, the criminal justice system, police activity, racial harassment, equal opportunity – or lack of it – and asylum policy. The first chapter explores the minefield of terminology, the 'labels' of race, something which it is important to get right not just for 'political correctness' but because words are still the primary way of communicating knowledge, ignorance, paternalism, prejudice and even hate. The chapter also looks at causes – why racism, where does it come from? The argument is that its roots are both economic and psychological; Christians might also describe it simply as an aspect of original sin. Finally comes the section on the fruits of racism, a description of the problem areas, most of which have already been highlighted by the case studies above.

Chapter 2 looks at the arrival of black people in Britain. It is only an overview, but it points the reader to a number of other sources where they will find greater detail. We are introduced to Olaudah Equiano and Ottobah Cugoano, doughty campaigners against the slave trade here in Britain. We hear of Mary Seacole and Harold Moody from the Caribbean, of Dadabhai Naoroji (first Asian MP) and Cornelia Sorabji. A remarkable number of those who strove for racial justice in these times were influenced by Christianity. This is also true in the stories of Frederick Douglass, Nat Turner and Sojourner Truth found in chapter 5 on the United States. The second chapter finishes with the arrival of West Indians in increasing numbers into post-war Britain. Chapter 3 tells the story of a north London church where the author was the minister between 1974 and 1987, and which welcomed many arrivals from the Caribbean and Africa in the 1960s and 1970s, some of whom subsequently became its leaders. It illustrates how much black and minority Christians have to give to the British Churches, if they will only let it happen.

The Churches in Britain did respond to the increasing arrivals of Commonwealth citizens, albeit rather little and rather late. Information about what was done by particular denominations appears in other literature, but chapter 4 of this book provides the first full account of the ecumenical response. It is about the Community and Race Relations Unit (CRRU) of the British Council of Churches, and indicates that the tradition of work in the areas of immigration, the criminal justice system and in helping the Churches understand what it means to have a permanent black presence in the UK began early. Throughout its 20-year life CRRU struggled for racial justice, then handed over the baton to the Churches' Commission for Racial Justice in 1992. It was my privilege to serve as Moderator for the last two years of CRRU, and for the first period of CCRJ's life. The Commission is integrated into the national structures of the Churches. As its Secretary, the author has had the opportunity to work with the 25 new Commissioners to try to focus the minds of the wider Church on issues like economic empowerment, racial violence and ameliorating the worst effects of immigration and asylum policy.

The fifth chapter brings in some perspectives from outside Britain, the US in particular. The following chapter also expands our horizons, with insights drawn from theologians in Latin America, Asia and South Africa. James Cone is the key black theologian on whom the book draws. Those who do not know his writings will hopefully be encouraged to read them after the snippets included here. Martin Luther King, Malcolm X and Alice Walker are among other African Americans to make their appearance in this chapter.

The theological undergirding of the book's approach is to be found in chapter 6. A concept of struggle is enunciated and proposed as an essential 'way of life' for any involved in living out the Christian faith in the racially unjust Europe and North America of the late twentieth century. The first short section suggests that racism as we understand it has existed more or less since biblical times, especially in the attitude of many Jews to the Samaritans. Insights are provided from liberation theologians to illuminate the situation in Britain today. The Christian response is the struggle for justice, also involving reconciliation, but justice first!

Finally, chapter 7 sets out an agenda for the rest of the century. We read of the four circles – individual, church/community, national and international – in which the struggle needs to be waged. We are reminded of the importance of inter-faith relations and the media, as well as providing a plan of action in the key areas referred to above, including criminal justice and immigration. The economic dimension, both at British and international level, is focused on. The racism underlying the global economic system is pointed to, and it is argued that the market and its damaging effects have to be vigorously and continuously exposed and challenged. Finally, a programme for the millennium – a Year of Jubilee – is outlined, picking up and developing the theme of Leviticus 25, upon which many Christian bodies are now beginning to focus in the context of the year 2000.

The Churches' Commission for Racial Justice (CCRJ) is happy to be associated with this book and we are grateful to colleagues in Church House for assisting in its publication. We hope it will be widely read in the Churches of Britain and beyond, to help white Christians in particular to engage in the struggle for racial justice. If they do, by the time the millennium comes this world might be looking a much better, happier and more just community.

Finally, a word about David Haslam. He is well placed to write this book for at least two reasons. His commitment to the pursuit of racial justice is an exceptionally strong one and he continues to be an example to us all in this. Secondly, his writing stems from his work over many years at the Churches' Commission for Racial Justice, and its predecessor, the Community and Race Relations Unit (CRRU) as Executive Secretary. I am grateful to him both for his work and for taking up the task of writing this book.

Revd Theo Samuel

CCRJ Moderator

Acknowledgements

This book emerges with thanks to friends and colleagues in many places, who have read the text, offered ideas and criticism, or stimulated and inspired in lectures, conversations and writings over a number of years. Associated with the Churches' Commission for Racial Justice – Theo Samuel, Pat White, Alastair Haggart, Richard Crowson, Trudy Thorose, Richard Zipfel, James Ozigi, and Leela Ramdeen; associated with CRRU – Gwen Cashmore and Janet Henderson; in the United States – Tyrone Pitts, Joe Agne, James Cone, Cornel West, Tim Smith, Jim Wallis; associated with the World Council of Churches' Programme to Combat Racism – N. Barney Pityana, Jean Sindab, Deborah Robinson and Bob Scott; in the economics field – Rob van Drimmelen, Peter Madden and Ulrich Duchrow; on inter-faith relations – Christopher Lamb and Philip Lewis; and of course the people of Harlesden Methodist Church.

Others who have helped with reading parts of the manuscript and editing include Judith Longman, Sarah Cooke, Sara Haslam, Cyril Rodd, Derek Winter, Colin Davey and Jan Winter. Thanks also to colleagues at Church House for facilitating the publication and in particular the Board for Social Responsibility, to David Sheppard and Theo Samuel for Foreword and Introduction, to Ben Birnberg, to Nadir Dinshaw for practical encouragement, and to Pauline Fielding, Mary Donovan and Judith Smith, who all insisted the title needed rescuing from the rather pedestrian original, *Church and Race.* Needless to say, I take full responsibility for errors and misrepresentations.

Grateful acknowledgement is made to the following for permission to reprint copyright material:

Assorted excerpts and six lines from negro spiritual from Cone, James, *Black Theology and Black Power*, copyright © 1969 by The Seabury Press Inc., reprinted by permission of HarperCollins Publishers, Inc; Cone, J. and Wilmore, G. (1993) *Black Theology: a Documentary History, Vol. I (1966-79), Vol. II (1980-1992)* (Orbis); Cugoano, Ottobah (1988) *Thoughts and Sentiments on the Evil of Slavery*, introduction by Paul Edwards (Dawson); Edwards, Paul (1989) *The Life of Olaudah Equiano* (Longman); Fryer, Peter (1984) *Staying Power: the History of Black People in Britain* (Pluto); Grant, Paul and Patel, Raj (1991) *A Time to Speak* (ECRJ/CRRU); Kipling, Rudyard (1940) *Rudyard Kipling's Verse: Definitive Edition* (Hodder and Stoughton) from 'The White Man's burden' is reprinted by permission of A.P. Watt Ltd on behalf of the National Trust for Places of Historic Interest or Natural Beauty; Marable, Manning (1984) *Race, Reform and Rebellion*

(Macmillan); Mason, David, Ainger, Geoffrey and Denny, Norwyn (1967) *News from Notting Hill* (Epworth); Miguez Bonino, Jose (1975) *Revolutionary Theology Comes of Age* (SPCK); *New English Bible* © Oxford University Press and Cambridge University Press (1961, 1970); Pope-Hennessy, James (1988) *The Sins of the Fathers* (Geoffrey Chapman, a Cassell imprint); Vaughan, David (1950) *Negro Victory* (Independent Press, now The United Reformed Church in the UK).

List of abbreviations

AGIN	Action Group on Immigration and Nationality
ARC	Asylum Rights Campaign
BCC	British Council of Churches
BCE	Before the Christian Era
BNP	British National Party
CAAC	Council of African and Afro-Caribbean Churches
CARJ	Catholic Association for Racial Justice
CCBI	Council of Churches for Britain and Ireland
CCME	Churches Commission for Migrants in Europe
CCMWE	Churches Committee for Migrant Workers in Europe
CCRJ	Churches' Commission for Racial Justice
CE	Christian Era
CEC	Conference of European Churches
CORE	Congress on Racial Equality
CPS	Crown Prosecution Service
CRE	Commission for Racial Equality
CRPOF	Committee for Relations with People of Other Faiths
CRRU	Community and Race Relations Unit
EATWOT	Ecumenical Association of Third World Theologians
ECCR	Ecumenical Committee for Corporate Responsibility
ECWGAR	European Churches Working Group on Asylum and Refugees
EDCS	Ecumenical Development Co-operative Society
EEBC	Economic Empowerment of the Black Community
EIRIS	Ethical Investment, Research and Information Service
ELR	Exceptional Leave to Remain
FITC	*Faith in the City* (The Report of the Archbishop of Canterbury's Commission on Urban Priority Areas)
EU	European Union

GATT	General Agreement on Tariffs and Trade
ICCR	Interfaith Centre for Corporate Responsibility
IMF	International Monetary Fund
IPPR	Institute for Public Policy Research
JCWI	Joint Council for the Welfare of Immigrants
MELRAW	Methodist Leadership Racism Awareness Workshops
MSC	Manpower Services Commission
NCBC	National Committee of Black Christians
OAAU	Organisation for Afro-American Unity
OECD	Organisation for Economic Co-operation and Development
PACE	Police and Criminal Evidence Bill
PCR	Programme to Combat Racism (World Council of Churches)
PSI	Policy Studies Institute
RAG	Racial Attacks Group
REEP	Race Equality in Employment Project
SAPs	Structural Adjustment Programmes
SCLC	Southern Christian Leadership Conference
SITC	*Staying in the City* (Bishops' Advisory Group for Urban Priority Areas)
SNCC	Student Nonviolent Co-ordinating Committee
TCNs	Third Country Nationals
TECs	Training and Enterprise Councils
TNCs	Transnational Corporations
TRJ	Towards Racial Justice
UN	United Nations
UNIA	Universal Negro Improvement Association
UPAs	Urban Priority Areas
URC	United Reformed Church
WCC	World Council of Churches
WDM	World Development Movement
WTO	World Trade Organisation

1

Setting the scene

Joan and Michael Danso made the mistake of falling in love when they were both visiting Europe from their respective home countries of Jamaica and Ghana in 1981. They spent most of the next ten years fighting to stay together, along with their three children, rather than be deported to a country totally foreign to at least one of them and which their children had never seen. Their battle included imprisonment in Holloway for Joan, while her baby was forcibly fostered, two periods of several months in sanctuary in an east London church, and an incredible degree of uncertainty for their children.

They are at least alive. In the eighteen months to the beginning of 1995 there were at least three deaths related to unannounced arrivals of immigration and police officers. In July 1993 Joy Gardner, who resisted forcible deportation and was handcuffed, restrained in a body-belt and gagged and had thirteen feet of parcel tape wound round her face, died as a result of her treatment (see Amnesty International report on the death of Joy Gardner, August 1995). In May 1994 Kwanile Siziba, a 27-year-old Zimbabwean woman, fell from the twelfth floor of a north London block of flats trying to evade officials looking for someone else. Then in October Joseph Nnalue, father of three, similarly died falling from a third-floor window ledge. He was hiding outside his bedroom window while immigration and police officers were questioning his wife and small children inside the flat. In June 1995 three police officers charged with the manslaughter of Joy Gardner were acquitted.

Rupert Taylor is a west London lay preacher. In 1984 he was arrested by Notting Hill police and accused of possessing drugs. He went through a nightmare, deeply troubled about losing his good name. Eventually he was able to prove his innocence. In 1991 a jury awarded him £100,000 damages, including £70,000 to express their disapproval of police behaviour. The sum was reduced on appeal, but Rupert Taylor believed at least he had cleared his name. This was thrown into doubt, however, when nearly eight years later the charges against the officer who arrested him were thrown out. Mr Taylor said he had lost faith in British justice.

1

Mrs Dhanjal was flying back to England from India via Damascus in February 1993, after a short visit to her extended family. She had lived in Shropshire for several years with her husband and two daughters. Changing planes at Munich Mrs Dhanjal was informed by an airline official, nervous of the £2,000 Government fine levied on carriers who bring ineligible passengers into Britain, that her documentation was incorrect. Not fluent in English, Mrs Dhanjal tried to explain that it was, but she was turned over to the German immigration authorities who strip-searched her, kept her without food or her medicine (she later fainted) and deported her next day. She spent five uncomfortable days in the transit area of Damascus airport before it could be officially confirmed that she had a perfect right to enter Britain, and she was flown back to her family.

Tony Paris is a young Cardiff-born black man, intelligent and articulate, but not a high achiever in educational terms. He existed through the 1980s in Cardiff's Butetown, supplementing his dole in whatever way he could. In February 1988 a young white prostitute, Lynette White, was brutally murdered in Butetown. Although police were originally looking for a white male, after several months without success they suddenly arrested eight local men, of whom seven were black. Five were charged with the murder of Lynette White, and three – including Tony Paris – convicted. They became known as the Cardiff Three. In Wormwood Scrubs prison, during the battle to prove their innocence, Paris described himself as a hostage, just like Terry Waite. In November 1992, after a four-year campaign, and an extraordinarily short appeal, the convictions of the Cardiff Three were pronounced unsafe and unsatisfactory, and they were set free. No charges have been brought against the police for wrongful arrest or malicious prosecution.

Paul (not his real name) is a Zairean. He came to Britain to escape persecution in Zaire but his asylum claim was rejected, and in January 1994 he was sent back. While in transit in Kenya his escort abandoned him. He says the Zairean ambassador in Nairobi warned the security forces at Kinshasa that he had been expelled from the UK, and he was arrested on arrival in Zaire, detained and tortured. In July 1994, with a friend's help, he managed to escape and reach Britain again, with his wife and child, but was taken into detention. The Medical Foundation for the Care of Victims of Torture examined him carefully, and found evidence which corroborated his story. He was suffering from severe headaches and depression. His wife was desperate to get him released, but his solicitor felt he was being detained by the authorities to try to conceal the growing evidence that it was not safe to return refugees to Zaire.

The stories could go on. I could relate the story of Marion Gaima, whose church supported her eight-year struggle for safety in Britain away from the dangers of

Sierra Leone; that of Geoffrey McKay, a black soldier, going AWOL from his British Army unit in Germany after endless racist abuse; that of the Rochdale Bengali couple who – long resident in Britain – finally proved their young son in Bangladesh was 'related as claimed' despite immigration refusals, only to be told he could not join them as he was now over 18; that of 'Asif Mohammed', born and bred in Birmingham, who changed his name to get a job as – despite his excellent qualifications – employers never called for interview someone named Mohammed; and that of Afghani refugee Ruhullah Aramesh, clubbed to death in south London in 1992 by young white men wielding iron bars, for asking them to stop taunting female relatives.

Such attacks, in many parts of Britain, are a deeply worrying phenomenon. Black Methodist teenager Stephen Lawrence was stabbed to death in south-east London in April 1993. In Neath, South Wales, in November 1994, 60-year-old Mohan Singh Kullar – roused in the middle of the night from the flat above his 'Costcutter' shop by stones at his window – was brutally attacked in the alley outside and died later from his injuries. In Scotland an African refugee was killed in 1992, and attacks continue. Even in Northern Ireland, where ethnic minorities are few and the Chinese community of about seven thousand is the largest, harassment and bullying takes place; this was reported by Shek Yung Lee, Chairman of the Chinese Chamber of Commerce, in a speech to Belfast businessmen in early 1994.

It does not take much to work out what all those who are the subjects, and in most cases the victims, of the above stories have in common. All are black or from minority communities, and all have experienced in a deep, personal and – for some – a vicious way the racism that remains entrenched in British society. Experiences like the above happen to some white people, including Irish activists and Bosnian Muslim refugees, but such behaviour is not institutionalised to the same degree as for black people, due to their particular visibility.

Racism should be as much a concern to Christians who live in Basildon as in Brixton, in Harrogate as much as in Handsworth, to the faithful who inhabit Macclesfield as well as those in Moss Side. Racism is a corporate more than an individual sin, and therefore involves us all, whether we like it or not.

This book is intended to help white Christians firstly to understand the depth and intensity of racism still present in our society, and secondly to respond to it. I believe we need to, and vigorously so, for unless Western Christians are engaged at some level – in both corporate and personal dimensions – in the struggle against racism, there can be no salvation, no wholeness, in society or in community life. It is interesting that quite often, when pressed why they continue to challenge racism rather than trying to ignore it, black Christians – like Olaudah

Equiano whom we shall meet later – will thoughtfully comment that they are doing it primarily for the sake of whites, who need to understand the depth of the trouble they are in. Whatever black Christians say, however, I as a white Christian am often worried, sometimes angered and frequently ashamed at the complacency, insensitivity and arrogance of white people. There is a great need for repentance, in terms of an active 'turning around', for white Christians to become committed anti-racists. Hopefully black Christians may also find something of merit in the book, especially in the historical chapters, as often what their parents have done is little-known in the wider Church.

In this introductory chapter I look at some of the terminology used in the race debate, explore where the notion of white superiority comes from and recount how the 'fruits' of white racism actually affect people. I focus on three of the sectors where racism is most influential – immigration policy, the criminal justice system and economic inequality. In a later chapter I detail 'church response' in these sectors.

In the second chapter I look back at the coming of black people to Britain and how long they have been here. I visit briefly the dreadful period of slavery, which still has vital lessons to teach us. It is a historical experience which every white person needs to absorb if they really wish to engage with both the individual and corporate dimensions of racism in our world. In learning about black resistance to slavery in England (and later in the US), we find a strong Christian faith often associated with it. Such belief, in the teeth of all experience to the contrary, should inspire faint white hearts as we contemplate challenging the powerful forces of racism still rampant in our world.

The next two chapters illustrate in different ways the response of the Churches. The first is the story of one local church where I was the minister between 1974 and 1987. The second recounts the ecumenical response to the first large-scale immigration of the 1950s and 1960s and describes Church activities from then until the 1990s in relation to the three key sectors referred to above.

Moving from the local to the international, many of those involved with the racial justice debate find much knowledge, wisdom and prophetic insight coming from the USA. Although one of the world's more racist societies, it has a myriad of people – black and white – working together and separately against racism. The history of the battle against slavery in the USA is littered with those who opposed it because of their Christian faith, many of them – as in Britain – black. The giant of more recent generations is of course Martin Luther King. His philosophy, activity and developing analysis are important to understand, and to transfer where appropriate to this side of the Atlantic. Malcolm X is increasingly recognised as another key figure in recent US history, and I have been much informed by the account of their contrasting but complementary views by James Cone, the black American Methodist theologian. The 'Perspectives from the USA' chapter contains an introduction to Black Theology, an essential perspective for white Christians to hear and absorb in order to participate in the search for racial justice.

I hope this chapter and others will act as an appetiser for reading what black Christians – whether from North America or elsewhere – themselves have to say. I believe however that it is crucial for white people to seek to offer some response.

Then comes some theological reflection. In the Bible, in human history and in contemporary experience examples can be found which demonstrate faith, repentance and conversion into new life. The motif of the reflection is the struggle for justice, and it draws on the writings of 'Liberation Theologians' from the countries of the 'South', whose work has still not been really absorbed into the practice of the faith in the 'North'. The question of whether reconciliation is possible is vital as, moving into the next millennium, we seek to understand the practice of the Christian faith.

Finally there is a chapter devoted to a future programme for racial justice work. It attempts to lay out some of the principal areas and goals for such work in the approach to the twenty-first century. It would be pleasant to assume that by the time we have reached that point racism would have been eradicated and Christians could turn hearts and minds to other challenges. However, so deep are the roots of racism that it may be with us a good deal longer. So the agenda is broad, but the Spirit is equal to it, as long as we allow Her to enlighten, encourage and empower us in the ongoing struggle.

Labels

The terminology in this area can be difficult, but it is essential to try to understand it, and to change descriptions from time to time, as understanding and consciousness grow. What is the relationship between 'race' and 'racism'? Should we call people 'black', or 'Asian' or 'African'? Does accepting the label 'racist' automatically condemn a white person? The word 'race' itself can cause much debate. Many would say there is only one race, the human race, and there should be no compromise with those who want to speak of different races. Black sociologist Paul Gilroy in *There Ain't No Black in the Union Jack* (1987) always uses 'race' with inverted commas, to signify that there is a question around it. He describes 'race' as a 'political category', rather than a biological one. He notes that it may be used in different ways, for different reasons, at different times, and believes it is 'important to compare and evaluate the different historical situations in which 'race' has become politically pertinent' (p. 38).

Gilroy goes on to describe how race in the British context has gradually changed in the post-war period, to acquire more of a cultural content. He believes it no longer has to do simply with colour, or the shape of hair or lips, but to do with nation, with 'Britishness', and says it may be possible for a person originating from Asia or Africa to become 'British', provided they leave their culture and historical identity behind. Not everyone would agree with him, but Gilroy feels race has begun to seem almost synonymous with nationality, and in the case of Britain, national identity seems 'bounded on all sides by the sea'. Psychotherapist Paul Gordon comments on how often human groups identify themselves over against an 'Other'. Lord Tebbitt has suggested that belonging to Britain is bound up with which side a person living in England supports in a cricket Test Match, Jamaica, England or Pakistan.

Conversely, when the chips are down, and the Argentines invade some sheep-farming rocky islands seven thousand miles away from Britain, 'race' or 'nationality' become elastic, and the Falkland Islanders, most of whom have never been to Britain, become more British than some born and bred here, but whose parents came from Africa or India. I shall return to the concept of 'British'.

Whatever 'race' means it clearly makes a difference. Racial characteristics create a disparity in the way people are treated. Racial discrimination, racial harassment, racial violence, all exist, and can be measured as social and economic phenomena. They are the physical expressions of 'racism'. Few British people now want to remove all black people, but they create other types of pressure, towards conformity. As Gilroy says 'Racism is not a unitary event.... It must be understood as a process' (p. 27). Also, racism defines the subject, rather than the object the focus must be on the perpetrators rather than the victims.

Having brought in the term 'racism' without actually defining it, it may be appropriate to restate two fairly widely-known insights. Firstly, racism operates at both the personal and the institutional or structural level, though the two are fairly closely related and the second is probably the more important. Secondly, the simplest, most common and still most effective definition of racism is 'prejudice plus power'. White American Joseph Barndt in *Dismantling Racism* (1991) says that if that is our definition it is essential that we have a way of measuring its intensity. He argues that there are three ways in which the power of racism can be measured – by judging a person's intentions, by determining the amount of legislation controlling racism or, most crucially of all, by measuring results. To measure such things is complex, but when it can be demonstrated that despite twenty years of our 1976 Race Relations Act, black unemployment remains at least twice as high as white, then clearly something is wrong.

Barndt believes racism is an individual issue but it is even more a condition, a structural reality, an ideology which carries the possibility of not just being prejudiced but of exercising that prejudice against its object, and with force if desired. An employer, an immigration official, a teacher or a police or prison officer may be prejudiced; each also has the power to put that prejudice into operation. It then becomes racism.

A complaint of the critics of the 'race relations industry' is that 'racism' is too strong a word, and they continue to try to either rubbish its usage or amend its meaning. Barndt accepts that the term can offend people and cause them to react defensively, and this should not be forgotten. However, he says that the most important reason for retaining not just 'racism' but 'white racism' is the tendency of white people otherwise to evade the issue. He cites the history of the USA in demonstrating 'the lengths to which we will go in order to avoid dealing with racism and its results'. He recalls the 1968 Kerner Report into the mid-1960s riots in the USA, which identified one of the main causes as white racism, and which was rapidly shelved. Barndt says that 'There is no soft, polite way to discuss the problem. The name which it must be given is white racism. To call it anything else avoids the real issue' (p. 40).

Other definitions of racism include the slightly more sophisticated one by Ann Sipko in *Naming Barriers/Claiming Possibilities*, in which racism has to do with the power to make and enforce decisions (who decides), access to resources (who has access to what), standards that are set for appropriate behaviour (assumption that white standards are best) and a misplacement of the problem (who really is the cause). A definition by the US Catholic Bishops in 1980 states;

> Racism is a sin: a sin that divides the human family, blots out the image of God among specific members of that family and violates the fundamental dignity of those called to be children of the same Father. . . [it] makes racial characteristics the determining factor for the exercise of human rights.

The 'new racism' here in Britain is more circumspect than the old. It links 'discourses of patriotism, nationalism, xenophobia, Englishness, Britishness, militarism and gender difference into a complex system which gives 'race' its contemporary meaning', notes Gilroy (p. 43). The 1980s/1990s brand of racism operates across the board, including some people and excluding others with varying subtlety. The word 'immigrant' is one example. Originally it was simply a descriptive term for Canadians, Poles, Africans, Swedes, Indians and anyone else who came into Britain with the object of settling here. During the 1960s and 1970s, however, it gradually came to be used of black people by all parties, and was seen as a synonym for aliens, invaders and – by some – social security scroungers. A similar change has happened in the early 1990s to the meaning of 'refugees', a change – courtesy of the popular press and certain Government Ministers – from people fleeing persecution or conflict to poor-country residents wanting to grab more for themselves as economic migrants, who are 'bogus' and 'fake'.

Another manifestation of the new racism focuses on Muslims as outsiders, especially the 'fundamentalists', the new 'enemy within'. Provided Muslims pray at home, or in a (preferably small) mosque, do their (low-paid) job, send their children to a C of E school – but no Islamic worship – all will be well. But should they wish to take Eid as a holiday, pray together at work or have the Imam take school assemblies, militancy is scented, and the tabloids are soon on the trail. None of these practices is British and all would fail Lord Tebbitt's 'cricket test'.

A variation on the Tebbitt test appeared in *Wisden's Cricket Monthly* in July 1995. An article by Robert Henderson suggested that black players, at cricket and by implication in other sports, did not try as hard as 'real' English players. Some sportswriters supported the idea that teams with a strong 'national identity' do better. Others pointed to the great performances of many 'polyglot' teams, at national and international level. One, Mike Marqusee, remarked that the problem is that racists are often 'perfectly polite, well-educated people', who may even be 'accomplished journalists'. The changing shapes of racism need constantly to be monitored. *Wisden* later issued an apology.

Peter Fryer, on whose seminal work *Staying Power* (1984) we shall draw also in the next chapter, defines the difference between race prejudice and racism thus:

> Racism to racial prejudice is as dogma is to superstition. Race prejudice is relatively scrappy and self-contradictory. It is transmitted largely by word of mouth. Racism is relatively systematic and internally consistent. In time it acquires a pseudo-scientific veneer that glosses over its irrationalities and enables it to claim intellectual respectability. And it is transmitted largely through the printed word. . .. The primary functions of race prejudice are cultural and psychological. The primary functions of racism are economic and political. (p. 134)

There is of course a deeper and darker aspect to racism, and this is highlighted by Anglican priest Ken Leech in his *Struggle in Babylon: Racism in the Cities and Churches of Britain* (1988). Leech believes that racism as an ideology, or belief-system, always contains the presence – passive if not active – of violence. 'Racism (as opposed to racial prejudice or discrimination) cannot exist apart from violence, for it presupposes the existence of a powerful group which is capable of enforcing its position' (p. 63). Leech demonstrates this with three illustrations – the historical association of racism and violence in the Nazi experience, the violence of imperial power in the twilight of the colonial era to prevent black liberation, and the institutional racism operating in Britain every day.

Leech is quite acidic about the record of the Church in co-operating with, and even encouraging, racist ideologies. As well as church endorsement for the system of slavery, which we will look at later, he says that the Church accepted the racism underlying the development of colonialism into a cohesive system, it provided the majority of members of the Ku Klux Klan in the USA and it contributed to the growth of Nazi activity in Germany, failing ever to denounce clearly and publicly the anti-Semitism of the 'National Socialists'.

Racism is sometimes described as a cancer, which needs to be cut out. Apart from being potentially hurtful to cancer-sufferers, this is probably a less accurate description than understanding racism as a kind of **corporate poison**, like something in the water, or the air, by which everyone is affected. It invades the mind gradually, sometimes not giving any signs of being present until triggered off by a particular set of circumstances. It may create hallucinations of pleasantness and wellbeing. It is present in all white people, even though some struggle against it. It may well be present in black people too, where they have some power, but few manifest the symptoms. When they do whites are the first to point it out, while seemingly missing the much more active symptoms in their own behaviour. Ubiquitous, the poison is very difficult to remove, and can certainly not be eradicated by a one-off 'surgical operation'.

Rather than surgery, treatment is much more a matter of a range of closely-monitored therapies, a careful mental diet of helpful books, magazines, radio and TV programmes; a calculated experience of really listening to what black people say, with a bias towards believing it rather than the opposite; healthy exercise of participation in anti-racist struggles or campaigns; rest periods for reflection and repentance. Such a regime may gradually rid our psyche of the poison, and help to provide our community and society with another defence against its destructive results. Personally I believe it is never entirely eradicated, but its effect can be minimised and its damage severely limited. The mutual solidarity of people in the struggle, particularly among those of different coloured skins, is in the end the most effective antidote.

However racism is described, whatever form it takes and whether it is overtly violent or not, Christians clearly ought to be against it. What terminology do we then use about ourselves? We can say we are in favour of equal opportunities; we can speak of moving towards racial equality; we can express a commitment to racial justice. Exception could not be taken to the first of these but experience shows it produces little. The second does require that structures be addressed, but the third has its roots in the biblical tradition, depends on commitment, indeed on faith, and expects change. Justice, or 'making things right', is something constantly sought by the prophets, and contains more of a dynamic than the rather passive feel of 'equality'. It is the mighty stream of '*tsedek*' (Amos 5. 24) or the '*dikaiosune*' by which Abraham is transformed into God's instrument (Romans 4).

A terminology debate has also gone on between the proponents of 'multiculturalism' and 'anti-racism'. Those who take the first approach stress the positiveness, the importance, of accepting the plural nature of British society, and ensuring that there is space for all to enjoy their own music, dance, literature, food, clothing and worship. There can be little argument with that.

The supporters of anti-racism, however, argue that it is necessary to go further, not just to create space and ensure opportunity, but to challenge all aspects of racism wherever it is found, and seek to eradicate it. Racism can be overt or covert; more often it is the latter, and sometimes it is quite unconscious. People simply do not realise that if you perpetuate the same old ways of teaching history, recruiting people for jobs, selecting candidates for the ministry or appointing Church stewards, then inequality will be entrenched, and nothing will change.

If practices remain unaltered we have to take responsibility for our racism. We Christians need to train ourselves as anti-racists, ready to spot the poison spreading – in ourselves or in others – and to halt it. The signs can range from the persistence of 'colour-coded' language – 'black' spot, day, sheep, economy, or whatever – through the use of the revealing phrase 'these people', to the complaint that we can't understand the African preacher. We forget that English is perhaps his/her third language (and how many do we speak?), and that what is needed is a bit of real concentration, and perhaps some judicious questions after the service.

Incidentally, in colour-coded language like the above examples, 'black' denotes judgement and negativity; phrases like 'black coffee' or 'blackout' are perfectly acceptable as they are purely descriptive. Anyone who scoffs at concern over colour-coded language should read the poem by a young black mother entitled *What Shall I Tell My Children?*, angrily questioning how she is to bring up her child in a world where everything bad is labelled 'black' and everything good 'bright' or 'white'. The importance of the influence and the terminology of colour, and the related place of Christianity, is described in Robert Hood's *Begrimed and Black: Christian Traditions on Black and Blackness* (1994). He remarks that historically, philosophically and aesthetically Christian thought has 'reinforced a subordination of blackness to whiteness', as a metaphor and later as a racial characterisation.

Institutional racism also needs to be defined, and tackled. A suggested definition is that **institutional racism** can be observed in the effects of a combination of historical inequalities and an ideology of racial superiority – either overt or covert – which between them result in particular ethnic groups being discriminated against both in the opportunities offered and the sanctions operated within a given society.

Joe Barndt believes the restraints of the 'prison of racism' are not so much created by individuals as by the corporate structures of the myriad of smaller institutions which then go to make up larger ones. The latter include Government (national and local), education, employment, the criminal justice system, health and social services and the media. He goes on:

> When we examine institutional racism the issue of power must once again be emphasised. Remember that racism is the power to enforce one's prejudices. As our nation oppresses its people of color, our personal bigotry and prejudice do not cause the primary damage. Rather the damage is done by racism which has been institutionally empowered and is administered in seemingly impersonal ways. . ... We [should] feel what it is like to be a person of color on the receiving end of educational, housing, welfare, police, labor, political, and economic institutional activity. (p. 77)

Barndt goes on to comment that such institutions do not only control and exploit, 'they do it in our name'.

Hence all white people are beneficiaries of institutional racism, whether we are aware of it or not. We benefit from it, but it corrupts us. It remains a poison, even if it offers pleasing hallucinatory effects. Ultimately, everyone suffers from racism.

Another dimension of the terminology in this area which can be something of a minefield is around the description 'Black'. Most people now in Britain who originated from Africa (either directly or via the Caribbean), and many from the Indian Sub-Continent, are reasonably happy with the description 'Black'. There are Asians from the Sub-Continent, from Malaysia and China, and people from

11

the 'Middle East', who are less so. Overall, just as racism is a political category, 'Black' is primarily a political colour. Activists for racial justice, whether from Nigeria, Jamaica, India or Kurdistan, have usually been happy to work under 'Black' as a generic term.

Those from these communities who are less happy to use 'Black' sometimes use 'Black and Asian', though that may exclude smaller communities. Another option is to use 'black and minority ethnic' as the adjective, on the basis that all of us are 'ethnic' communities, including white British, and in Britain certain groups are in a minority.

Many communities reject the use of 'minority' as a noun, i.e. 'ethnic minorities', feeling it belittles them. They argue they are ethnic groups, like the 'Anglo-Saxons'. In Britain they happen to be a 'minority ethnic group', over against the 'majority ethnic' whites. In India or the Caribbean, whites would of course be a 'minority ethnic community'. When using 'minority', however, it is important to remember that there are over one million Indians in the UK, already a third as numerous as the Welsh, and that in the world as a whole (as increasingly in the Christian Churches) white people are a pretty small minority. Modood in particular argues that restricting any description to simple 'Black' harms Asians, and in a 1995 essay lists seven reasons why. Most of them are related to the fact that 'black' is not a neutral term among 'non-white ethnic groups': for example, Asians are sometimes black and sometimes not black, depending on the speaker; 'black' distorts the analysis of what might need to be done and encourages too narrow a conception of racial discrimination, based upon colour rather than culture.

The North American 'catch-all' phrase is 'people of colour'. That does not seem to have caught on in the UK, though it has a good deal to commend it, in terms of avoiding over-use of 'Black' (which clearly Kurds or Moroccans physically are not) whilst at the same time using a single phrase conveying a sense of solidarity among all the minority communities who experience white European racism.

Some descriptions change down the years, and vary in use, 'Afro-Caribbean' being an example. Some of those who have come from the Caribbean, but originate in Africa, now prefer the term 'African Caribbean'. There are of course also 'Indo-Caribbeans', who originated from India, often as indentured labour, but mostly live now in Trinidad or Guyana (geographically South American but culturally Caribbean). There are Chinese Caribbeans and Anglo-Caribbeans also. In Britain we use 'Asian' to refer largely to people from the Indian Sub-Continent. In the USA 'Asian' refers to those originating from Japan, Hong Kong, Korea or other countries of the 'Far East'.

12

Also in the USA there has recently been a further development of thinking in which people give themselves hyphenated identities such as Asian-American, African-American or Native-American. A similar possibility for Britain has been suggested by Tariq Modood (1992), in *Not Easy Being British* published by the Runnymede Trust. Modood feels that 'British' is 'closely identified with "whiteness"', and that we need to broaden the concept of what British means. He says:

> What we need therefore, contrary to the reinforcement of ethno-centricity in the national curriculum, are ways to move towards a concept of Britishness that is not frozen in history and identified with only one or a narrow set of ethnicities, such as English, Welsh, Scottish and Irish, but can highlight the grounds of our commonality past and present, as well as our contribution through our differences. (p. 5)

Most activists in the field from the minority communities still seem most often to use 'black', seeing it as a political description which includes all who are the objects of racism.

Another debate swirls round the term 'Third World', which to some who come from outside Europe seems to carry a feeling of 'third class'. In any case, as they often point out, they are the 'two-thirds world' in terms of numbers, land-mass and natural resources. Sometimes the term 'the South' is also used but it seems more sensible, and accurate, to refer to 'the countries (or people) of Asia, Africa, Latin America and the Caribbean'. Such lengthy phrases may seem tiresome, but people's identities are at stake, and it is yet another aspect of racism that white people often want to speak of inhabitants of the rest of the world in short-hand. It is best to enquire, where possible, what people *themselves* wish to be called and, when in doubt, to use a broader and lengthier terminology which includes everybody.

A final comment on terminology needs to be made about the use of the phrase 'good community (or race) relations', especially by official circles. It is often used to justify a further piece of repressive activity or legislation. This is because the authorities usually see community relations from a white perspective, and what they appear to mean by 'good community relations' is something which panders to the more racist section of the community, for whom it is a code for keeping the blacks under control. When this phrase is used the question always needs to be asked, '*which* community?' The viewpoint here is that for Christians equality and justice must be the most important factors in race relations; genuinely 'good community relations' will always need to be based on justice.

Sometimes, in this book and elsewhere, 'Black' is written with a capital. This is to demonstrate emphasis, or particularity, sometimes, in contrast to 'White'. Usually when 'White' is used with a capital there is the connotation of an assumed imperialism or reminder of ever-present racism.

Reference has been made above to 'British' being used by certain sectors of society as a synonym for 'white' – or at least for those who pass the 'cricket test'. Modood argues that many black or Asian people now identify themselves with majority British cultural styles, while also maintaining some of their own. He believes that it cannot be right for a pluralistic society if 'individuals are pressed into narrow pigeon holes', just because of their colour or ethnic origin.

Leon Murray, first black Vice-President of the Methodist Church, in *Being Black in Britain* (1995) refers to the difficulties of young British-born blacks. 'This is their country', he says, 'and they have a right to be here . . . They are British and should be proud to be so'. But later he says that, amidst the pressures of our present society, they 'start to lose confidence from a very early age. By the time they are twelve or fourteen they no longer want to be part of the wider British society'.

A new (and tentative) definition of 'British' might be 'those who live or have lived in Britain (i.e. England, Northern Ireland, Scotland or Wales) and who – although in some cases having roots in or antecedents from other parts of the world – regard themselves as primarily of British social and cultural origin'. A 'British' person may then support whichever cricket team he or she wishes.

A brief word about 'numbers'. It is important to avoid responding to the 'numbers game' (i.e. how many black people are 'pouring' into the country) and the 'overcrowded island' argument as much as possible, as being in themselves racist. This is emphasised in the introduction to *Britain's Black Population* (Bhat *et al.*,1988), where one of the authors, Sushel Ohri, says 'there has been no shortage of attempts to use the "numbers game" as an ideological symbol to mobilise racist support and bolster racist attitudes against blacks' (p. 10). It should not be forgotten that even within Europe Holland has a greater population density than England and Wales, and Germany an equivalent one.

References to numbers and overcrowding enable politicians and journalists to blame black people, often in coded form, for a wide variety of social problems, including unemployment, homelessness and crime. However, while writing this book, at a speaking engagement with forty public school sixth formers – whom one expects to be relatively well-informed – I asked about the proportion of the black population in Britain. We started with 5 per cent, and few agreed; a good number thought it was 10 per cent, some thought 20 per cent and a few at least 30 per cent or even more. There were murmurs of disbelief when I said the first answer was right. Further incredulous noises followed my subsequent statement that in most of the previous twenty years more people had left Britain to settle elsewhere than had settled here. I added that of course most of those who had left were white, and most who came in were not, and received some nods of enlightenment in response. The effect of media disinformation plus racism is extraordinary and should never be underestimated.

Causes

Why racism? Why is it that such a negative and destructive ideology is so prevalent, especially in so-called Christian societies? There seem to be two main areas in which to seek answers, one in the macro, economic area, the other in the personal and psychological one.

There is no doubt that as Europeans began to learn more about the realities of the slave trade there must have been some public response. People could surely not have heard about the conditions of the journey, and the nature of the buying and selling at both ends, without opposition, or even outrage, being expressed. Therefore there had to be some justification for what was going on, some explanation which would put troubled consciences at least partly to rest. What more convenient explanation, especially given the African origins of the slaves, than that they were as akin to apes as to human beings? Africans were therefore not human in the same sense as Europeans (even the Spanish and Portuguese, who were problem enough). They did not feel the same loss at leaving their country, the same pain at leaving their families, as Europeans would. All this seems to have gone down well enough with those who had never visited Africa nor met an African, or who were beginning to benefit nicely from the trade, but wanted no qualms of conscience.

Fryer, whose description of racism was referred to above (p. 8), saw its primary purpose as economic and political. He believed it emerged in the oral tradition of Barbados in the seventeenth century, and 'crystallised in print in Britain in the eighteenth as the ideology of the plantocracy, the class of sugar-planters and slave-merchants that dominated England's Caribbean colonies. [Racism] emerged, above all, as a largely defensive ideology – the weapon of a class whose wealth, way of life, and power were under mounting attack' (p. 134). Fryer goes on to document the contribution of the Jamaica planter Edward Long, the travel writer Sir Thomas Herbert, Sussex vicar Edward Topsell and Scottish judge Lord Monboddo. Herbert described Africans as 'devils incarnate'. Topsell said that apes (and men who look like them) lust after women and Monboddo claimed there were men with tails in foreign parts who provided the 'missing link'. Herbert went so far as to describe African cannibalism in the following terms:

> Not satisfied with nature's treasures . . . the destruction of men and women neighbouring them, better contenting them, whose dead carkasses they devour with a vulture's appetite; whom if they misse, they serve their friends (so they miscall them) such scurvy sauce, butchering them, thinking they excuse all in a complement, that they know no rarer way to express true love than in making (not two soules) two bodies one in an inseparable union; yea, some (worn by age, or worme-eaten by the pox) proffer themselves to the shambles, and accordingly are joynted and set to sell upon the stalls. (quoted in Fryer, p. 141)

Fryer concludes that there were three basic ideas active in seventeenth- and eighteenth-century racist ideology: that Africans were closely connected with apes; that different-coloured people had different origins; and that humans could be hierarchically graded by skin colour.

Gradually, however, more white people met more black people, and more Africans came to visit or to settle in England. A few became Christian and were baptised. The more extreme notions of racist belief were challenged, although some have remained firmly fixed in the corporate white psyche. A number of Christians were prominent in this process of challenge, including George Fox (founder of the Quakers), Presbyterian preacher Richard Baxter and bishop's grandson Revd Morgan Godwyn, who had been warned off baptising slaves by the planters, as it would be like blessing a puppy or a 'black bitch'. It was Godwyn who, according to Fryer, in 1680 put his finger on 'the economic basis and role of plantocracy racism' in his book *The Negro and the Indian's Advocate*, written to 'prove the Negro's humanity' and to demonstrate that 'neither their Complexion, nor Bondage, Descent nor Country' could be a barrier to that humanity.

Fortunately the likes of Godwyn and others battled on, through the eighteenth century, against the prestige of philosophers such as John Locke and David Hume, and authors like Oliver Goldsmith. The latter laid the ground for the 'scientific racism' which is referred to later. The struggle went on through the nineteenth century. One incident highlights both its progress and the way the cognoscenti of England divided on the matter. This was the Morant Bay rebellion in Jamaica in 1865, when Governor Eyre's troops killed 439 blacks, flogged 600 others, murdered children and burned a thousand homes. A Committee who called for Governor Eyre's prosecution included John Stuart Mill, Thomas Huxley and Charles Darwin. Among Eyre's supporters were Thomas Carlyle, John Ruskin, Charles Dickens and Charles Kingsley.

So racism provided some kind of justification for slavery, indeed it almost went so far as to praise it, in certain quarters, as a Godsend for the African. As slavery gradually disappeared during the nineteenth century however, empire and colonialism took its place. There was thus a need to justify these periods of land-grabbing and exploitation also, so racism took on new forms and a more civilised style. By mid-century, says Fryer, the more liberal English person accepted 'Commerce, Colonisation, Civilisation and Christianity' as the best way forward for Africa. He goes on to report how the idea of 'trusteeship' developed, in which the older, wiser party (the Europeans) took responsibility for the 'attractive children' as Lord Lugard, a British administrator over Africans for thirty years, described them. Lugard notes the missionaries' view that Africans 'represented unregenerate mankind, sinful and unwashed' and says 'Britain marched across Africa with a clerical boot on one foot and a "scientific" boot on the other'.

Missionaries were therefore not without responsibility in these matters, although there were of course different approaches within the missionary movement. Some took the trusteeship line, while others both championed and worked with the abolitionist slaves to achieve their goal.

Overall the general approach was to take up the 'white man's burden', although Lugard, for example, freely admitted it was absurd not to admit that Western exploration into Africa was 'the satisfaction of [the West's] material necessities'. The phrase 'the white man's burden' may or may not have been coined by Rudyard Kipling at the end of the last century, but one of its best known appearances is in one of his verses from 'The White Man's burden':

> Take up the White Man's burden-
> Send forth the best ye breed –
> Go bind your sons to exile
> To serve your captives' need;
> To wait in heavy harness
> On fluttered folk and wild –
> Your new-caught, sullen peoples,
> Half devil and half child.

The 'trusteeship' approach to blacks in the imperial era was undergirded even by children's literature, and Fryer quotes from G. A. Henty, who described black people as 'just like children'. They are either laughing or quarrelling, they can be lazy or may work hard for a time, they can be clever to a degree but, according to Henty, are 'absolutely without intelligence, absolutely without inventive power'. It is not therefore surprising that the average educated English child grew up with a somewhat patronising attitude towards black people.

17

The study by Robert Hood referred to above (p. 11) researches the history of the Christian understanding of blackness. It explores the views of the early Christian fathers as the Gospel spread into north Africa and beyond, and the growing discomfort about black Christians and their origins. Hood's thesis is that Christianity has to take some of the responsibility for the reaction of Europeans to black people and thus for the roots of racism as we know it today. The negative legacy of blackness, says Hood, is 'firmly grounded in the Christian tradition and Christendom'. It is 'buried deep within our Western psyche and culture'. Hostility is related also to the spread of Islam across north Africa and into southern Europe. There is 'an unfinished symphony between the church and blackness'.

Racism, whether disguised or not, undoubtedly played its part in the opposition to freedom of countries such as India, Nigeria and South Africa. In some cases, like Zambia, threats had to be made, and in others, like Kenya, guerrilla warfare had to be used. In the former southern African colonies, Rhodesia and South Africa, armed struggle was required. There is no doubt that white racism, the arguments of 'kith and kin' and British economic interests, combined in these countries to support the whites and create a protracted struggle for liberation in which thousands of Africans (and hundreds of whites) died. Those involved in the anti-apartheid movement through the seventies and eighties were quite clear what lay behind the dissembling and prevarication of British Governments and British-based companies. It was a strong self-interest, combined with a belief that black people were incapable of running a country efficiently, or as profitably as was required.

The latter belief is particularly rich when one studies Africa today. It is littered with conflicts arising from the self-serving economic and political policies of the West. In the first half of the 1990s Zaire remained in turmoil around the Western-financed President Mobutu; Angola was suffering endless war promoted by Jonas Savimbi – figurehead over years for South African and US interests – who would not give up even when a relatively democratic election went against him; Somalis were shooting one another with arms mostly provided by the West; Mozambique seemed continually on the brink of collapse after decades of South-African-promoted brutality which Europe and the USA did nothing to stop; then came the horrors of Rwanda. None of this is to say that African politicians are without blame or responsibility, they are not, but their failures are constructed upon the selfishness of Western policies on their continent.

The modern form of colonialism requires raw materials from the countries of Asia, Africa and South America at as cheap a price as possible, and the repayment of crippling debts in order that Western economic development may continue to be financed. How is it that the average North American and European accepts a situation where our comforts are paid for by the hunger, poverty and disease of others? Part of the answer seems still to be racism. We do not believe that black and brown people feel as much hurt, suffer as much pain, experience as much distress as 'we' do. Or if they do, it does not really matter, because they are socially and intellectually inferior. Hence racism is still needed, at home and abroad, to justify white hegemony in an increasingly unequal, unjust and dangerously imbalanced world.

Much justification for the West's policies takes place in terms of the economic mistakes made after independence, the 'inability' of many Africans or Asians to run a modern economy, tribalism, lack of the right raw materials or infrastructure, failure to keep social costs under control, and unwillingness to grow 'cash crops' for Western markets. The facts – that poor producers of the South are played off against one another, that the inheritance of colonialism still creates all kinds of problems, that infrastructure is the wrong sort or in the wrong place, that less-developed countries need to grow food for their people before luxury crops for the West, and that the so-called Uruguay Round of the General Agreement on Tariffs and Trade (GATT) marginalised poor countries' problems in its six-plus years of deliberations – all these are largely ignored. 'We' organised the world this way, at considerable effort and cost ('we' say) because others lacked the ability. The prophecy of economic inequality is self-fulfilling. The macro argument for black incompetence has marshalled its evidence. The belief-system that incorporates racism is sustained.

And what of the personal, psychological area? Not that the psyche is only personal, or individual, and perhaps that is where some comment can be made. Psychoanalysis has had a good deal to say about the unconscious, much of which is created by what is passed on from generation to generation. Jung coined the term 'collective unconscious' which he saw as the place where 'psychic heritage and possibilities' were deposited. In the *Critical Dictionary of Jungian Analysis*, edited by Samuels *et al.* (1986), we are told that the collective is a 'repository of all that may at some time have been individually expressed, adapted or influenced' (p. 32). Vital constituents of the unconscious are archetypes, the 'primordial images' repeated throughout history in the human psyche. Archetypal patterns may appear in a variety of ways in human behaviour and are 'reinforced by traditional or cultural expectation'. To allow an archetype to be expressed may be to 'interact consciously with the collective, historical image' in a way which gives opportunity for the revealing of the past and the collective memory.

The psychological roots of racism may therefore be found in the fear of the dark and of the Other, and the association of blackness and darkness with evil and the devil may well be related to what Jung describes as the 'collective unconscious',

19

where what is individually expressed or experienced over generations is gathered. It may then be that 'primordial images' related to the archetypes deep in the human psyche feed a collective racism that has been encouraged in white communities by socio-economic factors. It may not be without significance that some white people who are mentally disturbed, in response to certain triggers, can release a stream of racist invective which is only just bearable in spite of their sickness. Even the great are not without blemish, however, and according to an essay by Farhad Dalal in the journal *Race and Class*, even Jung's work contains racist assumptions.

Fryer has a section on the 'demonology of race' in which he describes the charged meaning of the words 'black' and 'white'. He points out that blackness has traditionally stood for death, evil, sin and danger and gives other examples of the colour-coded language referred to above, such as the black arts, the plague (the 'Black Death'), blacklist, blackmail, and so on. Early Christianity also contributes to the 'archetype' of blackness, of potential evil. The devil is described as black in the early literature, and St Jerome wrote in the fourth century that 'Born of the Devil, we are black'. It does not take a wide knowledge of English literature to know that this theme appears in Shakespeare's Caliban and Othello too. So is the sense built up of blackness as synonymous with unpleasantness, wickedness and evil.

Paul Gordon is a psychoanalytic psychotherapist with long experience as a researcher on race. He observes in an essay in the *British Journal of Psychotherapy* that while race is in one way an 'empty category' and has no anthropological or biological validity, it has social and political validity of such importance that it can engender violence and even murder. Gordon believes psychoanalysis can help to explain why racism seems 'so persistent, so resistant to change, to legislation, exhortation and education'.

Gordon summarises psychoanalytic views of white perceptions or projections. They picture black people as a suitable target 'because of the association for white people of blackness with repressed fears and desires'. Blacks are rivals – siblings or oedipal fathers; they have great sexual prowess, they are foreign bodies, pollutants in the human race, even filth or excrement. For some racism is a psychotic state, and unintegrated personalities – individual or group – can pour their anxieties or hatred into the split-off section of the psyche which then focuses on the Other, the Blacks. Psychoanalysis alone cannot account for racism, says Gordon, although it should be part of the explanation. To understand racism one must include both the psychological and the political dimensions. Gordon quotes Robert Miles as saying that psychological fear of black people did not create or legitimate slavery. It was only when the economic and political imperatives required the denial of Africans' humanity that racism as an ideology arose. Gordon believes that psychoanalysis helps to explain racism and may ultimately assist in eradicating it. The damage inflicted on the black psyche by centuries of racism should not be minimised but the white psyche, with its fears, anxiety, self-doubt and self-hatred, must also be addressed.

All 'in-groups' react against 'out-groups', and seek to exclude or control them. The pathological nature of white racism, however, suggests a dynamic deeper than this, and one which is deeply damaging, not only to white or black but to the whole human race. It is in the end a spiritual issue, which has to be addressed for the spiritual health of us all. This has been a limited attempt to address the 'why' of racism. We now move onto its actual effects, as they are experienced in contemporary British society.

The fruits of racism

Racism clearly affects most directly the black and minority ethnic communities in our country and our continent, but its presence diminishes us all. This section seeks to illuminate those areas where racism is most demonstrable, and perhaps where white anti-racists can most importantly influence matters if they intervene. In speaking here of white anti-racists I am not referring so much to those committed people who already live and/or work in multiracial communities, and who are often already over-stretching themselves in concern and campaign, but to those who live in the suburbs, the country areas or the 'White Highlands', whose active participation is essential if inroads are to be made into the current power-structure, whether social, political or economic. We address three main areas – the effects of immigration controls, the system of criminal justice and in particular the activity of the police, and black economic empowerment.

THE EFFECTS OF BRITISH IMMIGRATION POLICY

This could of course be the subject of several books in itself. British immigration laws have become progressively tighter over the last twenty-five years, at least with respect to people from Africa, Asia, South America and the Caribbean. Controls have of course grown less stringent for people from west, north and central Europe, and may soon disappear altogether. While visa requirements were put on in the late 1980s for Nigeria, Ghana, India, Pakistan and Sri Lanka, they were removed in the early 1990s for Hungary, Poland and Czechoslovakia. From the beginning of 1995 the citizens of Sweden, Finland and Austria have had free access to Britain due to their citizenship of the EU.

This, in the context of the historical links of Britain with the Caribbean, the Indian Sub-Continent and both east and west Africa, and the fact that many British residents have ties of family or friendship there, is one of the more blatant contemporary examples of international institutional racism. Perhaps the sharpest way to demonstrate this is simply to tell some stories, in slightly more detail than those at the beginning of this book, to show what ordinary people have to put up with, as a result of economic inequalities in the world, and of immigration policies wrought out of a desperate anxiety that at least half the world wants to come and settle in Britain. After these stories, which are mainly about resisting deportation, we shall consider another group of people who are not inside trying not to be thrown out, but outside trying to seek temporary security within. These are asylum-seekers, the great majority of them from countries where there is civil unrest, persecution and in some cases open war.

Resisting deportation

Most of these examples from the last few years are ones in which either the former BCC Community and Race Relations Unit or the Churches' Commission for Racial Justice (CCRJ) have had some involvement and can vouch for what happened. They mostly involve 'overstayers', people who arrived in the country legally, and only much later became 'illegal immigrants', because for many different reasons they overstayed their allotted period. More stories can be found in the booklet *Breaking up the Family*, published by the CCRJ in September 1994.

The Danso family

This is the family mentioned at the beginning of this chapter (p. 1) as one of the examples of the problems caused by the racism in UK immigration law.

Michael, a Ghanaian who had obtained his Bachelor's degree in textiles, was in 1979 invited by the West German Textile Manufacturers' Association for a study visit. There was a military coup in Ghana and Michael applied for political asylum. In 1980 Joan left Jamaica for Germany to study the language and met Michael the following year. In 1983 Michael was able to return to Ghana to sort out his business affairs. He then applied and was accepted for a degree course at Strathclyde University and he made arrangements with his business partner in Liberia for funds to be transferred to Britain.

When he arrived at Strathclyde to check arrangements and ensure he could start the course on time, he discovered his partner had absconded to the USA with all the money. Joan had come from Germany on a visitor's visa to join him

22

and they sought to raise fresh funds for his course, and for a return home to enter afresh on the correct student's visa. In 1984 Michelle was born. The next year Joan was arrested for overstaying; she was granted bail but failed to report for fear of being deported without her baby.

In 1986 Michael and Joan were married. Later that year they were tracked down and arrested. Joan was sentenced to be deported, and imprisoned in Holloway jail. Eight-month-old Michelle was fostered, Social Services intervened and after two weeks Joan was released. Representations by the Joint Council for the Welfare of Immigrants (JCWI) and the local MP for Michael to be granted his student visa were rejected. In 1987 little Michael was born. From 1986 the family were required to report every week to the Immigration Department. Officials were pressing them to leave, and at one point said that if they could not agree where to go together they would be sent to separate countries and the children would be cared for here as 'Britain is a civilised society'.

During 1989 Michael was still hoping to obtain his student visa, in order to obtain the qualifications which would give him better employment opportunities back home. He had two or three years' sponsorship to support him. However, he was eventually informed that his application had been rejected. The family was claiming no state benefits, Michael and Joan earning money as and how they could. Due to the intricacies of the system and some poor legal advice the family faced being split, and finishing up on two, or possibly three, different continents.

By this time Michael had not lived in Ghana for ten years and had no home; he would be denied a job if he went to Jamaica. Joan did not want to go to a Ghanaian village, to live in a small house with Michael's mother, who spoke no English, and with very limited health or education facilities for her children. In fact she said she would rather leave them in Britain (the older ones had a right to stay) than take them to Ghana.

When it became clear that legally nothing more could be done one of the local churches, supported by the Newham Churches Immigration Support Group, decided to take their concern to its logical conclusion and offer them sanctuary. The family spent several months in sanctuary in 1989/90, received a stay of execution, came out, were refused again, went back into sanctuary, and finally after petitions, letters from local churches, national churches and MPs, articles in the local newspapers and the *Methodist Recorder*, along with some advice from a helpful immigration official, were given the right to stay. Having lived in a fairly small room in the church for most of two years, they returned to a rather mediocre council flat. They were delighted, and the children in particular did not know what to do with all the space. The Harold Road Church felt that at last all their sacrifice had been worthwhile. Michael has set up a charity group and is involved in community work in east London and Ghana which attempts to link the two.

The Tahir family

Mohammed, aged 32, and his wife Ghazal, aged 31, ran a grocery store in the small town of Blyth, in Northumberland. Mrs Tahir had been married to a British citizen in the UK in the early 1980s, but the marriage broke up and she returned to Pakistan. There she met Mohammed and eventually married him. She returned to Blyth, believing she still had her residential status, to run the family shop. However, because she did not return within two years, she was deemed to have lost her right to residence. By this time she had three children, Ameena (6), Marium (5) and baby Aroosh. The baby was born in the UK, the older two remembered little of Pakistan.

The Tahirs appealed against the refusal to allow them to stay but were refused. The threat of deportation brought enormous support from the local community. A petition attracted over 4,000 signatures, and the children at the local school wrote to the Queen. There was much publicity, even in the national press, about this family who seem to have taken seriously the prevailing enterprise philosophy and yet found themselves rejected. The local MP, Ronnie Campbell, sponsored an Early Day Motion in Parliament which attracted more than 200 MPs in support.

Despite all the protests a final deportation order was issued against the Tahirs at the end of 1993. In early 1994 Mrs Tahir became ill, partly it was felt, due to the emotional pressures the family was under. The order was suspended, but when she recovered in the middle of the year it was reimposed. The possibility of sanctuary was discussed with local churches, but a suitable and willing church community could not be found. Against the wishes of the local schools, the local community, the churches and the elected representatives, eventually the Tahirs left, reluctantly and in tears, slipping quietly away to avoid yet more of the public spotlight on their family. Supporters said that nearly a year later they were living practically destitute in one room in a small house in rural Pakistan, with little if any hope for the future, and no hope of returning to Britain under the current regime.

The Ogunwobi family

Sunday Ogunwobi arrived in Britain as a student in 1981. His wife Bunmi came soon afterwards. He undertook several courses and was still studying when their first child Deborah was born in 1987. She was born two months prematurely and was very small, and was still being treated at the beginning of 1994. Two years later Tunde was born; he also had medical problems, and was attending a weekly clinic during his first year in school. Sunday was continuing to study, Bunmi was supporting the family, and they did not claim any income support. Sunday had been active in one of the black-majority Churches, then transferred to a Baptist Church in north London, where he was made an elder and also became a governor of his children's school.

Meanwhile the Home Office had decided Sunday had been here too long, and refused a further extension of his student visa. An appeal was turned down and eventually a Deportation Order served. The family lost an appeal against the Order. By this time in March 1994 Bunmi had had baby Phoebe and Sunday had been offered a job with a new Church-based local employment project HELP (Hackney Employment Link Project), working with local young people to try to help them find employment. The children were still receiving medical treatment and after 13 years all the family's life was in the UK. In Nigeria parents had died and there was no proper home to go back to.

After urgent discussion, debate and prayer, involving the family's own Baptist congregation (which did not have a building), a neighbouring congregation (which did), immigration lawyers and the CCRJ, the day before his deportation Sunday decided to go into sanctuary as a last resort. After some weeks, during which observation (which she experienced as harassment) of the rest of the family by immigration officials increased considerably, Bunmi and the children joined him. The two congregations set up a support committee, which brought in representatives from other churches and other groups, and began both to raise funds and to campaign for the family to stay. After ten months of living in one room, and wide support from all kinds of people, in January 1995, the Home Office Minister responsible agreed to meet a delegation to discuss the family's case. A review was undertaken, but there was no change of heart. Their plight was known far and wide however, and when the Revd Jesse Jackson visited them in June 1995 and promised to take their case to the United Nations the family had spent 15 months in the church. By September 1995 Sunday had spent 14 years in the UK, a period usually attracting a 'long-residence concession'. However a 'fourteenth anniversary card' signed by over thirty church leaders brought yet another negative response from the Home Office. Sunday's reaction was to say that the family would stay in the church as long as was necessary. The family celebrated Sunday's second anniversary in sanctuary on 15 March 1996.

Asylum-seekers and refugees

The problems of Britain's immigration system relate, as mentioned above, not just to those who face removal from this country, but to those who seek safety here. The numbers of people heading for Western Europe increased considerably in the early 1990s, particularly with respect to Germany due to its admirably humanitarian Constitution. Arrivals reduced, however, in 1993 when the Constitution was amended restrictively, in the teeth of strong opposition from liberal writers, academics, politicians and Church leaders.

Conflicts around the world, in which Western countries often have some involvement, or even responsibility, have caused large numbers to flee their homes – Tamils from Sri Lanka, Kurds from Turkey, Iraqis and Iranians, Ethiopians and Eritreans, Somalis, Angolans and residents of former Yugoslavia. Due to air travel some have managed to get to Europe, to the apparent chagrin of the authorities in Western European countries. Hence a generalised reaction has evolved to characterise asylum-seekers as economic migrants or – even more unpleasantly – as 'bogus' or 'fake', 'swamping' or 'flooding' our countries in 'tidal waves'. Such language attempts to justify an increasing range of measures to prevent them from taking temporary refuge here.

It seems important to reiterate some basic facts about all this, in order that the necessary debate may be a productive one. Firstly, by far the majority of uprooted people stay within or close to their own countries. Secondly, less than 5 per cent of the world's refugees were in Europe in 1995, although that could rise if conflicts in central Europe escalate. Thirdly, poor countries support far more refugees than do rich ones; examples include the Afghanis in Pakistan, the Mozambicans in Malawi, the Ethiopians and Somalis in Kenya, the Tamils in south India, and the Rwandans in Zaire. Fourthly, although Germany may be said to have a problem, with some 450,000 asylum applications in 1992, Britain's maximum was only about 50,000, a much easier number to deal with.

In fact the number of asylum-seekers arriving in Britain then began to fall, due partly to obstructive measures such as the £2,000 fine on airlines for bringing in incorrectly-documented passengers and the measures in the 1993 Asylum and Immigration Appeals Act which reduced multiple applications, and partly to the message that has gone round the world regarding the inhospitable approach of the British Government. By 1994, in both Britain and Germany, these numbers had halved: in the UK the total was 23,765, though it has risen again to 44,000 in 1995 (Home Office figures). In early 1996 the Government brought in further restrictions, including the removal of benefits, to force certain asylum-seekers to leave. The refugee issue has to be addressed at the European level. For the Churches this is being done by the Conference of European Churches (CEC), in co-operation with the World Council of Churches and the Churches Commission for Migrants in Europe (CCME), based in Brussels. In a report published in 1991 staff members of these bodies outlined the developing situation, and the problems of the Churches in responding to it. One of them quotes the second-century Epistle to Diognetus: 'Christians are not distinguished from the rest of humankind. . .. They dwell in their own countries but only as sojourners. . .. Every foreign country is home to them and every homeland foreign.'

The report says we must try to create a European home for those who need, temporarily it is hoped, to leave their own countries. To do this the Church needs to keep before its members the obligation to serve one another, to serve the society we live in, and to act together to try to meet the wider needs of humankind. The report suggests that the Churches in certain countries may be helping to create the problem by not resisting vigorously enough particular forms of nationalism, and in others failing to solve it by not demanding more from their governments and their people. It is essential to humanise the situation. Even 25,000 asylum-seekers arriving in a year may sound a lot, never mind nearly half a million, as came to Germany in 1992. Who are these people? How are we treating them? Are some with good cases being turned down, and returned to areas where there is conflict, persecution and danger? It is essential for churches and Christians in areas where there are few asylum-seekers to familiarise themselves both with the issues and where possible with the people in question.

In 1992 the Asylum Rights Campaign (ARC) was set up to co-ordinate opposition to parts of the 1993 Asylum and Immigration Appeals Bill, before it became law. ARC through its members has access to a range of stories and experiences of asylum-seekers who have had a difficult time proving their cases to British immigration officials. Reports have been produced by Asylum Aid on the experiences of Iraqi asylum-seekers in the aftermath of the Gulf War, by the Medical Foundation for the Care of Victims of Torture on the treatment of those who have experienced brutality, by the Refugee Council on Nigeria, by Charter 87 on some very disturbing individual cases, and by Amnesty International on the contravention of international Conventions by the forms of detention of asylum-seekers being practised by the British Government. The Refugee Council and the Refugee Legal Centre also have considerable information both on individual cases and on the rapidly rising rate of refusals.

The whole system appears to have been tightened up, largely in order to exclude as many people as possible. The Asylum and Immigration Appeals Act of 1993, although providing an appeal system for all asylum-seekers, also puts in place a 'fast-track' system where those who arrive from what the Home Office regards as 'safe countries' can be deported within a matter of days. This has helped to reduce enormously the number of those granted 'exceptional leave to remain', a category which has previously enabled thousands of people from conflict-ridden countries such as Sri Lanka, Iraq, Iran, Somalia, Ethiopia and Zaire to stay in safety until things at home calm down. Increasingly the question will be not so much how asylum-seekers can be helped to stay here in safety, but how they can be enabled to get in at all, to have their cases heard. This became clear during 1993 especially with respect to refugees from former Yugoslavia.

Hence the mechanisms that want to keep out more 'immigrants' from Britain, while expelling at least some of those already here, are also at work in the approach to refugees. 'Good community relations', according to Government practices, seems to mean a minimum of arrivals, and very few granted refugee status – just 600 in 1994, with 2,500 given 'exceptional leave to remain' and 10,000 refused (Home Office figures). The hope seems to be that such figures will appease the racists, and social discontent will be minimised. The Government then used the high rate of refusals to announce further restrictions for 1996.

In the meantime there appears little willingness to address the other half of the equation, the causes of the conflicts that create the refugees. If European Governments are going to insist, from dubious motives, on refusing to admit more than a fraction of the world's refugees in the first place, whatever their predicament, more must be done to assist them where they are, and to act pre-emptively but sensitively, in full consultation with the United Nations, to try to prevent political, economic and social breakdowns. Every refugee would prefer to remain at home, if their safety and a relative minimum of living standards are reasonably secure.

POLICING AND THE CRIMINAL JUSTICE SYSTEM

A second area in which the fruits of racism can be shown to be thoroughly unpleasant is the operation of the criminal justice system, and in particular the front-line of that system, the police. The lack of professionalism, ongoing harassment and inability to apologise for mistakes in the approach of the police to black and minority ethnic communities (including the Irish) have been revealed in countless events over the last twenty-five years, and they do not seem to be decreasing. The notorious cases affecting Irish people include the Birmingham Six, the Guildford Four, the Maguire family and Judith Ward.

Cases related to Black and Asian communities include the Rupert Taylor and Joy Gardner affairs, mentioned at the beginning of this chapter (see p. 1), and the Tottenham Three. These were the three men found guilty of the murder of PC Keith Blakelock in the 1985 Broadwater Farm uprisings and then released. The campaign continues due to the procrastination of the Home Secretary in considering new evidence in another case for which Winston Silcott was imprisoned. There is Alban Turner, originally convicted for the Notting Hill Carnival murder on information given by someone who alleged he was forced to provide false evidence by police threats, and the Cardiff Three, released from murder convictions in 1993. A book soon to be published describes how South Wales police managed to convince themselves three young black men were guilty, despite having no real evidence. There are also the East Ham Two, two Tamils convicted of murder in an intra-community dispute, one of whom undertook two long hunger-strikes while in jail. At their second appeal the judgement, referring to one police officer's statement that he had heard screaming coming from the interview room, stated that it had become apparent that 'there were wholesale breaches of the Police and Criminal Evidence Act', and allowed the appeal. Several black people were released in 1993 and 1994 after having been convicted on evidence from Stoke Newington police; dozens have successfully sued police over the past few years. The saga of the West Midlands Serious Crimes Squad needs also to be mentioned, where 40 per cent of those complaining of wrongful conviction were black.

This section concentrates on the police, as it is they who have the most power on the streets. Once black people are arrested and charged it becomes increasingly difficult for them to demonstrate their innocence. Many say it feels as if it is for them to prove their innocence rather than for the police to prove their guilt. One important reference point of police racism is the small number of black and minority ethnic officers. Despite apparently strenuous efforts the service seems unable to attract or keep the number of officers it wants. At the end of 1994 there were still only just over 700 black officers out of 28,000 in the Metropolitan Police, below 3 per cent for a population which is over 20 per cent ethnic minority, and in some areas a majority (Metropolitan Police figures).

The most likely reason for this seems to be the prejudice that black officers have experienced, and their increasing unwillingness to put up with it. In a number of cases in the last five years quite heavy payments have been made to black or Asian police officers for racial discrimination in Nottingham, Kent, Liverpool and other places. One example was the £30,000 reportedly awarded to a black detective in the Metropolitan Police in early 1996. Many senior police officers continue to talk about the odd 'bad apple in the barrel', and the police being 'no more racist than the rest of society'. If the first is true why does the same kind of behaviour persist year on year, without such bad apples being removed? If the second is true something needs to be done because prejudiced police officers are in a much stronger position than almost anyone else – except perhaps immigration officers – to put that prejudice into practice.

In the years since 1980 there have been a whole range of incidents reflecting racist behaviour by the police. The victims range from young black men through families and elderly pensioners to celebrities such as athletes Linford Christie and John Regis and high-jumper Dalton Grant, boxers Maurice Hope and Nigel Benn, and footballer Garth Crookes. The issue is how police use their power. This can be shown in relation to their attitudes, and to the harassment and even violence for which they are responsible.

Even middle-ranking police officers such as Chief Superintendents, with oversight of multiracial areas, have exposed their prejudices in public comments. This happened in the late 1980s in Leeds and London. A leaflet was issued by Staffordshire police asking residents in Neighbourhood Watch areas to report on 'coloureds and their vehicle numbers'. There have been constant failures by senior police officers to acknowledge the seriousness of the problem, or to apologise when very destructive mistakes were made. One of the most unfortunate was by the Metropolitan Police Commissioner, Sir Paul Condon, in July 1995, with reference to 'black muggers' on London streets.

Such incidents and mistakes are mainly reported in the black press, but Linford Christie received national coverage when his autobiography was published at the end of 1989. He recounted how he had been called 'black bastard' by police, and when stopped while driving asked 'What's a nigger like you doing in an England tracksuit?'. Also police had raided his home seeking to arrest his brother for an alleged offence. He said his father was knocked unconscious, other family members were attacked and he was kicked in the testicles – and then fined £100 for assault. Christie later obtained a five-figure settlement from the Metropolitan Police over wrongful arrest for 'stealing' a rented car he was driving.

Minority newspapers regularly report on such awards and the following are examples of recent payments by police. In early 1994 after a long battle the police paid over £30,000 to the Scott family of Broadwater Farm, north London, for a police raid in which shotguns and rifles were used, and which caused the family 'anxiety, distress and humiliation'. Kent police paid £25,000 in an out-of-court settlement to a black electrician, Ricardo MacLeish, who claimed he was racially abused and beaten by police called to evict him from a public house. In July 1994 the Metropolitan Police paid £7,500 to student Foziat Ali in a settlement for assault and false imprisonment, 'with no admission of liability', which is the usual formula adopted. In 1995 the Metropolitan Police paid out public funds totalling £1.5 million in damages.

In mid-1995 Terry Akaijaye received £30,000 in a settlement for his treatment when in 1993 he went to a south London police station to report the theft of a car radio. He said he was questioned on his immigration status, arrested and taken home in handcuffs to produce his passport. Mr Akaijaye said he was very upset that, despite his being here perfectly legally, the police failed either to apologise or to discipline any officer for their actions. About the same time the Metropolitan Police paid £31,000 in an out-of-court settlement with Terry Prince and Marie Stewart, a couple who were charged with threatening behaviour, and Mr Prince additionally of assault, after an incident in December 1990. The two were cleared of all charges, and alleged that in fact the police had beaten up Mr Prince and knocked Ms Stewart to the ground. The police, while denying any liability, also paid the couple's legal costs.

In many such incidents people find it either too expensive or too time-consuming to sue, or are fearful of repercussions. Legal action may take years. After one long battle, in December 1995 black housing worker Rennie Kingsley accepted £76,000 damages after being arrested in 1990 on drugs charges by Stoke Newington police. Nine others have also received damages. Then in March 1996, a Hong Kong-born Streatham hairdresser, Kenneth Hsu, was awarded record damages of £220,000 for a claim of violent assault by police during an arrest in 1992. One officer told him he was 'the first Chinky' he had arrested. No disciplinary action was taken against any officer involved.

The following month a 29-year-old black man, Daniel Goswell, was awarded damages of £302,000 by a jury in a civil action. Mr Goswell told the jury he had complained about lack of police activity over an arson attack on his home. He was then handcuffed to police officers, when another officer hit him on the forehead with a blow leaving a permanent scar. The officer was sacked, but reinstated by the Home Secretary when he appealed. Such occurrences infuriate many in the black communities. The Metropolitan Police has said it will appeal in both the Hsu and Goswell cases.

There are also cases of even more serious police violence. As well as the cases referred to above, in February 1990 widow Thora Rose accepted £130,000 after an eight-year court battle over the death of her husband as he was being escorted to a psychiatric hospital. Mrs Rose, with two small children, was forced to sue. Eventually the police made a settlement offer it was too hard for Mrs Rose to refuse. It came just two weeks before the case was finally to come to trial, seemingly in order to prevent all the publicity of the courtroom.

The number of deaths in police custody in the last few years, many of them black people, gives considerable cause for concern. A list of such deaths is included in *Deadly Silence: Black Deaths in Custody* published by the Institute for Race Relations in 1991. In July 1994 Mark Harris was reported to have committed suicide in a Bristol police station. The inquest in November 1994 recorded an open verdict. The Coroner remarked that the family were left 'none the wiser' about what actually happened inside the police station. The Cardiff-based family have therefore continued to campaign for a full review of the case.

More recent deaths include Shiji Lapite – who died within thirty minutes of being arrested by Stoke Newington police in December 1994, Brian Douglas, dying in April 1995 after his skull was fractured while south London police equipped with long-handled batons were apparently trying to arrest him, and Wayne Douglas (no relation) who died in police custody in Brixton in December 1995. In the Lapite case both the Crown Prosecution Service and the Police Complaints Authority indicated they could find no basis for action against the two officers known to be involved, but in January 1996 an inquest jury brought in a verdict of 'unlawful killing'. It remains to be seen whether any charges will be brought or, like a similar verdict in the case of Omasase Lumumba, killed in Pentonville prison in 1991, it will be ignored by the relevant authorities. Ibrahima Sey, a Gambian asylum-seeker, died in custody at Ilford police station in March 1996. CS gas was reported to have been used in the arrest. A post-mortem examination stated that Sey died after a period of exertion and was suffering from hypertensive heart disease. His family disputed this, saying Sey was fit and active. A Police Complaints Authority enquiry into the circumstances surrounding his death began almost immediately and was continuing as this book went to press.

The police response to racial violence is often criticised by the black community. In late 1994 three police officers from the Manchester community liaison department were suspended for alleged racist attitudes which according to a former colleague included referring to those they were supposed to be supporting as 'wall-to-wall shit'. The officers were later exonerated.

The current law on racial violence is relatively weak, and efforts were made in 1993 and 1994 to get it strengthened. This is an item for the 'agenda of the twenty-first century' referred to in chapter 7. That chapter also makes suggestions about what should be done in other parts of the criminal justice system.

One necessary area of progress, as with the police, is the active participation of black people in the different sectors of the system. A small amendment added at the last moment to Section 95 of the 1991 Criminal Justice Act provides the basis for a helpful monitoring of what is actually happening. The measure was proposed by Baroness Flather, a Conservative who is the only Asian woman peer, and gives the Secretary of State power 'to publish such information as he considers expedient' to assist those working in the justice system in their duty not to discriminate by 'race or sex or any other improper ground'. If this power is properly employed it can provide a regular survey. For example the 1994 report announced that in March 1994 'there were believed to be four ethnic minority judges, eleven recorders and nine assistant recorders', and that from

June 1992 to June 1993, 5 per cent of magistrates appointed were black. Because of the historical preponderance of white magistrates this is a much lower rate than is necessary if a representative target of 6 per cent is to be reached. The National Association for the Care and Resettlement of Offenders (NACRO) reported in 1994 that only 2.5 per cent of prison staff were from minority ethnic communities.

The result of the present system is the highly disproportionate numbers of black and minority people in prison. Throughout the first half of the 1990s some 16 per cent of the male prison population was black, while among females in 1994 it went as high as 29 per cent, partly due to women being used as 'mules' – drug couriers – from overseas. Excluding foreign nationals the figures in 1993 were 12 per cent of males and 14 per cent of females. In some London prisons 40 per cent of prisoners were minority ethnic; the figure reached 55 per cent in one remand institution (NACRO figures). This has required a cultural change in prisons, which the Prison Department claims is happening, including matters of food, language and religion. The Department has a Race Relations Policy which is publicly displayed in all its establishments. However, as with all policies, the effectiveness is in the delivery, and the defensiveness of officials who point to the policy as if it were the answer suggests either naivety or duplicity, neither of which is acceptable. As elsewhere the small numbers of black staff indicate the extent of the problem. There has been some progress in the police, prisons, judicial training and other areas of the criminal justice system over the last ten years but much remains to be done.

UNEMPLOYMENT

One way in which majority groups in any society maintain their position and power is by denying an economic basis to minorities. If this happens minority groups are prevented from feeling that they genuinely belong. This can lead to an unwillingness to contribute to a society, a sense of boredom or alienation, or to growing feelings of frustration and anger which seek to gain revenge on the majority community. To avoid such negativities minorities need to be able to build an economic base. There are two main avenues to this in present economic structures, these being equality of employment and access to capital, though it is suggested by some that black people will only achieve adequate economic justice through a fairly basic shift in economic structures. Such a move would require a change in values from those worshipping an entirely free market to values of equality of opportunity, condition and distribution as well as wealth creation. In the following section we shall deal primarily with equality in employment, important as it is particularly for young people in the minority communities.

The problem is not of course new. A major research study in the 1960s, which was written up by W. W. Daniel (1968) as *Racial Discrimination in England*, delineated the problem. Its chapter on a survey of one thousand 'immigrants' began thus:

> Difficulties with regard to employment, often directly linked to discrimination or prejudice, are the most widespread single source of disappointment with life in Britain for coloured immigrants. The discrimination they face individually and collectively in employment is the factor most frequently mentioned to explain why they think some kind of colour bar exists in Britain today. (p. 57)

The chapter goes on to describe the personal and statistical responses to the survey, and the level of overt rejection black people (usually then known as 'coloured') experienced. The survey went so far as to send three people with the same qualifications for the same forty jobs, one white, one black and one Hungarian migrant. The white Englishman got 15 offers and 10 refusals, the Hungarian 10 and 23 and the West Indian 1 and 37. The survey's conclusion was that not only were black claims of discrimination justified, but it was the most able black people who experienced most discrimination.

The Department of Employment kept statistics on unemployment rates and in 1979 commissioned a further survey by the Policy Studies Institute (PSI), published under the authorship of David Smith in 1981 as *Unemployment and Racial Minorities*. From the statistics it was fairly clear that by 1970 the rate of unemployment among minorities and the 'host community' was about the same, although the rate for young Afro-Caribbean men was twice that for young whites. However, when unemployment began to rise in the late 1970s and early 1980s minorities were shown to be more vulnerable. Figures in 1977 showed 9.6 per cent unemployed among minorities compared to 5.2 per cent for whites. The 1979 PSI report commented that the main reason for higher black unemployment was a low status in the workforce, among groups where unemployment always struck harder.

The survey concluded that the experience of unemployment always hits the poor and already economically disadvantaged the hardest, and minorities were affected most severely. In 1979

> unemployed Asians and West Indians tended not to ascribe their difficulties to racial discrimination or prejudice, and tended not to react to their misfortune in an extreme or violent manner. It remains to be seen whether the response of the minority groups will change as unemployment continues to rise and to affect them even more than the rest of the population. (p. 160)

The study was published a few weeks before Brixton, Toxteth and Handsworth erupted in the most vigorous outbreaks of disorder in England this century.

The Radical Statistics Race Group published their second edition of *Britain's Black Population* (Bhat *et al.*) in 1988, and offered a sharp analysis of the black predicament. One of the issues the Group looked at closely was black unemployment. The 1981 edition had already found high levels of unemployment among blacks, and listed possible reasons such as lack of qualifications and the effects of recession. The second edition rejects these reasons. It cites the successes of local authorities which have adopted a positive approach through equal opportunities and other measures. The Greater London Council, for example, doubled its black and minority staff from 6 per cent to 12 per cent by such means between 1982 and 1984. The Group concludes that 'blacks have been, and are, discriminated against in every sphere', and goes on:

> the real explanation for the overrepresentation of blacks in unemployment statistics is due to racism both at an individual level and at an institutional level. It is this racism which enables white people in power to abuse their position and ensure 'unequal' processes apply in practice when it comes to employment, promotion, redundancy or treatment of black employees. This is the single most important explanation why blacks have continuously suffered adversely in the labour market, irrespective of the market situation. (p. 95)

The Group goes on to make a number of suggestions for positive action, a theme to which we shall return in the final chapter.

Among some employers, such as the Civil Service, there have been attempts at positive action and by mid-1992, 5 per cent of employees in the Service were black, against 4.2 per cent in the working population as a whole. However the number of black and Asian executive officers was only 3.6 per cent and of senior managers only 1.82 per cent. Most black people (80 per cent) were to be found in the lower clerical grades, as were 71 per cent of Asians, but only 50 per cent of whites. In September 1995 it was reported in a *Guardian* article that a Cabinet Office advisory panel had found the Service still to be a bastion of prejudice, with only 61 black and minority employees at Grade 5 (from a total of 2,850), and only one above it (out of 1,005). Of the 61 only six were actually career civil servants as opposed to consultants on contracts.

It is a common assumption that discrimination in employment no longer exists, because of the 1976 Race Relations Act. An important study on the effectiveness of the Act, written by McCrudden, Smith and Brown, was published by the PSI in 1991, entitled *Racial Justice at Work*. The study sought to analyse what success, if any, the legislation had had. The main measures made available by the 1976 Act were bringing individual complaints to a tribunal, and the formal investigation of a company. The purposes of these, according to the PSI, included assurances to minorities their concerns being addressed, the improvement of channels to address them, the changing of unfair practices and the establishment of standards of public and private behaviour. The needs of individuals were being taken into account, but the necessity for structural change was also recognised.

The study reports on the degree of success of the methods of formal investigations and of individual complaints, referring to the role of the Commission for Racial Equality (CRE), and gives case-studies of employers who have had action taken against them. It concludes that fear of bad publicity was more effective than legal powers and that overall the 1976 Act has failed in its prime aim of eliminating racial discrimination in employment. It believes there should be a requirement for ethnic monitoring above a particular size of workforce. It also suggests a change in terminology to 'equality of opportunity' or 'equality of employment'. This would require the introduction of positive action, of targets and of monitoring, in a way the term 'equal opportunity' does not. The playing field needs first to be levelled; only then may positive action mechanisms become redundant.

The PSI followed up its 1991 study with another in 1993 by Trevor Jones entitled *Britain's Ethnic Minorities*. This was based on an analysis of the government's Labour Force Survey data from 1984 to 1990 and appeared to demonstrate that certain minority groups are achieving much better than others. It found that a higher percentage of young people of African Asian, Indian and Chinese origin entered higher education, and that they obtained more qualifications and achieved the same proportion of professional jobs as whites. At the same time most male workers from the African Caribbean, Pakistani and Bangladeshi communities remained in manual employment. These differences in achievement bear out the point made by Tariq Modood, that there are quite substantial differences between minority groups. Jones concluded that the diversity he found among and between different ethnic groups meant that it no longer made sense to regard minorities as a single group. There is no longer a simple contrast, he stated, 'between relatively well-off "whites" and poorly-off "blacks"'.

Black unemployment in British society remained much higher than white into the 1990s, being 22 per cent for ethnic minorities in 1993, compared to 10 per cent for whites. It was 35 per cent for Pakistanis and Bangladeshis. For women it was 7 per cent for whites, 21 per cent for all ethnic minorities and 37 per cent for Bangladeshis and Pakistanis. These figures may even represent under-reporting by young people. The unemployment rate in Greater London at the end of 1995, with all the attempts by the authorities to massage the figures, was 9.5 per cent, and in many inner London boroughs with high black populations like Lambeth, Southwark, Tower Hamlets and Haringey it approached 20 per cent, rising to a maximum of 22 per cent in Hackney. The problem was acknowledged by the Government in January 1995 with the release of Labour Force Survey figures which showed that 62 per cent of young black men in London between 16 and 24 had no job. A TUC report published in October 1995 confirmed that unemployment was still well over twice as high for blacks as for whites, 18.8 per cent for blacks and 8.1 per cent for whites.

Person for person, unemployed black people have higher educational qualifications than unemployed whites: for example, there are disproportionately more black than white graduates without work. In addition it appears to be more difficult for black people to obtain training and promotion, and it is still the case nearly twenty years after the Race Relations Act 1976 that very few black people can be found in senior positions in organisations or companies in all sectors of society.

The Churches themselves, and their agencies, employ quite a number of people, and have some influence over a much wider range of employment by, for example, sitting on boards or committees. They do not appear to have a record much better than any other institution, and that is a situation which must be addressed.

Some of the ideas raised in *Racial Justice at Work* were proposed in the Second Review of the 1976 Act put forward by the CRE in 1992. The Churches' Commission for Racial Justice (CCRJ) supported the Review's proposals, but – like the CRE – grew very disappointed when after 18 months the Home Office again refused to consider any form of compulsory ethnic monitoring, even for large employers. This would be the most effective and significant move towards equality of employment, and the commitment of any Government to economic racial equality can only be measured by the way it responds to proposals such as ethnic monitoring.

This section has dealt primarily with the lack of equality in employment rather than 'access to capital'. In order to enable the black and minority ethnic communities to obtain equality of capital access certain mechanisms will have to be adopted, including forms of positive action, and monitoring. Equal opportunity statements by themselves, whether in terms of capital access or employment,· rarely alter anything.

Both church and commercial investors could take positive action to overcome discrimination and enable access to capital for black enterprises. One idea put forward in 1994 by the CCRJ to the Social Justice Commission set up by the Labour Party was for tax or other incentives to encourage banks, building societies and other financial institutions to ensure their lending bore some relation to either the racial balance of the local community or that of the country as a whole. For example, as the minority population is of the order of 6 per cent, if a bank demonstrated that 3 per cent of its lending in a particular year was directed to minorities this would bring a certain degree of financial recognition. If it was 4 per cent it would be more, 5 per cent yet more and so on. Similar 'sweeteners' might be offered to building societies or banks in areas where there are 10 per cent, 20 per cent or even 30 per cent minorities. Financial institutions could also receive some recognition for not withdrawing from inner-city areas or outer estates, as so often happens. Schemes may be difficult to administer, but unless something is done, injustice will remain, and grow.

The degree of inequality in British society in the 1980s and early 1990s has increased considerably. Two reports issued in June 1994 demonstrated that in the twelve years between 1979 and 1991 the number of people living below half the nation's average earnings has shot up from three million to eleven million. The poorest 5 per cent were 15 per cent poorer in 1991 than in 1979. Millions of children live in poverty. As black and minority people are normally over-represented in the poorer sections of society there is little doubt they will be disproportionately present in those sectors referred to above. It is in some ways surprising that such inequalities have not led to greater social breakdown. Nevertheless fragmentation in terms of crime, education and health indicators, and – in many communities – despair is plain to see. However it should not be for this kind of negative reason that Christians speak out for social and racial justice. Christians promote equity because it is God's will, and because it is right. We shall need to be pressing in the final years of the twentieth century, particularly in the context of the new Europe, for justice in immigration, penal and economic affairs.

2

The coming of black people to Britain

'There were Africans in Britain before the English came here.' So runs the first startling sentence of Peter Fryer's *Staying Power* (1984). It appears that soldiers from North Africa came in the Roman armies of occupation, before the Angles, Saxons and Jutes landed from what is now North Germany and Scandinavia to become the forebears of the English. Remains of a young African girl buried near Norwich around 1000 CE were recently discovered. There was a black trumpeter, with turban, portrayed on the parchment roll of the Great Tournament of Westminster, dated 1511. Other occasional evidence of black people in these islands is cited by Fryer, prior to the beginnings of the trading and colonial era in the mid-sixteenth century, after which increasing numbers of the inhabitants of many parts of the world were brought to Britain as either slaves or curiosities. We shall read in this chapter both of some of the extraordinary individuals and of the growth of consciousness and resistance in the black communities, drawing out in particular any points of interest to Christians. According to Fryer the first group of Africans came in 1555,

> before we had potatoes, or tobacco, or tea, and nine years before Shakespeare was born. Queen Mary was on the throne, had recently married Philip of Spain, and was much occupied with having heretics burnt. Some of her subjects were more interested in getting rich than in arguing about religion, and it was the pursuit of riches that caused them to bring here a group of five Africans. (p. 5)

The slave trade began in earnest soon after this. It was accompanied by all kinds of suggestive myths that black people were carefree, idle, had large appetites of all kinds, and were 'inherently inferior, mentally, morally, culturally and spiritually, to Europeans. They were sub-human savages. . . English racism was born of greed'. Savages or not, the numbers of black people brought to Britain gradually increased. As well as house-servants and possibly prostitutes, some of them became recognised as able entertainers. This in turn brought criticism that the country could not support these extra mouths (the population was about three million) and in 1596 Queen Elizabeth I was sufficiently moved to send an open letter to the Lord Mayor of London and the mayors of other towns, suggesting that any 'blackamoors' resident should be transported home forthwith.

This first attempt at repatriation was not however particularly successful, and from the mid-seventeenth century the numbers of black house-servants and slaves began to rise fairly rapidly. One way this is known is the number of advertisements which began to appear in newspapers, reporting runaway black slaves and offering rewards for their return.

Folarin Shyllon, himself from West Africa, in his book *Black People in Britain 1555–1833* (1977), reproduces an advertisement from the *London Gazette* in 1688:

> A black boy, an Indian, about 12 years old, run away the 8th inst. from Putney, with a collar about his neck with this inscription: 'The Lady Bromfield's black, in Lincoln's Inn Fields'. Whoever brings him to Sir Edward Bromfield's at Putney, shall have a guinea reward. (p. 11)

Shyllon cites many other such cases. It seems that black resistance to white domination began early in England, even if it only took the form of running away from slavery. Sometimes this resistance took a religious form, but with brutal results:

> Katherine Auker asked the Middlesex sessions in 1690 to discharge her from her master, a Barbados planter called Robert Rich, who had brought her to England about six years before. When she had herself baptized – a ceremony widely but wrongly supposed to confer freedom on slaves – her master and mistress 'tortured and turned her out; her said master refusing to give her a discharge, she could not be "entertained in service elsewhere"'. (Fryer, p. 23)

The eagerness for baptism was demonstrated even earlier in the reports of the first black person to be baptised in Haringey in 1610, Walter Auberey from Sudan. The first black resident of Bristol to be similarly blessed in 1645 was Frances, a 'Blackymore maide'; thirty years later Ann Atkins, 'a dark woman', was baptised into the same church. However, it seems baptism produced spiritual rather than temporal liberation. Shyllon quotes Thomas Bluett stating in his

1734 volume about an African slave that the Bishop of London had declared that 'baptism made no sort of change in the political estate of a [Black]'. He also quotes a number of examples from Revd Morgan Godwyn, who has been mentioned earlier (see p. 16), describing how in 1680 many Africans then in Britain were denied baptism by their masters, who threatened clergy to prevent them baptising their slaves. In one case where a slave had the temerity to seek baptism his master immediately had him transported to America where, 'according to general custom there, he shall never more hear of Christianity'. Shyllon comments:

> There is a curious irony here. The English had sent missionaries to Africa to 'civilize' and baptise the 'savage' and 'heathen' Africans. . .. Now that black body-servants of planters and captains of slaving vessels were arriving in England, the 'civilized and Christian' country, they were hunted and hounded, tortured and turned out into the streets, or bundled into prisons for undergoing baptism and becoming full members of the Christian church. (p. 19)

These little difficulties were a modest sideshow, however, to the massive slave-trade as it grew up based in Bristol and Liverpool. While the history of that trade is not fundamental to the theme of this book, an understanding of its vast scale and the wealth built from it is necessary to comprehend the relationship today between white and black, particularly black people of African origin. Also, it was this trade which was indirectly responsible for African Caribbean people coming to Britain in the twentieth century – because they had no employment in the West Indies. Fryer describes in much detail the business enterprises in Bristol, Lancashire and London which grew from the wealth generated by the slave-trade. It is a salutary experience to read of them, to recognise the cruelty of the trade, the wealth it created from human suffering, the foundation it laid for British industrial development and the justification for it by all social institutions including the Church.

There is however some encouragement for Christians in that much of the opposition to slavery came also from Christians, black and white. The roots of Christian resistance to racism are important, reminding us of the message of the Gospel despite its being unheard by some of those prominent in the Church. In this chapter, after reminding ourselves of the nature of the slave trade, and the involvement of at least some supposed Christians in it, we shall examine some of the other parts played by Christians – primarily black ones – challenging racism, during the slave-trade and subsequently. Their role may become an inspiration as the struggle against racism continues in the present day.

Slavery and racism

Bristol was more or less built on the commerce in slaves and sugar. Its activity peaked in the 1730s, with up to fifty sailings a year, taking cheap manufactured goods to West Africa, then carrying as many as 17,000 slaves annually from there to the West Indies. An average profit from a voyage was £7,000 to £8,000, a princely sum in those days. Liverpool was founded on the trades in slaves and cotton, some of its proceeds being absorbed into the fledgling Manchester cotton industry. There are differing estimates as to the takings. One estimate puts Liverpool's proceeds between 1783 and 1793 at £12 million, though James Pope-Hennessy in *Sins of the Fathers* (1988) states:

> The net profit to the town of Liverpool on an aggregate of 303,737 slaves sold was almost three million pounds. . .. This was the golden harvest which accounts for all – for the fetid, feverish weeks on the African coast, for the vile and dangerous Atlantic crossing, for the sordid scramble in the Guinea-yard, for the callous division of Negro families. (p. 145–6)

Whether it was £12 million or £3 million, the extent of Liverpool's investment in the slave-trade was considerable, and outstripped that of Bristol and London.

> At this time in Liverpool there were ten merchant houses of major importance engaged in the slave trade, together with three hundred and forty-nine lesser concerns. . .. Shipbuilding in Liverpool was gloriously stimulated by the slave-trade. . .. Loaded shop-windows displayed shining chains and manacles, devices for forcing open Negroes' mouths when they refused to eat, neck-rings enhanced by long projecting prongs . . .. thumb-screws and all the other implements of torment and oppression. (Pope-Hennessy, p. 146)

In Bristol the clergy apparently got directly involved, and one observer commented in 1732 'the very Parsons at Bristol talk of nothing but Trade, and how to turn the Penny'.

Bristol parsons however did not have a monopoly. Liverpool Council actually commissioned a priest, Revd Raymund Harris, to write a pamphlet entitled *Scriptural Researches on the Licitness of the Slave-trade, shewing its conformity with the principles of natural and revealed religion, delineated in the sacred writings of the word of God*. It is quoted in Fryer as follows:

> As their 'most obedient And most humble Servant', Harris 'most respectfully inscribed' this work to the mayor, recorder, aldermen,

and bailiffs of the town. According to Harris, the trade was 'in perfect harmony with . . . the principles and decisions of the Word of God respecting *Right* and *Justice*'. Even in Liverpool it was just as well to know that God was on your side, and the council awarded the author £100 out of the public purse 'for his late excellent publication on the subject of the Slave Trade', in recognition of the 'advantages resulting to the town and trade of Liverpool from the said publication'. (p. 57)

In addition one of Liverpool's slave-captains had begun in the 1750s to study for the ministry. His name was John Newton and his writings give us a good deal of insight into slavery. He later wrote a number of well-known hymns, including 'Amazing Grace' and 'How Sweet the Name of Jesus Sounds'. Newton was reportedly converted in 1748, although he already had something of a religious background, but the fact that he was able to continue as a slave-captain for several more years after that date indicates the attitudes of most Christians of the time towards slavery. He kept journals, which became one of the most useful insights into the realities of the trade during the mid-eighteenth century. The journals have been edited by Bernard Martin and Mark Spurrell as *The Journal of a Slave Trader (John Newton): 1750–1754*. Among their quotations from the diaries are the following:

> 21st March 1753: [Newton] thanked God that he had been led into 'an easy and creditable way of life';

> 21st February 1754: after listing some of his blessings Newton wrote in his diary of the 'disadvantages of being obliged to pass so much of my time in this distasteful climate and employment';

> June 1756: he recorded how he had to leave the trade through illness, and wrote 'thus I was brought out of a way of life, disagreeable to my temper and inconvenient to my profession' (i.e. of the Christian faith). (p. xii)

In between these evolving entries Newton commits his voyages to God, holds public prayers on board, meditates on Sundays upon Holy Communion and undertakes daily personal prayer and Bible-reading. He appears to have been relatively humane as a captain and a slave-trader but that did not stop him putting Africans in irons to transport them, and using thumb-screws and neck-yokes on any caught plotting subversion.

Later he admits in his pamphlet *Thoughts upon the African Slave Trade* (1788) that the trade itself was bound to brutalise its participants. The pamphlet was written some thirty years after Newton had left slaving, when he was Rector of St Mary

Woolnoth in London, and was his effort to 'throw my mite into the public stock of information'. He did it so that those then debating the future of the trade would be better informed and 'this stain on our national character will soon be wiped out'.

Newton describes firstly the number of English seamen lost in slaving, and secondly 'the dreadful effects of the trade upon the minds of those who are engaged upon it', including the vicious behaviour of many of those involved. He only later gets onto the effect on the slaves themselves. Newton does however state his considered views that the Blacks – as he often calls them – are not inferior to Whites, and are sometimes superior. He says in his pamphlet 'I have lived long and conversed much, amongst these supposed savages', and goes on to describe how he has slept safely in an African village in a house filled with trade-goods but with no locked doors or guards. Again he says, the Africans, who do themselves have slaves, treat them fairly and are not allowed to injure them. On the other hand, 'our people' consider Africans as a people 'to be robbed and spoiled with impunity', and to be 'cheated in the number, weight, measure or quality of what they purchase, in every possible way'. Not only that, says Newton, in some areas of Africa the people have established a fair and just social order and although there are wars between the local peoples he believed that most of the wars would stop if the Europeans ceased to tempt Africans with the slave-trade.

In the body of his pamphlet John Newton goes on to recount the appalling means by which the slaves were transported. He perceives the object as being to cram as many in a ship as possible, but without threat to the crew and therefore locked together in irons. Up to a half died on the journey, he says, and even when they arrived in the West Indies their joy was short-lived as they were soon absorbed into the dreadful conditions of the plantations. He summarises the debate going on in Antigua at the time (1751) as to whether it was cheaper to treat slaves well so they worked on into old age, or to work them rigorously with a minimum of food when, if they died after a few years, they could be replaced with new ones. The planters apparently believed the latter more economic. This debate is also mentioned by Pope-Hennessy, who supplements Newton's account for us and quotes a doctor of the time recounting a method of slave-sale called the 'scramble', in which it is decided between captains and purchasers that all the 'Negroes' shall bear the same price.

> 'On a day appointed' [the doctor writes] 'the negroes were landed, and placed together in a large yard belonging to the merchants to whom the ship is consigned. As soon as the hour agreed on arrived, the doors of the yard were suddenly thrown open, and in rushed a considerable number of purchasers, with all the ferocity

of brutes.' The theory of the scramble was that any Negro, Negress or infant you could lay your hands on was yours to buy. 'Some instantly seized such of the negroes as they could conveniently lay hold of with their hands. Others being prepared with several hand-kerchiefs tied together, encircled with these as many as they were able. While others, by means of a rope, effected the same purpose. It is scarcely possible to describe the confusion of which this mode of selling is productive'. Violent quarrels among the purchasers broke out. The Negroes themselves were so appalled by this bestial onslaught that several clambered up the walls of the yard and 'ran wild about the town'. (p 106)

It was not only the selling which was utterly demeaning but the subsequent treatment of those who resisted. Pope-Hennessy quotes Sir Hans Sloane, 'eminent physician, botanist and creator of the Herb Garden in Chelsea', on slaves being castrated, whipped (followed by salt or melted wax being poured in the wounds), fitted with iron collars with inward-projecting spikes, thrown into vats of boiling cane juice or nailed to the ground and burned alive. Children who were deemed a nuisance were simply killed, with minimal punishment for the perpetrators, or even none at all.

Resistance to slavery – black and white

Someone who brings a contemporary Christian insight to bear on the slave system from the inside, as it were, is Olaudah Equiano, himself sold into slavery from what is today Nigeria. He spent some years in the West Indies then, obtaining his freedom, travelled to London where he spent most of his later life – although finding time and opportunity to visit the Caribbean, Canada and the Mediterranean. In 1789 when Equiano was about 45 he published his own life-story as part of the battle against slavery, which he opposed both as a Christian and because of his own personal history. He often uses the nominal Christianity of the slavers and planters to expose and challenge their activities.

In his book Equiano gives account of his capture, his journey on a slaver to Barbados, his purchase by an English naval officer, Captain Pascal, and his consequent further travels and experiences. One of his great complaints is that despite his having been a faithful servant to Pascal for a number of years, having even met some of Pascal's relations in England, and with finally some hopes of purchasing his freedom, Pascal sold him almost at a whim. He had to struggle again from nothing to earn his freedom, and then make his way to England to confront Pascal as to why he had used him so ill. He has better treatment from

Pascal's female relations who, when he gets to London, put him up and help him find employment in his free condition, a process which eventually leads to his writing his autobiography. This is now available, edited by Paul Edwards, as *The Life of Olaudah Equiano, or Gustavus Vassa the African, Written by Himself* (1989). Gustavus Vassa was a name given to Equiano by Captain Pascal.

Early in his account Equiano describes the 'scramble' in much the same terms as Pope-Hennessy, but adds a poignant personal anecdote to his account about two brothers, who had come on the same ship as himself, being sold to different owners. 'It was very moving on this occasion to see and hear their cries at parting. Oh, ye nominal Christians! might not an African ask you, learned you this from your God?' (p. 27). Equiano is clearly, despite his experiences – many of them at the hands of white Christians – himself becoming a Christian, and this makes his comments at different points of his story the more devastating. He remarks on the beatings given to slaves by their 'Christian masters', or supposedly 'Christian' sailors gratifying their passions on girls as young as ten, and on the Assembly of Barbados which decreed that

> if any man shall out of 'wantonness, or only of bloody-mindedness, or cruel intention, wilfully kill a negro . . . he shall pay into the public treasury fifteen pounds sterling . . .' And do not the assembly which enacted [this] deserve the appellation of savages and brutes rather than of Christians and men? (p. 73)

Equiano further details incidents in which he was cheated or abused by whites, describing them as 'these tender Christian depredators'.

When, despite the obstacles created by so-called Christians such as Captain Pascal, Equiano is finally able to buy his freedom, he likens it to Peter's deliverance from prison recorded in Acts 12. He goes on to describe his personal search for faith, which at one point included observing the practices of Muslim Turks. He seems almost to despair of Christianity, no doubt due to the many experiences of racism in the various stages of his life, experiences which lead to what Paul Edwards calls 'thinly concealed rage'. However he perseveres in his quest and in 1774, some years after he had become free, he begins to attend Westminster Chapel, still to be found in Buckingham Gate in central London. After initially being considered unready as a communicant he is finally accepted into the fellowship, and describes his experience as being 'born again'. He continually refers to the providence of God in his writings, and at one point visits the Bishop of London, seeking to become a missionary. But, despite commendations from those who thought this was the way forward for missionary work, Equiano reports – apparently ironically – that 'from certain scruples of delicacy, [the Bishop] refused to ordain me'.

Philip Quaque, born in Ghana in 1741 and brought to England in 1754 by the Society for the Propagation of the Gospel (SPG), was more fortunate. According to Folarin Shyllon, after being educated in Islington and then in 1759 baptised there, Quaque was ordained deacon by the Bishop of Exeter in 1765, then priest by the Bishop of London. He did not, however, serve the Church in Britain, but worked for the SPG in Ghana for the next fifty years.

Equiano concludes his extraordinary story with a Christian affirmation. He says 'I early accustomed myself to look for the hand of God in the minutest occurrence, and to learn from it a lesson of morality and religion.' He adds that, after all, the importance of any event is related to its teaching us 'to do justly, love mercy and walk humbly before God', quoting Micah 6, verse 8. The often negative or disinterested reactions Equiano received to his efforts to challenge slavery from both secular and religious quarters demonstrate the racism already active in English society, and makes his Christian commitment the more remarkable.

Another African writer on the slave trade was Ottobah Cugoano, whose 1787 work *Thoughts and Sentiments on the Evil of Slavery* was republished in 1969. It tells how men, women and children on their arrival in the colonies were stripped naked before the planters 'for the brutal examination of their purchases'. Fathers, mothers and children begged not to be separated. Cugoano was born about 1757 in a Fante village in what today is Ghana. Carried to Grenada in the West Indies at 13, he was eventually brought to England and set free in 1772. His book is sprinkled with biblical quotes and engages in theological argument on why there is no justification in the Bible regarding slavery (indeed he cites the opposite). He challenges both the idea that Africans as 'sons of Ham' are destined to be hewers of wood and drawers of water, and the idea that the 'mark of Cain' is upon Africans in any negative way. He offers his grateful thanks to God for his deliverance from slavery and the 'divine revelation of the only true God, and the saviour of men' (p. 13).

One group that may have been responsible for the degree to which ex-slaves became committed to the Christian faith, despite their experiences, was the Quakers. Towards the end of his autobiography Equiano describes a visit to some Quakers, with an address of thanks from the 'poor, oppressed, needy and much-degraded Negroes' for their benevolence and labour in seeking to break the yoke of slavery and 'to administer a little comfort and ease to thousands and tens of thousands of very grievously afflicted, and too heavy-burdened Negroes'. Both Fryer and Pope-Hennessy also draw attention to the importance of the Quaker role in seeking to abolish slavery. Quakers presented the first anti-slavery petition to Parliament in 1783. However, Fryer also points out that thirty years earlier, in Bristol, there were as many as 84 Quaker slave-traders. Among them were Alexander and David Barclay, who partly from their earnings created what has since become a large and well-established international bank.

In May 1787 a Committee for the Abolition of Slavery was set up in London, and according to Pope-Hennessy all but three of its members were Quakers. One of the three non-Quakers, and perhaps the most able and effective of the whole group, was Thomas Clarkson who, having won a prize at Cambridge for a Latin essay on slavery, decided to give up his own clerical career and seek a solution to the problem posed by his own essay. Clarkson and his Quaker friends expended enormous amounts of energy, overcoming the opposition of merchants, bankers, ship-owners and much of the Church and State, in order to abolish slavery. Wilberforce took much of the limelight, but Pope-Hennessy believed it was Clarkson who was the driving force and the true radical, highlighting also his links with the emerging working-class movement, and his support for the aims of the French Revolution.

It is of some encouragement to note that, despite the silence of much of the Church on slavery, or even its tacit support, at least some Methodist missionaries in the West Indies did have ideas of undermining the slave system. Certainly John Wesley – influenced by the Quakers – opposed it. Pope-Hennessy believed the Methodists were stirred up partly because, in islands where Roman Catholicism held sway, slaves were better treated, being given Saturday to do their own work and Sunday to rest and worship. However, the Methodists were resented by the planters 'who feared that their doctrine that all men were equal before God would disturb the uneducated mass of Negro slaves' (p. 131). This belief in equality, and its practical outworking, was one of the factors that led eventually to the destruction of the slave system. It must be noted however that in *Capitalism and Slavery*, published in 1944, Eric Williams – later to become President of Trinidad – argued strongly that slavery largely defeated itself, for economic reasons and because the slaves themselves undermined it. Equiano makes a similar argument in his book; the abolitionists in their campaigning were simply riding the tide of history. Either way it is a very sorry period in the history of the countries of western Europe, and their 'Christian' civilisation.

A fundamental and contemporary question

One conundrum we are inescapably left with is that which Pope-Hennessy raises towards the end of *Sins of the Fathers*, 'How was it that cultivated and literate Europeans – professing Christians at that – could totally blind themselves to the foul nature of their profession?' (p. 262). He points out that even those who participated in the trade, and later became active Christians, give little clue; 'John

Newton's journal, memoirs and letters provide no answer to this basic question'. That is largely true. The nearest Newton gets is to plead an early life of 'difficulties and hardships', when he was almost a slave himself, and a degree of ignorance, 'the slave-trade was always unjustifiable, but inattention and interest prevented for a time the evil from being perceived' (p. 100).

Equiano does not help us greatly here. He has his tongue in his cheek from time to time as he refers to 'European superiority' and how the whites failed to give the Africans a chance by teaching them and educating them into their own knowledge and skills. He satirically urges Europeans to remember that their ancestors were once 'like the Africans, uncivilized and even barbarous', and asks if therefore *they* should have been made slaves:

> Every rational mind answers, No. Let such reflections as these melt the pride of [European] superiority into sympathy for the wants and miseries of their sable brethren, and compel them to acknowledge, that understanding is not confined to feature or colour. (p. 14)

Equiano pursues a kind of moral investigation, without ever really asking Pope-Hennessy's sharp question. It is to Cugoano we must turn for a more penetrating analysis. He challenges the falsities which underlie the philosophy justifying the trade, and which pretend that 'Africans in general are a set of poor, ignorant, dispersed, unsociable people, and they think it no crime to sell one another, and even their own wives and children' and that they want 'a better state than ever they could obtain in their own native country'. Cugoano believes this 'specious pretence is without any shadow of justice and truth' (p. 21).

Cugoano goes even further than accusations of lying and suggests that, far from black people being the devil as many whites believed, the reverse is true, at least of those engaged in the slave-trade.

> When I meet with those who make no scruple to deal with the human species as with the beasts of the earth, I must think them not only brutish but wicked and base . . . and if such men can boast of greater degrees of knowledge than any African is entitled to, I shall let them enjoy all the advantage of it unenvied, as I fear it consists only in a greater share of infidelity and that of a blacker kind than only skin deep. And if their complexion be not what I suppose it is at least the nearest in resemblance to an infernal hue. (p. 5)

Cugoano is clearly saying that the ideology of those who gained from slavery (which he later defines as all Britons) is the real evil, and that that ideology contains a very substantial dose of racism.

He is also devastating in his remarks about the failure of white Christians to live up to their calling. He writes of the wickedness of white people, who contrary to Scripture have 'endeavoured to keep the Black People in total ignorance as much as they can, which must be a great dishonour to any Christian government'. He believes an end to slavery would open up the way to a Christian world, for 'while the horrible traffic of slavery is admitted and practised, there can be but little hope of any good proposals meeting with success anywhere'. Were it abolished and 'the righteous laws of Christianity, equity, justice and humanity established in the room thereof, multitudes of nations would flock to the standard of truth . . . and count it their greatest happiness to be under the protection and jurisdiction of a righteous government' (p. 143).

The importance of racism in the intellectual underpinning of the slave-trade must not be underestimated. Fryer notes how fortuitous it was that in 1774, just as the British were beginning to set up the colonial system, Edward Long's *History of Jamaica* should appear – a book Fryer describes as pivotal in the turn to 'pseudo-scientific racism'. He quotes Long's reasons for his support for black slavery:

> That the trade in slaves and in goods produced by slaves was immensely profitable, not only to the West Indies, but to Britain itself, and that it greatly enriched Englishmen in all walks of life; that West Indian slavery was on the whole a mild and benevolent institution, and that slaves were better off than the lowest classes in Britain; that Negro slavery was inevitable and necessary in certain regions of the world; that the slave-trade benefited and helped civilize Africa; that virtually all the slaves were originally convicted criminals; that in every mental and moral way Negroes were absolutely inferior to white men, and that the most constructive thing which could happen to them was to be compelled to work productively. (Fryer, p.160)

Fryer adds drily that Long only missed out two arguments, the economic one that if Britain did not do it other European nations would fill the gap and take the profit, and the religious one, that black people were the cursed children of Ham.

Long's attitudes were formative for the racism that undergirded Britain's policies and activities towards its colonial peoples for nearly two hundred years. There were other supporters for them: the Swedish biologist Linnaeus, the German medical professor Blumenbach, the Dutch anatomist Camper and the Manchester physician Charles White. Fryer quotes White in a lecture stating that the white European is the 'most beautiful' of humans; 'No-one will doubt his superiority in intellectual powers; and I believe it will be found his capacity is naturally superior also to that of every other man' (p. 168). Such views speak for themselves.

Beliefs like these shore up and help to maintain the lack of concern felt by most Europeans today over the shameful and vicious inequalities of the modern world. Shyllon makes a revealing and specific link between the attitudes that sprang up around the slave-trade, and immigration policies in modern times:

> The undeniable truth is that racism has been a way of life ever since the first black arrived in Britain. The fact of the matter was that, when the importation of blacks into England had reached substantial proportions, men were proposing the same panacea as today to combat the Black Peril. Then, as now, Government was urged to stop further immigration or, more precisely, further importation of blacks into the country. Then, as now, Government was urged to introduce fiscal measures to get rid of the blacks already here, and stem the flow into the country of those still out- side. And twice, in 1596 and 1786, blacks were actually expelled. (p. 105)

In the context of current attitudes to black families already here, and to asylum- seekers and refugees, Pope-Hennessy's penetrating question as to how a supposedly Christian society could fail to see the oppression and exploitation of slavery has a decidedly contemporaneous ring.

Black communities in Britain

It was the growth of the black communities, of both slaves and free men and women from the late seventeenth century onwards, particularly in Bristol, Liverpool and London, which led to the beginnings of mutual self-help among the nascent black population. Perhaps it was these signs of independence which led to the anxieties of the white authorities. Indian servants and 'ayahs', or nannies, began to be brought back by British families who had been in India. Lascars, or seamen, were also used by the East India Company and others to provide cheap crews for ships from Asia, and then dumped here after their ships unloaded.

By the late eighteenth century there were an estimated 15,000 to 20,000 black people in England. London's black community was involved in discussion groups about its own situation and in organising social events with entertain- ment in London's taverns. English racists were complaining about the 'incredible number' of black people, who had clubs to support those who were 'out of place', i.e. unemployed.

Black people were normally, of course, in service. Occasionally they aspired, or were encouraged, to seek more independent work, so that as early as 1731 London's Lord Mayor had to issue a Court Order forbidding black apprentices. African and Asian women became house-maids, seamstresses, nannies and laundry-maids; some were forced into prostitution. Black people soon found opportunities for a better life by becoming entertainers and musicians; as long as two hundred years ago regimental bands had their black drummers and trumpeters. Even for blacks who sought this path to security, racism reared its ugly head – although not without resistance. Fryer reports:

> An anecdote tells how a black military bandsman was strolling down the Strand when he was accosted with the question: 'Well, blackie, what news from the devil?' He knocked the questioner down, remarking 'He send you that – how you like it?' (p. 88)

Leadership which developed in the new black community in Britain was often Christian-inspired. Ottobah Cugoano was advised to get baptised so he could not be enslaved again. His writings typified the new spirit of independence. He declared that black slaves had not only the moral right but the moral duty to resist, and he pointed the finger of judgement at every man in Britain, especially those of eminence and power such as nobles and clergy. Cugoano was the first African to demand the total abolition of slavery, a position hardly any white abolitionist had taken. Towards the end of his life he announced his intention to open a school 'for all such of his Complexion as are desirous of being acquainted with the knowledge of the Christian Religion and the Laws of Civilization' (p. 177).

The presence of black people in Britain has been a long one. Their activity as a community began centuries ago and they were vigorous from that time both in opposing slavery and racism, and in demanding equality. This resistance to the oppression which was propagated under the auspices of the British Empire continued into the present century. In *Staying Power* Peter Fryer recounts the stories of five black people who kept alive the legacies of such as Cugoano and Equiano. William Cuffay was born in Chatham in 1788 and after becoming a leader of the Chartist movement was transported for life to Tasmania. Mary Seacole, born in Kingston, Jamaica in about 1805, sought like Florence Nightingale to become a nurse in the Crimea in the 1850s. Ira Aldridge was born the son of a minister in New York in 1807 and despite racist reviews became a famous actor on the London stage. Samuel Coleridge-Taylor was a great musician, born in Holborn in 1875, who died at the tragically young age of 37; his compositions were greatly praised by Elgar among others. Born in Bombay in 1825, Dadabhai Naoroji became the first Asian elected to the British Parliament in 1882.

The story of Mary Seacole, a quite remarkable woman, is told in her autobiography, *The Wonderful Adventures of Mrs Seacole in Many Lands*, first published in 1857 and edited by Ziggi Alexander and Audrey Dewjee for its second edition in 1984. She travelled widely, coming twice to Britain, and opening a hotel in Panama, before returning via Jamaica to Britain in 1854. She fought for official sanction to go and assist the injured and sickly soldiers of the Crimea, but was refused. Eventually, aged 50, she set up a business with a relative, bought medicines and home comforts and opened the 'British Hotel' between Balaklava and Sebastopol in 1855. Fryer says that almost the entire British army soon knew of 'Mother Seacole's', where you might get everything from 'an anchor down to a needle'. The soldiers were her 'sons' and she was their 'mother'. She often went out under fire to minister to wounded troops, and was made famous by a war correspondent who recounted her work in some of his reports.

Mrs Seacole was the first woman to enter Sebastopol when it fell and she ministered to injured troops there. There is little in her book which gives a clue to her motivation, but it appears to have had a religious basis. She speaks of her conversations with young soldiers about to go into battle, and although they spoke lightly, at bottom she knew they were serious. 'I felt it to be so, for I never failed (although who was I, that I should preach?) to say something about God's providence and relying upon it; and they were very good . . . they would listen very gravely' (p. 191). This is one of the few glimpses into what inspired this extraordinary woman. When she returned to Britain bankrupt, senior Crimean veterans organised a four-day musical festival in her honour and for her pocket at the Royal Surrey Gardens in Kennington.

Phyllis Wheatley, who was born in West Africa around 1753, also made an impact on the anti-slavery struggle. She arrived in England in 1772 and her poem 'Hymn to Humanity' was published in the London daily *The Diary* two days after Wilberforce moved his first Commons motion against the slave trade. Women were therefore among those who contributed to the development of black identity and organisation in eighteenth- and nineteenth-century Britain, and some were prompted by Christian teaching.

Naoroji, the first black British MP, demonstrates the contribution which Asians began to make to nineteenth-century British society. He came to Britain in 1855 and was appointed Professor of Gujerati at University College, London. Fryer's account tells of how he also set up his own business, began to 'agitate against the discriminatory system of recruitment to the Indian Civil Service' and in 1865 helped to form the London Indian Society. He first fought a parliamentary seat in 1886, and although he had to put up with racist opposition even within his own party he won Finsbury Central for the Liberals in 1892.

There were other Asians who had cultural and political contributions to make to British life who visited the country for short periods but, according to Fryer, they never really liked it here. Among the reasons may be the attitudes which led the then Prime Minister, Lord Salisbury, to say of Naoroji, 'I doubt we have yet got to that point of view where a British constituency would elect a black man' – a remark which may well have got him elected – and Sir William Lee-Warner, a former Secretary in the India Office, to refer to a young Indian radical in the 1905 discussion on India's future as a 'dirty nigger' (Fryer, p. 268).

One Indian who made an impact on English society was Sake Deen Mahomed. He became an officer in the East India Regiment in 1780, came to England, settled near Cork in Ireland, and married a local girl. In 1801 he moved to Brighton, then a health resort, and after some setbacks set up 'Indian baths' which specialised in treatment of rheumatism. He was given a seal of approval by King George IV as his 'shampooing surgeon', published a book in 1822 and was buried in Brighton in 1851. Mahomed's story is told in *Ayahs, Lascars and Princes* (1986) by Rozina Visram.

Most of those coming from the Indian Sub-Continent during this period were servants. As early as 1709 an advertisement appeared in a London newspaper stating that 'A black Indian Boy, 12 years of Age, fit to wait on a Gentleman', was to be 'disposed of' in Finch Lane. There are other such adverts, for the purchase or sale of servants, or for news of those who had escaped. Queen Victoria was herself interested in Indians, and had several Indian attendants and an Indian teacher, Abdul Karim.

One particular group of Indians popular among the emerging English middle classes were nannies or 'ayahs'. Many were brought back by families of soldiers or merchants who had lived in India. Only too typically some of the ayahs, as well as servants, sailors and seamen, were left destitute in the streets of London when their services were no longer required. Visram quotes the concerns of missionaries who worked for the London City Mission, and sought to alleviate some of the misery. She quotes one Joseph Salter, writing in the *London City Mission Magazine* in 1858:

> At one house I found 28 ayahs. . ... The boxes of the ayahs generally form their bedstead, and they are all placed close together, to prevent them rolling out. The parlour with a shopfront has lost its door but its absence in supplied by a screen. . . . There have been windows in the door, but they have all been broken in the drunken riots of the ayahs.

The cost of this palatial accommodation was 16 shillings a week, no mean sum, and those who could not pay it were thrown out onto the streets. The London City Mission itself eventually set up a home for ayahs.

The situation for Asians on London's streets in the nineteenth century was similar in some respects to that of today. Henry Mayhew (1861) quotes an Indian street musician he interviewed, who stated: 'I put up many insult in dis countree. I struck sometime in street. Magistrate punish man dat left mark on my chin here. . .. De boys call me black dis or de oder' (quoted in Fryer).

There were protests from the enlightened establishment about the dumping of poor Asians and their treatment on the streets. However as the century progressed so did some Asians. Indian students began to arrive. Some were very well received but others left Britain seared with what one called 'that cold aloofness which is ladled out with spoonfuls and condescension to those like me who do not belong to a pure white race' (quoted in Visram, p. 26).

There were other politicians too. Mancherjee Bhownagree came to Lincoln's Inn to study law. After returning home for a time he settled permanently in England in 1891, and in 1895 won the Bethnal Green parliamentary seat for the Conservative Party. Bhownagree was knighted in 1897, and retained his parliamentary seat until the Liberal landslide in 1905. Sharpurji Saklatvala was born in Bombay in 1874 and educated at a Jesuit college. He came to Britain in 1905, joined the Independent Labour Party and then the Communists. In 1922 he won Battersea North for Labour, lost it, and in 1924 won it back as a Communist. He campaigned for Indian and British working-class emancipation until his death in 1936. Naoroji, Bhownagree and Saklatvala are perhaps the best known of many from the Indian Sub-Continent who have made forceful contributions to British public life in the last 150 years.

Another commentator on English life around the turn of the century was Cornelia Sorabji, who came as the first woman law student in an English university to Somerville College, Oxford, in 1889. She wrote a book about her experiences, *India Calling*, published in 1934. She was the daughter of Revd Sorabji Karsedji, a Parsi convert to Christianity, who maintained his family's commitment to Indian language and culture, Cornelia continuing to wear her sari. She wrote of being occasionally assailed by dear old ladies trying to convert her in 'Pidgin-English' – '"Calcutta Come?", "Bombay Come?"'. 'Only once', she says, 'did I try to undeceive a proselytising old lady. She regarded me reproachfully, "But you look so very heathen"!'. Ms Sorabji also had a revealing encounter with a local clergyman when she was in England during the Boer War. After a church meeting he came to visit her.

He advanced with arms outstretched, 'It's so good to see you', he said, 'so like Home!'. I'd never seen the man before, and said, 'Do you know India?'. 'No! But it's so like Home to see you. I've been working among the Coolies in South Africa!'

In a wider context there are a number of historical figures with African or Asian blood who are not often recognised as such. Some – men *and* women – are documented in *The World's Great Men of Color* (1946) by J.A. Rogers, and include St Benedict, Alexander Pushkin, possibly Beethoven, Alexandre Dumas (*père*) and Alexandre Dumas (*fils*), Robert Browning, Makeda (Queen of Sheba), Cleopatra and Nzingha, warrior Queen of Matamba in Angola. Hence people from Asia and Africa have been making a contribution to Britain and the wider world for centuries, and at every level. Folarin Shyllon wrote in 1977 that black people would

> march prospering whatever the obstacles . . .. Even if our petty bour-
> geois disown us, or criticise or denounce us. . . we will march on.
> They are the pimps and the slaves. We who have assumed the awe-
> some task and burden of black liberation are the free men. (p. 220)

Into the twentieth century

The black communities in some of Britain's major cities therefore had a history of at least two hundred years behind them when the nineteenth century came to an end. In the last section of this chapter we take a few glimpses from a Christian perspective into black contributions to Britain since 1900, and into the reactions to them.

When the 1914–18 war broke out black people found themselves welcome in Britain for the first time. They were needed in the chemical and munitions factories, in addition to the armed forces. Soldiers from Africa and the Caribbean fought on many fronts. The British West Indies regiment, whose rank and file were almost entirely black, lost 1,250 men and were awarded over sixty medals. Some 1,400 black seamen from Cardiff were lost at sea, or died as a result of exposure, during the conflict. Rosina Visram recounts some of the contributions of Indian soldiers in Europe's wars, including the 1.4 million troops who fought in the 1914–18 war, numbers second only to those from Britain itself. More than 64,000 lost their lives and twelve won Victoria Crosses. In his *India in Britain* (1984) Kusoom Vadgama describes both the contribution of India to the war, in terms of soldiers and finance, and the life in the Brighton Hospital where, he says, many Indian soldiers died of their wounds. There is a shrine at Patcham to the memory of Sikh and Hindu soldiers where, according to Vadgama, there is a unique annual pilgrimage and memorial service, led by the vicar of Patcham.

Indians also made a major contribution to the Allies' fighting forces in the 1939–45 war. According to Vadgama there were 2.5 million volunteers, the largest voluntary army ever formed. By 1945 over 36,000 were killed or missing, 64,000 had been wounded and 80,000 taken prisoner. Thirty were awarded VCs, and Vadgama has a photograph of three of them arriving at Buckingham Palace in 1945 for their presentations, surrounded by admirers.

Sadly black people's sacrifices towards winning the 1914–18 war were soon forgotten, as they were later, in 1945. Black seamen were no longer required, and some from other parts of the empire were left stranded in Britain without the means to return home. In 1919 riots took place in Tyneside, and then in Liverpool, where over 500 black servicemen were stranded. In the latter city many black people were forced from homes and seamen's hostels: the reporting in the *Liverpool Courier* about 'pimps and bullies' was similar to that in some of the British press today. An editorial at the time of the troubles is quoted by Peter Fryer, saying that 'the average Negro is nearer the animal than is the average white man', and that whites 'regard [the black man] as part-child, part-animal, and part-savage'. Also 'many of the blacks in Liverpool are of a low type . . . they insult and threaten respectable women in the street, and are invariably unpleasant and provocative' (p. 302).

Ernest Marke, whose memoirs of seventy years in England, *Troubled Waters*, were published in 1986, and who died in 1995, was in Liverpool as a young man at the time of the 1919 racial attacks. He reports a conversation with an older black man who tells him, 'We should have let them fight their own war. . . . Whether they is Germans, English or even Turks they all got white skins'. His friend concludes:

> If you should walk out of this room right now together with a German and meet one of them gangs outside. . . they'll beat the hell out o'you, and let the German go. They wouldn't want to know whether you fought in the bloody army, navy or flying co. You know why, Buster? it's because you're black, black! (p. 29)

Marke later describes the aftermath of the riots and how three police officers beat him up and brought false charges against him. He defends himself, persuades the judge and the jury, and is acquitted. Much of his anger is dissipated by two old white ladies who patted him on the back, said 'God bless you son', and stuffed five pounds in his pocket.

Fighting also took place in Newport and Cardiff in South Wales. Here the black community had to face the ransacking and burning of houses, gunfire from white ex-servicemen and beating by mobs in the streets. Fryer reports that there was a much more determined and organised attack on Cardiff's black community over several days, and that the whole of the city's police force was concentrated in the cordoned-off area that *The Times* actually referred to as 'nigger town'. Apparently soldiers from the Welsh Regiment were secretly drafted into the city as a precaution.

There was also a serious riot in Cable Street in Stepney, East London. The *Manchester Guardian*, pontificating about the riots, blamed black people for seeking to defend themselves against what almost amounted to lynch-mobs. Perhaps the final straw came for blacks when, despite their war-time sacrifices, it was decided no black troops should be allowed to participate in the July 1919 'Victory Parades'. Decisions like this were fuelled by attitudes such as those of Sir Ralph Williams, former governor of the Windward Islands, who justified the attacks on black people in a letter to *The Times*, stating that

> to almost every white man and woman who has lived a life among coloured races, intimate association between black or coloured men and white women is a thing of horror . . ., what blame . . . to those white men who, seeing these conditions and loathing them, resort to violence?

It seems that those with influence and wealth in whatever century have taken the same attitude to black people when the need for servants, labour or cannon fodder was satiated.

During the early decades of this century certain Churches were beginning to ponder together around racial questions faced by the missionary societies abroad. In 1910 a World Missionary Conference was held in Edinburgh, and J.H. Oldham was appointed Secretary of the Conference of British Missionary Societies (CBMS). After a series of meetings and correspondence with Dr Norman Leys, who had been dismissed by the Colonial Office for criticising its activities after 16 years practising in East Africa, Oldham began – from the headquarters of the CBMS then set up in London's Sloane Square – to raise these activities with the Government.

Revd Elliott Kendall, writing about Oldham, says that he found himself in the forefront of the movement in London to oppose labour policies in East Africa, by bringing pressure to bear on Government and educating public opinion. By so doing he created a prestigious position for the Conference of British Missionary Societies which, says Kendall, was subsequently to be exercised with considerable effectiveness on issues of justice in the world.

The Church campaign finally bore fruit, and the Government accepted that when African interests and those of British settlers in East Africa conflicted, 'the former should prevail'. Perhaps it was easier for the Churches to champion black interests in Kenya than in Liverpool or Leeds. Any opposition they offered to the first immigration legislation in 1905 was ineffective. Steve Cohen in his booklet *From the Jews to the Tamils* (1988) points out that our present immigration laws were largely shaped through the experience of legislation which sought to keep out Jewish refugees earlier this century. He comments: 'The first ever comprehensive immigration controls, the 1905 Aliens Act, were enacted precisely to deny entrance to Jewish refugees fleeing pogroms (massacres) and discriminatory legislation in Russia and Eastern Europe' (p. 12). It was some decades later that similar forms of exclusion began to be applied to black people.

Meantime, however, students had become one of the largest groups of the population originating from outside Britain. Visram recounts in *Ayahs, Lascars and Princes* how young Indians wishing to become part of the civil service in their own country had to journey to England. This process brought, among others, Gandhi, Nehru and his daughter Indira Gandhi, to study in London. By the beginning of the twentieth century there were around 500 Indian students here – remembering that until independence in 1948 India also included Pakistan and Bangladesh. By 1930 the largest group of overseas students in British universities was from India, 1,800 out of over 5,000. Associations were set up, both in particular universities and nationally.

Many Indian and African students did experience racism. According to Visram they found that 'being looked down upon as a "black man", or otherwise insulted and abused, was a common experience'. When an Indian student was elected President of the Oxford Union one London newspaper commented that the office was no longer what it had been. Even D. H. Lawrence, supposedly progressive in other ways, wrote in 1916

> I become more and more surprised to see how far higher, in reality,
> our European civilisation stands than the East. . . has ever dreamed
> of. And one is glad to *realise* how these Hindus are horribly decadent
> and reverting to all forms of barbarism in all sorts of ugly ways.

Lawrence made these comments after being decidedly unimpressed when Rabindranath Tagore won the 1913 Nobel Prize for Literature. Such experiences and attitudes did not bode well for the creation of a genuinely multiracial society as more and more students, soldiers and workers arrived in Britain.

However, black people were here to stay, and that included participation in public life. One successful initiative was the 'League of Coloured Peoples' created by Congregationalist Dr Harold Moody. Moody came to Britain in 1904 from Jamaica, aged 22, to study medicine at King's College, London. After qualifying in 1910 he found getting work very difficult due to his colour. He remained a committed Christian and although an effective public speaker he prayed before each meeting and offered his speech to God. He became chair of the Colonial Missionary Society in 1921 and later president of the London Christian Endeavour Federation. He used these to assist black people who, due to racism, were finding it hard to get lodgings or work. He built up a network of other successful middle-class blacks, and with some of them formed the League in 1931. Its aims, quoted from David Vaughan's biography of Moody, *Negro Victory* (1950), were:

> To promote and protect the Social, Educational, Economic and Political Interests of its members; To interest members in the Welfare of Coloured Peoples in all parts of the World; To improve relations between the Races; and To co-operate and affiliate with organisations sympathetic to Coloured People. In 1937 a fifth aim was added, To render such financial assistance to coloured people in distress as lies within our capacity. (p. 55)

Moody toured England, speaking mostly on Church platforms and pointing out the contribution black people would make to British society, if given a chance. When he heard of the state of black people in Cardiff in the mid-1930s he called for opportunities for employment and training, especially for black teenagers. He commented: 'the economic condition of our people in Cardiff is simply appalling and it is to be hoped that the Government and city authorities will quite soon apply themselves seriously to this problem'. He noted that the Churches were working in the area and he had tried 'so far without avail, to awaken the Christian conscience of our organised religion to tackle this human problem' (p. 79).

Moody goes on to say that he is not asking for money. His fellow countrymen have their pride, and 'it is the urgent duty of the Christian Church to make a real study of the spiritual, social and economic conditions of the coloured people in this country with a view to providing an effective solution'. If it does not, it is failing to solve 'this pressing problem of race'.

Moody continued his campaigning for equal treatment both during and after the war. In 1940 he had a long letter published in *The Times* which later became a pamphlet entitled *Racial Freedom – British Tradition and the Colour Bar*. In it Moody attacks the 'Nazi creed of racial discrimination' and points to the Christian basis of what he believes to be a British commitment to equality:

> The true British tradition is a Christian tradition and the prejudice which erects a colour bar or prompts racial exclusiveness is a

denial of Christian principles. Fundamental to any Christian view is the conviction that God is the Father of all men and that Christ died for all. In the Christian fellowship all racial barriers are done away – 'Ye are all one in Christ Jesus'. (quoted in Vaughan, p. 114)

For his statement Moody obtained the support of all the major Christian leaders of his time. His biographer Vaughan writes, 'the League [of Coloured Peoples] was his life. . . and he was the life of the League'. And so it was until his death in 1947.

Although criticised by whites and even black radicals, and never reaching more than 300 in membership, the League did have some influence. In 1940 Moody took on the BBC over the use of the word 'nigger', bringing forth an apology. Not all was victory, however. One of the League's Bulletin editors, Peter Blackman, having come to Britain to study theology, experienced racist attitudes in the Church of England. He left the Church and turned to Marxism. There was therefore, in a variety of forms, a small but partly politically-aware black presence already in Britain when the new wave of immigration began, by invitation, in 1948. There was also a long experience of white racism, even in those institutions which by their calling should have known a lot better.

The sense of determination and adventure required to leave one's homeland for another some 5,000 miles away, not knowing either what was at the other end or whether one would ever return, should not be underestimated. Behind the statistics of the early arrivals from the Caribbean around 1950 lies much anguish, separation and in some cases eventual desolation. The kind of atmosphere on the boats is very well captured in George Lamming's novel *The Emigrants* (1980), which traces the experience of some of the early arrivals. The single member of the group of men who has a clear plan about what he is going to do in England (though it soon falls through) is Higgins.

> The men shook their heads in a mutual acknowledgement of Higgins' good fortune. For the first time they seemed a little uneasy about the future. Higgins was the only one who knew with any certainty what was going to happen to him. He made it clear in any conversation because he wanted them to feel the same. . ... He was afraid for those who didn't know what they were going to do in England. . ... A silence had fallen over them. (p. 71)

The one man who has been in been in England before warns the others of what to expect. In England people do not notice one another; whether hungry or rich they keep it to themselves.

> You see this the minute you put foot in London. The way the houses build was the people doan' have nothing to do with one

another. You can live an' die in yuh room an' the people next door never say boo to you no matter how long you inhabit that place. It ain't like home. (p. 75)

Nevertheless, for many from the West Indies there was no other choice.

The first five years of immigration brought less than 6,000 West Indians, although there was a demand for their labour and at that point a certain kind of welcome on the mat. Subsequently the rate rose to about 20,000 a year and by 1958 those who had come totalled about 125,000. London Transport had begun recruiting in Barbados in 1956 and Britain was eagerly welcoming doctors and nurses from India and the Caribbean. Mr Enoch Powell, who was later to make such political capital out of immigration, was a Conservative Minister in 1956-7, and again in 1960-63. Neither as a Minister nor when outside the Government did Powell oppose immigration at that time, according to Paul Foot in *The Rise of Enoch Powell* (1969). Between 1960 and 1963 Powell more than once paid tribute to the contribution of overseas doctors and nurses to British hospitals. 'During Powell's régime at the Ministry of Health, Health Service recruitment drives for doctors and nurses in the West Indies and from India and Pakistan were not slowed down in any way' (Foot, p. 38). It seems that only when racism became politically opportune did Mr Powell take up immigration issues.

By the mid-1960s some 50,000 Commonwealth citizens a year were arriving. Some were from the Indian Sub-Continent, perhaps 55,000 by 1958. All were British citizens by the 1948 Nationality Act, having the right to come to Britain and stay if they wished for the rest of their lives. They came of course because there was insufficient work at home, and no unemployment benefit. A quarter were non-manual workers, and nearly half were skilled labourers; only a comparative few had no skills. They arrived to face racism, in a variety of manifestations, from employers, landlords, unions, the Churches and the general public. Not all had such negative experiences but certainly many Christians – Baptist, Methodist, Anglican, Catholic, Moravian, Presbyterian – were unpleasantly surprised to face reactions in local churches which ranged from a grudging welcome to a request never to come back again.

The new wave of racial attacks on black people – the worst since 1919 – began in 1958, though there were then still less than 200,000 in the entire country. Nottingham and north-west London were worst hit, mostly by young white fascists on the rampage. There were voices of reason. Fryer quotes Tom Driberg MP, Anglican and Chairman of the Labour Party, who told the 1958 Trades Union Congress,

People talk about a colour problem arising in Britain. How can there be a colour problem here? Even after all the immigration of the past few years, there are only 190,000 coloured people in our population of over 50 million – that is, only four out of every thousand. The real problem is not black skins, but white prejudice. (p. 380)

But these voices could not really expect to be heard in the already-disadvantaged communities where the newcomers sought the necessary cheap accommodation. David Mason of the Methodist Team Ministry set up in Notting Hill in the early 1960s wrote in *News from Notting Hill* (1967) that the increasing number of West Indians and Africans, coming into the area between 1950 and 1960, created apprehension and prejudice. He said that the basic factors sparking off the August 1958 race riots were:

(1) The failure of the local community to make the necessary emotional and practical adjustments to take into its system thousands of newcomers from overseas.

(2) Bad housing, high rents, Rachmanism projected – wrongly – on the West Indian.

(3) Racial prejudice – as deep rooted in Britain as anywhere else.

(4) Smear propaganda of the lunatic fringe of the British political underworld. (p. 7)

Through the following months there was street-fighting, attacks on black cafes and other meeting places, racist graffiti on the walls and considerable tension in local communities. The attacks finally brought a death. In May 1959 Kelso Cochrane, a West Indian carpenter, was stabbed in the chest beneath a railway bridge by a gang of white youths; his murderers were never found. It was these events that brought into being the Notting Hill Team Ministry, which was perhaps the first serious attempt at a fresh form of urban mission in the new multicultural British society.

David Mason describes the initial effort to haul the small local Methodist community around to see the missionary opportunities on their doorstep.

There were thousands of West Africans and West Indians living in Notting Hill; hundreds of them were Methodists. Although a small minority had always attended the Sunday services, there had been no great influx of new members, as there should have been. . . .. A systematic visitation campaign was begun. . . .. The Minister ransacked the church vestry for clues to any immigrant families with whom the local Church had contact, but who had drifted away.

> Sunday School parents were called on. Lay people undertook to get
> to know particular West Indian families. . ... Two rather shabby
> vestries were redecorated and equipped to form one large church
> office open every morning . . . this proved an essential factor in the
> work. Everyone knew that the church office was manned, the door
> open and so they called in. (p. 15)

His account goes on to describe the various initiatives which took place – the
Adventure Playground, the Social Council, the Housing Trust, a psychiatric
patients' club and the Portobello Coffee-Bar Project. The congregation also grew,
both in numbers and variety of nationalities.

While this kind of activity was developing at local level the 1962 Immigration
Bill was brought in, despite a rearguard action by black organisations and campaigns like Fenner Brockway's 'Movement for Colonial Freedom'. This
confirmed the second-class status of black people, and gave 'carte blanche', as it
were, to employers, agitators and even the police to put black people in what
fearful and ignorant whites felt was their place. Peter Fryer says the police also
felt liberated. Previously they had to appear neutral. Now they could go 'nigger-
hunting'.

> In December 1963 the British West Indian Association com-
> plained of increasing police brutality stemming from the passing of
> the Commonwealth Immigrants Act. In 1964 the Pakistani com-
> munity alleged that the wrists of Pakistani immigrants were being
> stamped with indelible ink at a police station in the course of a
> murder investigation. (p. 391)

It was soon after this that the 1964 General Election took place and Peter
Griffiths won Smethwick for the Conservatives on the slogan 'If you want a nigger neighbour, vote Labour'. Labour won the election but although it soon
passed a 'Race Relations Act' which sought 'conciliation' for racial discrimination in a public place, and set up the National Committee for Commonwealth
Immigrants and the Race Relations Board, to many it was too little, too late. The
veteran anti-racist commentator A. Sivanandan writes in *A Different Hunger:
Writings on Black Resistance* (1982), 'To ordinary Blacks these structures were
irrelevant, liaison and conciliation seemed to define them as a people apart . . .
when all they were seeking were the same rights as other citizens'. (p. 17).

Black organisations came into being, examples being CARD (Campaign Against
Racial Discrimination), set up at the suggestion of Martin Luther King when he
visited Britain in 1964, and RAAS (Racial Action Adjustment Society), a more
militant organisation led by Michael X. They were not, however, sufficient to

prevent Labour's 'Kenyan Asian Act', rushed through in a week in March 1968, or the Tory Immigration Act of 1971 which stopped all new immigration dead. On the face of it, this 1971 Act was no more racist than any other, but things had changed. According to Sivanandan,

> There was something else in the air. The philosophy had begun to change, the raison d'etre of racism. It was not that racism did not make for cheap labour any more, but that there was no need for capital to import it.

Here we have a reminder of the crucial importance of the economic factor in the whole question of race and immigration. This is something to which we shall return. In the meantime, how did the Churches respond to the new black presence among them, first in another London Methodist congregation not far from Notting Hill, then at a national level?

3

Race in a pastoral context: the Harlesden story

Black people have brought, and are continuing to bring, many gifts and contributions to the Churches in Britain. In some areas local churches would have died out, were it not for their presence. In others they provide new dimensions of ministry and fresh beginnings, based on a genuine faith that God is present in the church community and God will find the way forward. Perhaps this can best be illustrated – at least in part – by the experience of one local church where the black members became the majority of the congregation, and were thus able to demonstrate effectively their gifts and insights in an atmosphere relatively free from prejudice and resistance. The story illustrates the life that can arise in a multiracial church when all are able to play their part, and the ministry to the community that may result. The church of the story is Harlesden Methodist Church, in north-west London, where I greatly benefited from being the minister between 1974 and 1987.

The neighbourhood

Harlesden is in the southern half of the Borough of Brent, separated from Wembley in the northern half by London's North Circular Road. It is an area with one of the highest proportions of black people in the country. In the Harlesden area most of these are African-Caribbean or African; Wembley has a greater share of Asians. The area, a mile or two north of Notting Hill, became popular with the black communities in the 1950s and 1960s, with its large formerly middle-class houses providing homes for big families or easily converted into two or three flats. There was plenty of work on the nearby railway, on London Transport and in local factories and hospitals. It was within fairly easy reach of other parts of inner London, where family or friends might be situated.

The population of Harlesden is around 30,000, including the Stonebridge council estate, rather notorious for its social problems, and now becoming a Housing

Action Trust. It was laid out and built by people who had no intention of living there and without necessary resources or community infrastructure. It is a mix of high and medium-rise flats, and terraced houses, with a few permanently run-down shopping areas and neighbourhood 'facilities'. Many of the young people have little hope of a decent job; some are tempted by petty crime.

The rest of the community is primarily the middle-class housing from the turn of the century; it used to have smaller 'railway cottages' around the Willesden marshalling yards, but a good many of these were demolished to make way for the Stonebridge estate. Employment was found in what was then the public sector – local and health authorities, transport, communications and energy – and in the Park Royal industrial estate with its dozens of small factories. There were larger factories, such as Walls, but the latter was taken over by Unilever, and gradually 'run down' for 'economic reasons'. When I took over from my predecessor in 1974 he commented that you would know the economy was in trouble if ever unemployment became a problem in Harlesden. But of course in the 1980s it did.

The shopping centre traditionally had a mix of smaller shops with two or three chainstores. Until the mid-1980s it was given a 'touch of class' by Marks & Spencer, and there was talk of Sainsburys coming in to a newly-built shopping mall. However, with the economic decline of the area due to national policies in the 1980s, it became uneconomic for large stores to move into or even to remain in such areas. Sainsburys built a hypermarket a mile away and Marks & Spencer believed it could make higher profits elsewhere, an issue addressed later on (see pp. 85–6).

There was a tradition of thriving community organisations in the Brent area, and this was encouraged by the Council which, during the 1970s, funded hundreds of local groups. The black and minority communities were increasingly demanding their rightful share of services, jobs and resources. It was a lively and stimulating area to live in, where resources were increasingly directed towards those who had less, public housing was built for low-income families, and community organisations received proper support. The same was true at the London level with the Greater London Council, until it was abolished by a Prime Minister who seemingly found it difficult to countenance redistribution of resources. It was modest Council grant support which enabled local Churches to be effective in the community.

The local churches included Anglican, Baptist, Roman Catholic, URC-Moravian and several black-majority congregations. Like many such communities the ecumenical co-operation was patchy. Involving the black churches was difficult; the clergy fraternals were mostly during the day, and the black pastors usually had a paid job to go to; there were also theological and cultural differences. The need for at least the pastors and clergy in such areas to get to know and understand one another better remains paramount. One initiative which the clergy fraternal did undertake was to challenge the rising level of local homelessness. In 1981 the number of homeless families in Brent was approaching a thousand. Many were in bed and breakfast 'homeless hotels'. The clergy facilitated illicit media-visits into some of the dingy, under-resourced and occasionally dangerous premises. They challenged the then Minister of Housing, the late Ian Gow MP, to visit the area. He came, horror was expressed, but the number of homeless families continued to increase. The churches put on Christmas parties for the children, cooped up in their tiny rooms. As Brent has only been able to build a handful of new homes annually over the last decade, due to Government restrictions, the problem remains.

Nationally the Churches were more cautious than they should have been about the deteriorating social and economic health of communities like Harlesden. The Archbishop of Canterbury's Commission report *Faith in the City* in 1985 did momentarily register top-level church concern. However, the type of sustained witness about poverty, homelessness and racial discrimination which should have burst forth from a combination of inner-city and suburban churches has never really materialised. A theological understanding of salvation, or wholeness, of life which includes jobs, homes and access to decent education and health services is still lacking. This only begins to materialise when the Churches participate in the ongoing struggle for justice, a subject addressed further in chapter 6.

The Methodist Church

Harlesden Methodist Church was founded in 1869 in what was then a village on the stage-coach route from London to Harrow and beyond. The coaches changed horses at the Crown Inn across the High Street from the church, and the church's oldest member, Miss Wright, born at the end of the last century, recalled seeing horse-drawn buses come up the High Street. Before she died Miss Wright was persuaded to write a series of articles about 'old Harlesden' for the church newsletter, which produced some lively conversation among the more recent arrivals.

By the turn of the century a small church building had given way to a larger one, and the congregation had also moved on to larger things, although the premises suffered in the 1939–45 war, and a new church had to be built. The size and wealth of the membership between the wars, and the bringing together after Methodist Union of four congregations, led to the development of sizeable ancillary premises. These were a boon in the community ministry era of the 1970s and 1980s, before the gradual demolition of local government led to the loss of funding for such activities. At its centenary, in 1969, however, the Church was able to boast a relatively new church building, seating up to 300 people, a large hall, several meeting rooms and half a dozen 'Sunday School classrooms'. These became ideal small offices for community projects which were just starting up and needed a base. In the mid-1970s a brilliant scheme by a local structural engineer put an extra floor into the old hall, giving a youth centre downstairs and a new hall and coffee-bar upstairs, thus creating further possibilities for community use.

The congregation, which in the 1960s had sustained a membership above 150 when many in similar areas were declining quite rapidly, largely held its own. As white people moved out of the area, either for economic reasons or to get away from the encroaching black presence (as they saw it), they were replaced by new members from the Caribbean and from Africa. Keith Johnson, who was minister between 1964 and 1974, had made a point of welcoming the new arrivals, and visited assiduously. This had led to the message going out that black people were welcome at Harlesden Methodist Church, so they came. By 1974 the congregation was perhaps 85 per cent black, although the leadership was not. Some white people, mostly elderly, had stayed on, adjusted to the new surroundings, enjoyed them, but held on to their church offices. A few younger ones were coming in, partly because the church was building up a reputation for an active multiracial ministry, which included community initiatives – and wider political action. In one two-year spell a third of the members left, for a variety of reasons, but all were replaced.

Harlesden, like many inner-city churches, evolved a worship style which was a mixture of structure and informality. The structure was that of the Methodist Sunday Service with praise, thanksgiving and confession early on, a central section given over to 'The Word', and a final period of response, with intercessions, offering and hymns of dedication and commitment. Within that structure however came opportunities for different people to participate, with perhaps the children or choir leading some singing, stewards reading or taking prayers, biddings being sought for intercession and occasional short plays or dramatic readings. It was good preparation for what has now become known as 'all-age worship'.

After the initial section, the worship was opened up to the 'Notices and Concerns'. After the steward read the formal notices, which were as often about activities outside the church as inside, anyone present with information to give or a concern to share was invited to contribute. This led both to an opportunity for those who had hardly ever spoken in public to have their say, and also to the congregation getting a wider sense of what was going on in the community, and who was involved. Notices would vary from the next meeting of the local anti-apartheid group to a campaign against hospital closure, and from information about a member going for an operation to a pressing invitation to the Monday Prayer and Fellowship group. Visitors were welcomed from different parts of the world and those travelling asked for a blessing on their journeys. It was a time during which the church really became a community and although the Concerns often went on for twenty minutes (to the despair of those who thought an hour for the Lord on Sundays was enough), the occasional effort to restrict it led to failure.

The Concerns were also a time when important matters could surface, and they were then heard by the whole congregation rather than just the few who attended the committees where decisions were usually made. The Notices were also something of a barometer of the Church's thinking. One of the discussions which went on among the newer members from Africa and the Caribbean was around terminology. The older people called themselves 'coloured' and found it difficult to adjust to the younger generation's 'black'. On one occasion a senior steward giving information about some upcoming meeting said it was particularly for 'coloured people'. 'Black!', corrected several voices from the congregation, and from then on 'black' it always was. When I paid occasional visits to often larger suburban churches, it was hard not to reflect on how insular and indeed boring were the church notices. They seemed peripheral to the interchange which should always be happening between the church and the community of which it is a part.

The 'Notices and Concerns' usually concluded with the 'Peace', during which the children left for Junior Church, friends who had not met for a while hugged one another, visitors were introduced to their neighbours, the minister was informed about sick friends and potential baptisms and, one suspects, some child-minding and shopping arrangements for the following week were made. Because of the Peace no visitor left the church not spoken to, even if they had evaded the greetings of the eager door-stewards, and some experienced the movement of the heart which brought them back again, and again, in the future. From time to time people were encouraged to exchange names, which always helped those who had memory difficulties, or were relatively new. When the Peace was over, and it was time for the Word, there was always the sense of a genuinely united and expectant community, ready to hear what the Lord had to say.

Harlesden always sought a variety of preachers. There were exchanges with other Methodists and local churches of other denominations. There was also development of local preachers and the introduction of black church leaders from elsewhere. It was rare that half a dozen Sundays went by without a black preacher. We kept in touch with the Methodist and ecumenical grapevine to know who was visiting, especially from the Caribbean and Africa. Early Caribbean contact sprang from a month's visit in the mid-1970s to several London churches by a Caribbean team which included the then President of the Methodist Church in the Caribbean, Revd Claude Cadogan, and Revd George Mulrain – later to teach mission studies at Selly Oak College. This was followed by other Caribbean Presidents and District Chairmen, and by African leaders such as Revd Stanley Mogoba, Secretary of the South African Methodist Church.

The high-spot of this programme was the visit in 1984 of the Revd Jesse Jackson, then having a tilt at the US Presidency. On a brief trip to London he had expressed the wish to preach in a primarily black church, and Methodist MP Paul Boateng had arranged the trip to Harlesden. It was an occasion the church – packed to the doors, with loudspeakers on the forecourt – will never forget. It was an evening of great affirmation for many black people who had stayed with the church despite its failures, and who were still too often denied leadership in the traditional British churches. Such occasions are by definition rare, and it remains important for all churches, whether set in multiracial or predominantly white areas, actively to recognise and to celebrate the reality that we are not just multiracial in the pew but in the pulpit and behind the Table as well.

One of the initial difficulties regarding black participation in leading worship appeared to be lack of experience. This may have been because those who came to the UK from Africa and the Caribbean tended not to be from the leadership of their churches back home. The latter were perhaps more likely to be ensconced in secure jobs and had less need to emigrate to better themselves. Hence ways had to be found to build confidence and enable involvement. This was done to some degree by the Notices and Concerns, referred to above, and by invitations to read or lead prayers. However the real breakthrough came with the introduction of 'Members' Services' once a month on a Sunday evening. Attendance at evening services had declined to a dozen or less, and there was a discussion as to whether to end them altogether. Those who attended, some of whom had Sunday shift work, were unhappy, and the idea of 'Members' Services' emerged. A small group would plan the service; the 'sermon' might be an address by one of the group, or two or three shorter contributions on the same theme, or a discussion led by one person. Those who participated supported one another, and soon the numbers had increased, with sometimes over twenty on a light evening. In addition, some who had begun by helping to lead evening services began to contribute in the mornings as well, and could give an occasional contribution which inspired and encouraged, and expanded their own confidence.

'Worship Assistants' became an accepted group in the church, and their experience was useful when there was a house-group to be led, or a contribution made to a District Committee or even to the 300-member District Synod when it met. Leadership in worship became a training ground for other things, as it had been for the early trades unionists when the chapels were active among the nineteenth-century miners and agricultural labourers.

FELLOWSHIP

Fellowship was a vital element in building up the Harlesden church community. A strong sense of community, of being 'one-with-another', gradually became a vital factor in the church's life, but it had to be worked for, and was created in a number of specific ways in addition to those referred to above. One such initiative was the church 'Weekend Away', which began to take place in October or November each year. It was usually attended by between 35 and 45 members of the congregation, and held at one of the Methodist hotels which offer a cheap off-season weekend. The group would set off around 6 p.m. on Friday, often waved off by other members unable to travel. On arrival there would be supper and a short introduction to the theme, then evening prayers. Saturday morning saw a speaker and some group work, the afternoon a visit of the kind mentioned below and the evening a social occasion with a concert of variable quality but great fun! Sunday morning was worship either in a local church or the hotel – the former occasionally leading to some raised eyebrows when forty black people suddenly appeared in the congregation. After lunch a round-up session testified to new insights and experiences, old friendships deepened and new ones formed. The age range was broad; similar youth weekends for 30 to 40 youngsters in the late 1970s had prepared the younger members for this type of event.

Sometimes there was a speaker, sometimes the senior members led the event themselves, with the help of the minister or another theologically-trained member. The afternoon visits were aimed at exploring a little Christian history. When the weekend was in Bournemouth, a visit to Tolpuddle chapel and the story of the Methodist local preachers transported to Australia for their efforts to organise an agricultural trades union was a revelation to many. A trip to the New Room at Bristol, where Wesley had worked, was another experience, especially the upper window whence he listened to his preachers, and – so the story goes – interrupted them if they did not get it right! Such weekends led to a 're-creation' in body, mind and spirit, and not just for those who travelled; the experience was shared fully with those unable to attend.

After two or three years the feeling developed that the weekends could be developed further. Few Caribbean or African people went on holiday – not least because they were saving money for the occasional (sometimes emergency) visit home. Many had seen comparatively little of the rest of the UK, never mind Europe. Also, knowledge of Christian history was quite limited; Luther and Calvin were hardly known and even the name of John Wesley brought puzzlement to a few faces. The initiative for a 'Church Holiday' came from one of the first black stewards, Iris Livan, who had seen visits to the Holy Land advertised and was very keen to go. The minister's response, thinking this would take some time to organise, was that if we could get a group of eight we could make enquiries. Within a week Iris was back with eight names, so then we began in earnest. Eventually, in January 1982, a party of 50 left the church for Tel Aviv and Jerusalem. Our preparation had included introductory sessions from the Church Missionary Society Middle East Secretary, and the local PLO representative, just so that we were aware of the contemporary Israeli–Palestinian relationship as well as the past. The visit was a great success, with visits to many of the holy places. There was a service of blessing by the Jordan, and the interesting experience of floating on the Dead Sea, which even some of the larger members insisted on doing – as no swimming costumes had been brought – in their underwear.

On the holiday 'day off' we created our own programme, hiring an Arab bus and going out to the then occupied West Bank to visit projects in a Palestinian refugee camp and a Christian Palestinian leader. One visit, to a Women's Centre, led to the best inter-faith lesson I have ever witnessed. A group of West Indian women, packed into the modest office of the Centre's director, heard first about the nature of the Israeli oppression, then of anxiety about how the young were drifting away from their roots, how their faith did not seem to matter, how they never attended prayers and how the lack of opportunity in education and employment was turning some of them to drugs and violence. The nods and murmurs of agreement swelled as the story was told, and as we returned to the bus the conversation was loud and animated about the similarities with black youngsters back home, especially about having no time for religion. When our guide gently pointed out that our hostess was a Muslim the silence was palpable, as it sank in to dedicated Christian women how similar to theirs were the concerns and fears of the Muslim women of the West Bank.

The next year saw a visit to Yorkshire, discovering, through ruined abbeys and still-alive great churches such as York Minster, something of the origins and growth of Christianity in these islands. Sometimes on this and other trips those brought up long ago in Jamaica or Guyana would say 'I remember hearing about this in my history/geography/English lessons, we learned far more about

British battles/rivers/novels than about our own'. Subsequent years saw travels to Italy, Switzerland and what was then the German Democratic Republic (GDR). In 1983 a pastor from Leipzig, Revd Ulrike Birkner, had spent part of a year's study in England at the Harlesden Church, examining the links between liturgy and mission. When she finished her placement it was with a warm invitation to come and visit her congregation in Leipzig, when she returned home. In most churches that would have produced a gracious smile and a friendly 'maybe'. By this time, however, the Harlesden church had got the travel bug. The fact that the GDR was then a 'communist country' behind the 'iron curtain' seemed not to deter people at all. It may have been something to do with having had to up sticks and travel 3,000 miles or more from your home, often alone, to start a new life in a foreign country. What is a few hundred miles across Europe, in a coach full of friends, after an adventure like that?

So, somewhat perhaps to Ulrike's surprise, she received a letter stating that forty members of Harlesden Methodist Church were preparing to take her at her word, and pay a visit. It was a long and tiring coach journey, but the inimitable spirit of the community came out at a rather isolated East German border post when after twelve hours of travelling the inevitable delays took place, as the small immigration office struggled to cope with 14 different types of passport. The grim-faced border guards began to search through the bus, ignoring all attempts at conversation. One of the more anarchic Jamaican members decided to test whether they really could not understand English. 'You know what's in there?' she asked as a guard took hold of her bag, 'my underwear!' (except she used a rather more direct description). The guard spluttered with suppressed mirth, and the rest of the search was conducted in a lighter vein, though we were relieved when every passport was returned, including that of our cheekiest member.

The week was very informative. We learned about the Reformation, paying homage at the church door at Wittenburg to which Martin Luther nailed his theses, singing his hymns in English and German, and visiting museums which played up his commitment to the workers, as befitted a communist state – while omitting to mention his desertion of the peasants. We shared a memorable communion service in a packed Leipzig church. Then there was the reception at the Methodist headquarters in Dresden, drawing forth the observation from some that they had thought there were no Christians in East Germany, let alone a lively Methodist Church. We learned too of the effects of the fire-bombing of Dresden during the war.

When we discovered Catholics and Baptists as well as Lutherans the talk turned to the deceit of Western propaganda. 'Communism' was seen to be not all wicked. Even the local Christians, some of whom put up with a lot from the régime, pointed out the cheap housing, fuel, basic foodstuffs and children's clothes, the free nursery places for working mothers and the low unemployment (a tenth of the UK rate at the time). There was also the downside, the lack of freedom to speak, the control of decision-making, the persecution of some Christians. But the freedom of worship and fellowship, the protest movement even then linked to the churches, the relative equality of society and the sense of solidarity with poorer countries did not fail to leave its mark.

Subsequent years saw holiday visits to Ecumene, the Methodist-Waldensian centre near Rome, and to the Ecumenical Centres of Geneva – the World Council of Churches headquarters – and Agape in the Italian Alps. In Rome there was a look at the Colosseum, where some early Christians were martyred, and at the catacombs, wherein the early Church kept the faith. Such experiences seemed to speak volumes to black Christians, some of whom had their own experience of marginalisation by the Churches when they first came to Britain. We discovered again what it might mean to be persecuted for our faith, and realised how far the Church in Europe is from persecution. At Agape we learned how the followers of Waldo, the son of a rich Lyon merchant who began to take the Gospel seriously, were hounded from their homes and forced to take refuge to the east in the upper Alpine valleys. They came to be known as the Waldensians, and now form with the Methodists the largest Protestant church in Italy. This history helped our understanding of the continuing battle for the soul of the Church, between the values and powers of 'the world', and a commitment to the righteousness and shalom at the heart of the biblical message.

The visit to the World Council of Churches gave a vision of a Church committed to listening to and empowering the poor. No wonder, we thought, the WCC is not popular with some of the religious establishment in London, Frankfurt and Washington. A further dimension of our visit to Geneva was an introduction to John Calvin, who formed much of the church life in Geneva in the Reformation period. His view of predestination and his rather stern ideas of the Christian life were discussed and dissected. On the whole, lively Caribbean Christians seemed to prefer the earthiness of Luther, although due perhaps to their 'missionary upbringing' there seemed at least a suspicion of sympathy with Calvin's views on recreation and morality.

One other visit undertaken was to the island of Iona, to the ecumenical community established largely by members of the Church of Scotland through the vision of George Macleod. The spirit of that committed and open-hearted community emanates from the modern Iona. For the Harlesden members Iona, site of the landing of Columba as he brought Christianity to the north of Britain, gave a new perspective on Christian history. Away from manoeuvrings between

Church and State, the execution of kings and archbishops and the burnings of Catholics and Protestants, the wildness of Iona recalls the simplicity and privation out of which the Gospel message came. We pictured the monks sheltering under the rocks as they sought to build some refuge from the inhospitable climate. We stood before the ancient Celtic crosses, carved and raised to remind people of Christ's death but also his rising for the world. We marvelled at the ancient abbey, constructed far from 'civilisation', but then as now a place of pilgrimage for those wanting to discover more about the world, themselves and their God. It was amazing to us all to find South Africa, the Middle East, racism and the arms trade all under vigorous debate and to enjoy the songs and the spirituality of Latin America, Asia, Africa and Scotland in the Abbey's daily liturgy.

Such holidays were not unlike the pilgrimages of old, although admittedly more comfortable. The elements of learning, discussion, fellowship and devotion were all present. There were also the stories to tell when we returned, so that soon the whole church felt as if it had been through the catacombs, toured the World Council of Churches' headquarters or prayed on a boat in the stillness of Galilee. Church weekends, or holiday-pilgrimages, develop a great sense of fellowship and comradeship for a church community.

At the more mundane level there was of course the need to develop the day-to-day and week-to-week church spirit. In the mid-1970s the church had a Women's Meeting (slightly untruthfully known as 'Harlesden's Brightest Spot'), a kind of Guild that functioned sporadically and an annual discussion about ecumenical Lent groups which then sometimes actually took place.

The progress of the Women's Meeting was interesting to watch. When I arrived in 1974 it was 100 per cent white, and led by a kind and competent lady who had done this for some years. When she died, one of the older white ladies took over, and things continued much as before. The older members, however, began to move away to live with their families, and some with their Lord, and numbers began to dwindle. Some of the black women, nearing retirement, were clearly the Brightest Spot's future, but somehow none of the attending members could quite bring themselves to give the personal invitations which could make the difference. General invitations were given out in church, but the black women clearly felt these were not directed at them. Then one of the lighter-skinned Caribbean women, who also sang in the choir, ventured along one Monday afternoon. She became established, and just as attendance had begun to approach non-viability, it began to pick up again as more black members joined.

Within quite a short time the group had become 90 per cent black, and the leader had gone to another church, apparently a more congenial environment. One white member stayed on as secretary for some time, ensuring traditions were retained. 'They don't always know what to do', she would confide. Eventually she handed over responsibility, while keeping a careful eye on developments. Like all us white leaders in predominantly black churches she was treated with the grace, deference and affection none of us entirely deserve.

At the same time this was going on the black folk still at work, especially the women, expressed a need for a more spiritual time together, some kind of evening fellowship. Would the minister start one? No, if that was something the members wanted why did they not – like the early Methodists – organise it themselves? From the initial discussions it took about two years for the Prayer and Fellowship Group to be formed. During this period there seemed to be a lack of confidence, odd among people who took considerable responsibilities at work and with their families, to organise a regular church gathering without 'the minister'.

Eventually the step was taken and a group of between ten and twenty members began to meet on Monday evenings. Turns were taken to lead; members would arrive late (sometimes straight from an evening shift); favourite hymns were chosen, spoken about and sung. Prayers were said, for the church, for family members, for the sick and troubled, and for zones of war and poverty around the world. The meeting became the spiritual centre of the church and many times what began there as informal conversations bore fruit as to who might become a steward or what the topic should be for the Weekend Away. The minister attended from time to time, and resisted being urged into the role of 'leader', reminding the members that they heard plenty from him on a Sunday and this was his chance to listen to them.

Alongside the friendly but deeply spiritual atmosphere of the Monday group a Church Fellowship met monthly on a Wednesday, led by a former Methodist minister and circuit steward and one or two of the black stewards. It was replaced during Lent by a series of Lent Meetings, or ecumenical house-groups with the URC-Moravian church and occasionally with Anglicans, Baptists or Catholics as well. It was one of the weaknesses of local ecumenical relationships that broad-based annual Lent house-groups were never really a success.

The sense of togetherness and of caring among the whole church community was expressed in many other ways, including by the Neighbourhood Wardens who delivered the church newsletters, the sick visitors and the gatherings at weddings, funerals and other rites of passage. When a family member died, even back at home, members would gather at the relevant home for several evenings. When one died locally the church would be packed for the funeral. I often wondered what the undertakers made of it – at a white funeral there was often only a handful present, but when it was a black person they could hardly get the coffin through the throng. Such expressions of solidarity seem clear signs that Christ is present in his Church and the Incarnation is real.

PASTORAL WORK

There were two dimensions to the pastoral work of the church. One was the normal work of visitation and support, the other had wider ramifications, arising out of the fact that the membership was primarily black. With regard to the first there was an ongoing expectation, especially among the African and Caribbean Christians, that visits by the minister were what kept people coming to church. However, when the church and its minister were involved in a wide range of community, national and even international activities, that was not always possible. Another system needed to be developed to supplement what the minister could do, and whatever contact and support members got through worship and fellowship on Sundays. In addition leadership was emerging within the church community, and this needed to be encouraged and given an outlet, rather than stifled.

Hence the system of 'Neighbourhood Wardens', already tried out in a series of inner-city areas in both the USA and the UK, was discussed, debated and finally adopted. Some fifteen members agreed to take an interest in between five and a dozen households in the streets or flats close by their home. This included taking around the church newsletter when it came out every couple of months. It gave an opportunity for those with some connection with the church to get to know at least one senior member a little better, and for that member to invite them to special events when these took place, or to let the minister know when there was need for ministerial contact. In addition the sense of fellowship in the community did translate in a quite remarkable way to the wider group of people on the 'community roll', and although people who turned up only on high days and holidays were gently teased as to their whereabouts the rest of the year, they usually grinned apologetically and took it in good part.

The chronic situations of domestic strife or long-term sickness which are a part of all Christian pastoral work were of course an ongoing component of what went on in Harlesden. The pastoral crises of accidents and sudden death were there too. The crises in this particular church community however also involved how to deal with police raids which took place early in the morning, members of the youth group being accused of drug-dealing and families who either could not get certain members into the country, even for a visit, or were faced with deportation, either of individuals or in some cases of the whole family.

One example of a police raid took place soon after 7 a.m. when the parents had gone to work and teenage children were on their own in the house. Several officers banged on the door, accused a male teenager of being involved in burglaries, and announced they were searching the house. The older daughter was awake enough to ask about a warrant. They waved a piece of paper and proceeded to ransack the whole place. Nothing was found, so they issued a warning as they left, saying they would continue to watch the boy. In a second example the hammering on the door came later in the day. The youth concerned was out, so they insisted on searching his room, sure that something illegal would be found, although it was not. In another incident a young man had come from the Caribbean to spend some time with his aunt, a church member. A neighbour heard noises from the flat, forgot there was a visitor staying and informed the police. Watching when they arrived she saw the boy, realised her mistake and rushed out to apologise. The officers nevertheless searched the flat, saying they were looking for drugs, and questioned the young man on his immigration status. The neighbour was outraged, and told the police so. With advice from the minister, the member made an official complaint. A senior officer arrived and tried to persuade her to withdraw the complaint. He said he would make sure such a thing never happened again. Afterwards the lady remarked resignedly that she felt too pressured to do anything other than drop the complaint. It is essential in such circumstances to have a lawyer or other professional person present.

These kinds of invasions were traumatic, and enormously resented, especially when the usual result was that nothing was found. It never seemed to happen to the white families with whom the church had contact, although no doubt it does so happen from time to time. Perhaps then, however, the police are more polite. A further police incident involved one of the most gentle and pleasant of the youth group being violently arrested for carrying drugs. He was sitting in a friend's car when the police arrived and accused them of possessing drugs. His friend tried to escape, reinforcements were called and the boys were grabbed and thrown into a van. The minister spent several hours at the station with senior officers and was promised that in all probability the charges would be dropped. This never happened, though when the case came to court the officers failed to appear and it was dismissed. Meanwhile the boy had lost his job and his family had suffered considerable pain and disgrace.

Incidents like these led the church to seek meetings with the local Superintendent to hear the police point of view, and invite officers to an informal exchange of views in the manse. One meeting was held, and a frank exchange took place with parents, many of whom had had their children stopped and searched or subjected to some kind of indignity by police officers. They said they knew the police had a difficult job, but some of what went on was not good enough. They thought they had been heard. However when the police were invited to a second occasion they never managed to answer the invitation, and a good community initiative fell through. Unpleasant though some of these incidents were, however, they were not as bad as when an African member of a neighbouring church was stopped by police in his car, accused of stealing it, racially insulted and kept for several hours at a local police station. The church was incensed and a few weeks later, to the astonishment and embarrassment of the police, twenty members of the church turned up outside the station, with notices and placards, and stood for an hour in silent protest. In subsequent conversation with church leaders the Superintendent promised that such behaviour by police officers would be ended forthwith. With legal support the member won substantial compensation.

The immigration service was another structure which haunted church members, in a less directly oppressive but no less destructive way. One Caribbean family were divided because the parents and one son had the right to remain in Britain, but a second son did not. In his early sixties the father had a stroke, the wife needed to remain at work to pay the bills, and there was no-one to keep the old man company during the day. The first son had a good job to hold down; the second son back in the Caribbean was unemployed. He had spent one longish period in Britain, immigration had finally refused a further extension and he had gone back. Now the family needed him but the immigration department suspected, despite all the medical evidence and the family's promises to cover all his expenses, that it was a ruse to get him back into Britain. So mum had to go part-time, and dad had to stay on his own, with occasional visits from family friends. If ever I asked about the second son in his hearing he would break down and cry, pitifully.

The biggest immigration battle the church had to fight was over the Djima family, originally from Nigeria. Like other families referred to in chapter 1 they had been in Britain many years, and had become overstayers. Ben and Lydia had however become self-sufficient, and two of their children were old enough to be British citizens, so the church found it very difficult when someone informed on them and the authorities decided they would have to go. A petition was started, the local Council was lobbied, there were public meetings in the church with reports in the newspaper and the local MP, Paul Boateng, was brought in. Immigration officers arrived unannounced at the family home to try to pressure the family into leaving; Lydia phoned a church member who was horrified to hear the altercation going on over the phone, and hurried round to calm things down. The congregation talked about giving the family sanctuary, and indeed that might have come to pass. However after two years of pressure, resistance and campaigning, the Home Office relented. Sadly two years afterwards Ben Djima suffered a fatal heart attack. Many felt it was the result of all the pressure when the deportation fight was going on.

The pastoral ministry in multiracial communities almost inevitably becomes also prophetic, and a style of confronting the structures which deeply affect people's lives has to be evolved. It is possible – as some Christians do – to sigh, to call it the Lord's will and to subside into pious prayer. It is also possible to explode into prophetic prayer, which empowers engagement with racist structures. This also requires a broader engagement, calling on the wider Church for sustenance and support. Activities include everything from resolutions to the national Church Conference or Assembly to letters and articles in denominational newspapers and often uncomfortable correspondence and meetings with those in authority. And then there are the nasty letters and heavy breathing phone calls, especially after publicity in the local press. Pastoral ministry in inner-city areas has interesting and sometimes costly ramifications.

LEADERSHIP

As already suggested, leadership already present among black church members was beginning to assert itself in various ways by the late 1970s. The development of the Prayer and Fellowship Group, the organising of church weekends and holidays, the planning of the Members' Services on Sunday evenings, playing the organ and leading the choir, the taking of responsibility for the Women's Meeting, all demonstrated that skills and abilities already existed. But black people were still not part of the real decision-making. When I arrived in 1974 there was one black steward, though she was soon followed by one or two more. Articulate white members continued, however, to dominate the Church Council and the key committees.

Black members continued to display some diffidence in these areas. This seemed to be a function of the 'mystification' of church offices, especially anything to do with financial or secretarial skills. White leaders, even unconsciously, encouraged these perceptions and would constantly imply that no-one else really wanted to do their job. Black people sometimes had to be persuaded there was no special magic associated with becoming a senior steward or committee secretary. It often needed to be made clear that such tasks did not necessitate a special 'professional' level the communication of information about decisions made and the subsequent progress, and some forward-planning, were the key aspects of leadership.

It was the building up of teams of stewards which produced the most specific breakthrough in the gradual changes in the power-structure. While there were a couple of white stewards, even with two or three black ones, little seemed to change. However, when it was decided to increase the number of stewards to eight or ten a fundamental change took place. We caused some raised eyebrows at District Synod among the representatives of suburban churches with their morning and evening teams of two each when we said airily that we had ten stewards and the number was rising!

What this did was provide a pool of leadership which contributed its gifts in particular ways, as and when necessary. If a Sunday dinner was to be organised for the visit of the President of Conference, the stewards with professional catering experience came forward. If the Notices were to be read those who were more practised in reading presented themselves. When the Weekend Away had to be organised someone else would offer and when a spokesperson was needed for a local health or housing rally another team member took it on. Several times 'duty rotas' were tried, but several stewards worked shifts including weekends and others had young families, or more grown-up ones, who could suddenly demand attention, occasionally in Barbados or Nigeria! Flexibility was needed, and usually achieved. When someone was absent another team member would take their place. There were occasional mishaps, but everyone survived, and a collective leadership became a very positive experience.

One of the crucial aspects of this process was training. This included reading lessons and/or using the microphone effectively, drafting minutes of meetings, discussing the skills of drawing people into discussion in a house-group and exploring the broader structures of Methodism. One tactic used when no-one could be found to take on a task was to ask two people to do it, which helped in confidence-building and exchange of skills. One helpful idiosyncrasy of Methodist structures in the development of leadership is the 'six-year rule', requiring office holders normally to step down after six years. It remains quite astonishing how many people, while grumbling over their particular yoke, will nevertheless refuse to put it down, or how many verbally committed to the principles of equal opportunity suffer from sudden amnesia when their appointed time is up – or have not trained a potential replacement.

One challenge for white leaders in multiracial churches is looking for and working with those from the minority communities who have the ability to take posts but not the experience or confidence. We had our difficulties at Harlesden, and when periods of office came to an end, and black folk spoke out warmly of the service rendered, white folk sometimes felt that was a call to stay on. A turnover of office holders, and a balance in key positions between the different sections of the community, makes for a healthy church, not to mention the importance of 'role-models' for youngsters growing up in the church.

THE LOCAL COMMUNITY

It seems essential in times when the Church has little status in the local community, except for what it creates by its own witness and example, that we seek to make visible the truth of the Gospel by what we do rather than what we say. When we speak we are often talking only to ourselves, so it is better to demonstrate our faith by the actions we undertake, the use to which our buildings are put, the purposes of our financial appeals and the messages which appear on our notice boards. The Harlesden church sought to develop a spirit which showed that we felt we belonged in the local community and we wanted to be as open to it as possible. Behind much of our outward-directed activity was the idea of prophetic service, *diakonia*, linked with *dikaiosune* (righteousness). The church wanted to serve but also wanted to relate our activities to the most needy in the locality, and the most exploited in other parts of the world – and to explain the reasons why.

One way of serving was the use of the fairly substantial buildings and their situation fronting the High Street. Good usage meant that in 1974 there were already present the Harlesden Advice Centre, ideally placed in a disused chapel at the front of the church with High Street access, a full-time day nursery, the Samaritans' headquarters and a church youth club meeting one or two nights a week in the Hall. The Advice Centre had developed an expertise in problems of housing, benefits, debt, employment and immigration. It also campaigned about issues of local concern, and served those of all faith communities and none. The day nursery had been set up initially to give the young working mothers related to our church, both married and single, somewhere safe to leave young children. Support was negotiated with Brent Council to upgrade the facilities and soon there were three full-time and one part-time staff serving a fairly well-equipped nursery and preparing children from a range of nationalities, some from quite deprived backgrounds, for school. Fees were kept down, to accommodate low-wage families.

During the 1970s the church tried to develop youth work in the Tavistock Youth and Community Centre, named after the road alongside the church. Eventually the Council granted funding for a full-time worker and several part-timers, enabling a five-day week opening to try and reach some of the tougher neighbourhood youngsters. This led to some interesting experiences, with illicit late-night discos (at one of which I faced a drawn knife when insisting it had to close), pot-smoking sessions and secreted stolen goods. It was not an easy period, but while not suggesting in any way the police were conniving at offences, they displayed a fair degree of tolerance, apparently taking the view that at least they knew where the youngsters were if they were doing their thing in the Tavistock.

After a time the Samaritans moved out and gave us the opportunity to initiate something new. For some time baptisms had been increasing, and by the beginning of the 1980s there were three or four a month. This gave contact with an increasing number of young mothers, a proportion of whom were single. Once more the church began to look around for some 'pump-priming' finance, to start a Young Mum's Project where the mothers could meet. Before long we were able to appoint a part-time worker, with a couple of small rooms to work from. The mums were not keen on coming to church every Sunday, but the fact that the church provided them with this facility kept them in touch and meant they regarded us as 'their church', so they were often back for Christmas, Easter and other festivals – and the next baby's baptism too.

In due time the Mums' Project came of age and evolved so that it needed, and obtained, larger premises. Others took its place, such as the Black Mental Health Project. A small South African trust, the Luthuli Foundation, used a room for some time and several other community organisations started with offices on the church premises. What we provided was never in good enough condition for what was really needed, but at least it was a base from which people could start.

Church members participated in all these activities in a variety of ways, most commonly by serving on the Management Committees, but also as volunteers and by working to keep the premises in reasonably good order. That was not easy, and the rather plush surroundings of some suburban churches brought a degree of envy when we visited elsewhere. Although Methodist ministerial salaries are much the same everywhere, the conditions of Methodist buildings are not; inner-city church buildings often deserve better support.

Another use of our premises was by 'black-led' congregations, churches from the African or African-Caribbean communities, often attended by those who had not found a welcome in white-led churches. Four such congregations made their homes with us, one or two of our members occasionally attending through invitation or interest. Occasionally requests for the use of the Church for nights of fasting or other important services were granted. It may be that a discerning approach now needs to be taken to such churches. A tradition of inclusive leadership may need to be encouraged, rather than offering a roof to any group which splits from another, and the importance of ecumenical relationships also needs to be stressed, although that requires greater effort by white-majority churches.

One very serious debate took place in the Church Council after a request by a local Hindu community, growing but still without a temple, and being too large for the church hall, to use the church on several week-nights to celebrate Diwali. For some reason there were problems with local authority buildings, schools being in session at the time. After much discussion it was decided this was not possible. National Church policy that it could not be done was noted but it was the congregation's feeling that hospitality to other faiths could not extend thus far. One argument in favour was that it would enable us to get to know our Hindu neighbours better, for we knew little of them yet shared many problems, but it was not enough.

The church did however offer a 'High Street' platform for public debate on matters of local concern, including the housing crisis, health service cuts, world poverty and General Election hustings. Speakers from a range of opinions were invited to such meetings, though smoking was banned, people had to watch their language and some activists were clearly doing what they hadn't for years in coming into a church. Their anxieties were calmed by the posters round the church walls, which usually included protests against apartheid and the arms trade, and encouragement to support Central America or to save the environment. This poster pattern was replicated on the board outside, by posters urging changes in Government policy, supporting local campaigns, offering contemporary theological education (e.g. 'God is in the struggle against apartheid – are you?'), as well as inviting passers-by to join us at Christmas or Easter events. It was by these means that the church sought to become a catalyst for community concern – the leaven in the lump, and a signpost to a more just society – like a city set on a hill.

One local campaign that the church initiated came in the early 1980s when at just a few weeks' notice Marks & Spencer, for years the prime shop in the High Street, announced it was closing down. The news came in August when a number of people were away and the closure period was half over before the first protest could be mounted. Community leaders were well aware of the importance of 'M & S' to a local shopping centre like Harlesden. It brought in shoppers who would otherwise go elsewhere, and the trade of the whole High Street would suffer. Also, the last thing any High Street needs is a large boarded-up store, and there were reported to be no buyers in view.

A petition was launched, and a letter written to the Company Chairman asking on what grounds it was withdrawing from a community where it had been making money for seventy years. To locals the shop always seemed well-patronised, even though it now heavily emphasised 'bargain counters'. Two Saturdays of petitioning brought in several thousand signatures, and the letter brought an invitation to head office. Followed by TV cameras a coachload of objectors went to make their views vociferously clear to a courteous but immovable director. We asked among other things why, when Marks was so prominent in 'backing Brixton', it was 'dumping Harlesden'?

We failed, though we hoped Marks might be more careful about closing other inner-city stores. The company refused to deny it was continuing to make a profit; it felt simply that more money could be made elsewhere. It was a sign of the times for local High Streets. The forces of the 'market' mean that even stores which have employed local people and taken their money for years will up and off. It all adds to unemployment and crime in inner cities. No wonder large stores are often first to be burned in rebellions against inequality, as in Los Angeles in 1992.

As well as a servant role the Church has a prophetic one. Its place in multiracial areas means it is well-situated to make its views known. If it becomes part of its local community, offering premises and a welcome to as many groups as it can, it develops some right to speak on behalf of the community, along with others working for Kingdom values of justice and equality. Such values, particularly when expressed in the race context, deserve a far higher profile in Church life and activity. In that sense the experiences of inner-city churches have something to offer the whole Church, so that the Gospel message for the contemporary world may be honed and sharpened. This may then make an impact on the structures of power and of institutional racism, which affect us all.

THE WIDER COMMUNITY

So, what about the effect of a local church on the wider community? I remember on a visit to Trinidad in 1977 being impressed by the symbolic value of a new church building which had merely columns where the walls would have been, thus allowing the welcome Caribbean breeze to blow through. This 'church-without-walls' was open both to the atmosphere and to those who passed by, demonstrating – hopefully – both the church's involvement in and its vulnerability to the wider world. A multiracial church has a considerable advantage over most other churches as it is already to some degree a church without walls, a community into which people from several different parts of the world have entered. Unless the community has a peculiarly closed mind this sense of the breadth and depth of the international community will enter into that church's life, and influence much of what it thinks and does. It was partly this which enabled Harlesden church to travel so far afield, and espouse so many wider causes.

One effect of Harlesden's multiracial character was a desire to seek links with similar churches, as well as those the church developed with suburbs and rural areas through being part of the London North-West Methodist District. Within this District there were perhaps a dozen churches like Harlesden, but around London as a whole it was more like fifty. Hence there developed an interest in what was going on in Brixton, Lambeth, Tower Hamlets and Peckham, as well as Harrow, Watford, Berkhamsted and Aylesbury. The Methodist Inner City Churches Group (MICCG) was set up, primarily bringing ministers together but also enabling joint planning of events among multiracial churches around London. District links led to requests for the comparatively powerful suburban churches to support work around issues such as homelessness, racism in the police or maintenance of health services, but the response was rarely overwhelming.

Inner-city churches continue, however, to share their concerns, supporting one another in anti-deportation campaigns, opposition to racial violence or gathering for a visiting black preacher. Some churches also evolved joint schemes to develop black leadership. Harlesden instituted the Opportunity for Ministry scheme, whereby a young black person was given two years to test his or her vocation with a supportive congregation, if s/he felt offering for the ministry might be difficult from their own situation. The wider church gave financial support, and the first three participants in the scheme produced two candidates for the ministry and a church community worker. Thinking such as this did increase the number of black candidates for the Methodist ministry in the mid-eighties to two or three each year, though it seems to have fallen back a little since then. Although there are now more black ministers and clergy in all denominations such positive action remains essential in encouraging black people to fulfil their potential in the face of the institutional racism in white society, including in the Church.

Harlesden church always tried to be well-represented at the District Synod, held twice a year usually on a Saturday. Despite there being many multiracial churches few black people attended Synod, seeming to feel it was not their thing, but Harlesden usually supplied three or four representatives. There was a strange mixture of welcome and slight suspicion when our black members arrived. One of them said of such District occasions, 'Sometimes you go into a room and it's as if you had horns. The blacks have arrived!' That quote was taken from *A Tree God Planted*, an excellent account of the position of black people in the Methodist Church in the early 1980s, and giving a generalised picture alongside this particular one. Hopefully black Christians feel less like that these days, although as their presence spreads they may encounter such an atmosphere in more suburban or rural areas. Eventually a resolution was put to the national Conference urging Districts with multiracial communities to appoint *at least* one black person to Conference each year. That resolution led quite quickly to a regular average of 20 to 25 black Conference participants and is another example of the necessity of positive action to tackle structural racism. 'Good will' does not seem to work. Harlesden sent its first black representative to Conference in 1981; others have now followed.

One further means of being a 'church-without-walls' is by entering into twin-ning-type relationships with churches in 'almost white' areas. Harlesden, along with similar churches, tried this in a number of ways. One centred round young people, and interchanges were tried between the Harlesden youth group, quite sizeable in the late 1970s, and the youth section of one of the biggest churches in the District, some 25 miles from London. The arrangement proceeded rela-tively well at a rather superficial level, but when our young people began to talk about the issues which affected their lives – racism in school, overcrowded hous-ing, unemployment, harassment by the police – albeit in the context of studying what it means to follow Christ today – the welcome began to cool and the rela-tionship to become strained.

The same type of thing happened when the adults responded to an invitation from another church in the commuter belt. Tea, cakes and joint services were fine. But when our new friends were invited to hear an Asian minister speak, and explain just what happens to black people in British society, and what needs to be done about it – by white as well as black – interest waned. Not long afterwards our Church Council received a letter suggesting that priorities had changed for the months ahead, but they hoped to be in touch again in future. Meanwhile they would think of the Harlesden members as 'cousins', and we could pray for one another. The language did not go unnoticed; 'Christians are usually broth-ers and sisters', was one comment, 'now we're only cousins'. Such exchanges can be valuable but their basis needs to be fully thought through, by the leaders of all churches involved. There needs to be some kind of agreement or 'covenant', which makes a commitment both ways for a given time, and which has a proper programme and review system built in. Otherwise our 'almost white' churches may be denied a wonderful opportunity to hear the Gospel mes-sage brought by the new (black) missionaries.

SOLIDARITY

Inner-city churches, even if not the most wealthy, often exhibit the most soli-darity with the oppressed. Many of them are great givers; there is still a tithing tradition. There is also a feeling for those in need which is not often found in the rest of the church, perhaps because of the black community's own history. Black people also know, because of their roots, the exploitative economic relationships which still exist today – why is it that the wealthy countries will not pay a fair price for the goods of the poor? Hence the sermon about, or collection for, the oppressed or dispossessed always receives a ready response.

It is this kind of 'empathy' with those between a rock and a hard place which manifests the reality of the Incarnation in our contemporary world. If the

Church really believes that God was made human in Jesus Christ, then we all need to demonstrate that this is still happening. This can be done through that solidarity which gives money, offers prayer and organises action which strikes at the basis of the oppression. Even if it is only a petition about the withdrawal of a service for the mentally-handicapped, or urging the Government to increase the aid budget, one would think that every Christian would willingly sign. There were often a couple of such petitions gathering signatures at the back of the Harlesden church, but when they were taken to suburban churches they usually came back with but a few names added.

Giving was something Harlesden seemed always good at. When wealthier churches had long abandoned a '1% Scheme', giving 1 per cent of income for world development, perhaps thirty Harlesden members gave regularly. Part of the stimulus came from the church 'pilgrimages'. After returning from the Holy Land visit it was soon decided that a portion of the 1 per cent giving would go the Women's Centre on the West Bank where we had learned that inter-faith lesson. When the minister went on sabbatical in Nicaragua, and came back with pictures of a little Baptist school, with its open classrooms at the side of the church, and its pitifully small supply of educational materials, another portion was deposited there. Local campaigns of various kinds would also receive support.

During the 1980s the congregation had become increasingly caught up in the struggle against apartheid. Apart from posters on the church walls and leaflets and petitions at the back, members joined from time to time in picketing Barclays Bank and local supermarkets selling South African fruit. Much good educational work was done by these kinds of actions. Perhaps the most sensational was when, as part of a national anti-apartheid demonstration, church members picketed a Shell petrol station on the route of the march. That night a church steward was amazed to get a call from a relative in New York saying she had seen her on television, and asking what she was doing demonstrating out on the street at her time of life! She was able to explain the aim and purpose of the action, and encourage her family in the USA to join the Shell boycott.

As part of this commitment further portions of the '1% Fund' went to the ANC and to SWAPO in Namibia, at a time when most British churches would not give to the WCC Programme to Combat Racism, never mind direct to the liberation movements. What black people could not understand was why white church people were so reluctant to support the anti-apartheid struggle when members of the whites' own families had died in the war against fascism in 1939–45. Not only was there financial support but there was often a 'Material Aid for Women' box at the back of the church to collect soap, hygiene and sanitary products for South African women in the refugee camps. This had been inspired by Revd Jen

Sweet, a South African minister well-known and loved by the congregation. The Pan-Africanist Congress with offices nearby used the church hall for its fund-raising events.

Multiracial Churches have many insights and experiences to share with 'almost white' ones. When there are floods in Jamaica (or Bangladesh for that matter), or hurricanes in Dominica, or famine in parts of Africa, and when there are church members who know what it must be like, who have relatives or friends on or near the spot, or who can put across what must actually be happening, it greatly helps the church to be the Church. And when members have suffered from exploitative 'world prices' for the products their family works so hard to grow, from the effects of repaying the 'debt' to richer countries, and from what happens to those who resist these inequalities and fight back, the expectation laid upon Christians is much more easily understood. Hence the vital contribution that black members and multiracial churches have for the white Western denominations. They make it much easier to understand the modern missionary role, the fact that it is now focused here rather than there, that it involves a challenge to Western power-structures and our exploitative and environmentally-damaging standards of living. Such an understanding, of course, also brings the demand for sacrificial action.

The story of one multiracial congregation through the 1970s and 1980s can illustrate some possibilities for the local church of today. Whether it is use of premises, style of leadership, distribution of financial resources or prophetic action, there is much to learn from our inner-city communities. Harlesden was (and is) not perfect. Like the Early Church there were many disagreements. Some left because of them, others would not speak to one another for weeks. A few continued to complain at the length of church notices in Sunday worship; others grumbled at 'political activity', no matter whether it was Gospel-inspired. Overall however there was a spirit, a warmth, a vision, which the contemporary Church desperately needs. Most inner-city churches are very willing to share their message, and their fellowship, if the rest of the Church is willing to hear. But this may mean the uncomfortable rediscovery of a whole Gospel for a whole world, a Gospel which an all-white church could find it difficult to accept, and therefore preach and practise.

4

The ecumenical response

Many individual churches, like the Notting Hill and Harlesden Methodist churches mentioned above, responded positively to the arrival of black Christians from the Caribbean in the 1950s and 1960s, although many did not. Some of the responses felt by those black Christians are referred to, among other places, in *A Tree God Planted*, produced in 1985 by the Methodist Division of Social Responsibility, and *Church in Black and White*, published in 1994 by John Wilkinson, a Birmingham Anglican priest, and referred to in chapter 6.

Some of the white Christians who saw the need to make an active response in structural terms came together ecumenically in the later 1960s in meetings which eventually led to the formation of the Community and Race Relations Unit (CRRU) in 1971. This chapter recounts that process, and some of the themes and activities which characterised the Unit's work over the subsequent twenty years. It then records the setting up of the Churches' Commission for Racial Justice (CCRJ), and some of its early work. Other Christians were also contributing to the new situation, in their national denominations and their local churches, and that may need to be the subject of another book. However, the story of CRRU is a particular one, not only because it was an example of genuine, effective ecumenical activity when such relationships were less common, but because as well as a 'welfarist' approach to mission which may be still too common in the Churches, it addressed – however inadequately – questions of power. Also it engaged in the struggle for justice, it sought to educate the Churches for mission and it provided the victims with some modest resources for continuing the struggle themselves. The CCRJ has sought to continue that process, in a form more integrated with the Churches' own work.

How it all began

In 1962 immigration was a contentious political issue, as it has been ever since. It was the year of the first legislation limiting entry of Commonwealth citizens into the UK. The British Council of Churches (BCC) was in touch with its partner bodies in Canada, Australia and New Zealand, urging a common approach to their respective governments on the question. As a result of this a committee on migration issues was brought into being, which in due course gave rise to the Community and Race Relations Unit.

Also in 1962 Revd Daisuke Kitagawa of the Ethnic and Race Relations Secretariat of the World Council of Churches was surveying race relations in England. His report, noting the ambivalence in the UK between professed ideals and threatened interests, led to a discussion in BCC circles as to whether 'migrants wished to be integrated', and how 'integration must mean a process of change' for all.

A Working Party on 'Race Relations and Migration Questions' was set up, chaired by Methodist Revd Edward Rogers, which soon brought a recommendation that a 'Standing Committee' on the issues was required. Hence the October 1963 meeting of the BCC agreed to set up a Standing Committee on Migration, to 'gather and exchange information' and to study the problems and consider what contribution the Churches could make. The Standing Committee came into being in the spring of 1964, under the chairmanship of Edward Rogers, and the next year brought its first statement to the BCC Assembly on *Immigrants in Britain.* This called for an open discussion of the tensions caused by the arrival of 'immigrants', advice and pastoral care for new arrivals and the condemnation of any sign of prejudice or discrimination.

The statement also pointed out that colour was at the heart of the 'problem', and referred to the contribution immigrants were making to the British economy. It called for legislation against discrimination and a planned immigration policy. It urged the authorities to ensure that 'the coloured immigrant does not become a second-class citizen in Britain'. Hence the black people who had begun to arrive in greater numbers in the UK towards the end of the 1950s brought forth a fairly positive response from the Churches, at least in ecumenical circles. The response was less positive in other circles however and soon the Standing Committee found itself reacting to legislative initiatives which became the 1968 Commonwealth Immigrants Act.

Soon proposals began to emerge for a new organisation 'through which the churches jointly could operate in the whole field of community relations'. Such a body, it was said, should also be representative of the Roman Catholic Church and the 'Independent West Indian Churches'. Thus the ground was laid for one of the most effective areas of ecumenical co-operation in the last fifty years. There was even a suggestion it should include representatives of other faiths, though this was never actively taken up.

Edward Rogers recalls that the ecumenical atmosphere was assisted by the setting up of the World Council of Churches' Programme to Combat Racism at a

Notting Hill meeting in 1969. He also recalls that there was some resistance to setting up a 'Race Relations' body, but this was overcome when 'Community' was brought into the title. The Standing Committee on Migration had its final meeting in late 1970 and a 'bridging group' brought the Community and Race Relations Unit (CRRU) into existence in early 1971. Edward Rogers was its first Chair, Janet Henderson became Deputy Director and Douglas Tilbe, a Quaker, Director.

Its task was defined as the combating of racism and the development of good community relations, by the encouragement of local projects with grant support, education of the Christian community, advice to clergy and congregations in multiracial areas and keeping a watch on legislation, making representations where appropriate. There seems to have been little discussion with representatives from the black communities, however, in developing these terms of reference.

Christian Aid had begun its longstanding grant support of projects combating racism and overcoming racial discrimination in the mid-1960s, and continued that under the Standing Committee and then under CRRU. Funding was running at £40,000 per annum, a considerable sum in those days, and much larger proportionately than today. Christian Aid remains the most substantial contributor to anti-racist work in the ecumenical structures of the 1990s, under the Churches' Commission for Racial Justice.

The early years of CRRU (1971–5)

IMMIGRATION ISSUES

The first problem which engaged the attention of the new Unit was the 1971 Immigration Bill. The Unit issued a statement registering a 'fundamental opposition' to the Bill as it created 'insecurity and fear among the non-white population' and instituted the concept of 'patriality', allowing those who had a British grandparent to claim British nationality even if they had never been here, while denying it to many who had lived in the country for years. The statement said the Bill was 'indicative of a narrowly-conceived idea of British society, in which those of a different colour and culture are tolerated for the services they can render but not welcomed for the enrichment they can bring'. It pointed to the 'considerable racial element concealed within' the legislation, and opposed the limitation of family reunion and the 'wide discretionary powers' given to immigration officers. Hence the Unit began early the critical approach to UK immigration law it had for the rest of its 21-year life.

The statement led to correspondence with the Home Secretary, Reginald Maudling, and Briefings directed towards the different stages of the Bill. The latter, among other things, drew attention to the role of Mr Enoch Powell in creating anxiety and fear in the black population. In July 1971 CRRU co-ordinated a delegation of religious leaders, including Anglican and Catholic Bishops, the Secretary of the Methodist Conference and a Jewish rabbi, to a Home Office Minister. In a Briefing on the 1971 Bill the Unit raised 'the comparative position of Commonwealth immigrants and EEC nationals regarding future entry into the UK'. It pointed out that the latter would enjoy considerable advantages in respect of 'access to employment, rights of residence and the right to bring in dependents'. This has indeed proved to be the case.

The final Briefing for the Lords debate in October 1971 listed nearly a dozen improvements in the Bill gained from lobbying by CRRU and others, although its fundamental principles regarding right of entry and settlement, the need for work permits and the limitation of family reunion remained entrenched. The Unit continued to monitor the effect when the Act became law, and in June 1973 obtained the backing of the Council of Churches for a statement attacking the new practice of deporting people who had become 'illegal immigrants' under the 1971 Act. They urged an amnesty for those who had retrospectively become illegal. The following year much time was taken up with the arrival of some 30,000 Ugandan Asians expelled by Idi Amin. Many arrived penniless and the Churches raised £40,000 to help.

THE USE OF CHURCH BUILDINGS

The controversial issue of church buildings arrived on the Unit's agenda at the beginning of 1972. It set up an ecumenical working party on 'The Use of Church Properties for Community Activities in Multiracial Areas'. It included names of people active in such work for the following 25 years, Don Black (Baptist), Lewis Donnelly (Catholic) and Vic Watson (Methodist). It had to report on current practice in the churches, with a view to publishing an advisory report.

The working party looked initially at the use of churches by 'black-led churches', but also by other faith communities. By the end of 1972 its interim report was recommending that churches in use for Christian worship should not be made available for other faith worship, but church halls could. The report also said that the use of church buildings in multiracial areas should reflect a commitment by Christians to act with their neighbours of other faiths for the common good. The report was discussed by most major Churches. The Church of England got into some difficulty about it, supporting the proposition that buildings should be made available to minority groups, but opposing the sale of redundant churches to non-Christian communities. The Baptists and the United Reformed Church commended the report for study by local churches, the Catholics said it would take a long time to obtain a Vatican view and the Unitarians and Quakers said they had little problem with other faiths using their premises at any time.

The working party followed up the interim report with a further report in May 1973 of a 'three-area survey' of 50 per cent of the churches in parts of Bradford, Derby and Lambeth in London. This discovered that most church buildings are seriously under-used. Many Christians were 'fairly happy' with the use of the halls by other faith communities; the percentage rose when there were direct contacts.

The debate reverberated on for some time, but largely as a result of it many redundant churches were sold to become Sikh gurdwaras, Muslim mosques or Hindu mandirs. The working party produced its final report on 'The Community Orientation of the Church' in 1974, and this was remitted by the BCC Assembly to the Churches. The working party and its reports laid an effective basis for the Churches' thinking in this sensitive area and was undoubtedly partly responsible for the forward movement in the areas of inter-faith dialogue which led eventually to the formation of the Committee for Relations with People of Other Faiths, under the BCC, and the Commission for Interfaith Relations, under the Council of Churches for Britain and Ireland.

EDUCATION WORK

The Unit was fortunate enough to obtain an early grant from one of the Rowntree Trusts to employ a Secretary helping church people to accept that Britain was now a multiracial society. This meant, said the first Education Secretary Ruth Tetlow, 'facing and fighting racial prejudice in ourselves and others, as well as developing a concern for racial justice'. Work was built up through seminars and conferences, publications and links with secular bodies. The publications included a series of pamphlets on 'Black Churches', 'The Asian in Britain' and 'Migrant Workers in Europe', and three booklets on 'World Religions in Britain'.

Another dimension of the education work was the relationship with the Roman Catholic Church. There had long been a Catholic 'observer' on the CRRU Board and now the Catholic Commission for Racial Justice education worker began to work from the CRRU office. When Ruth Tetlow left in 1973 Gwen Cashmore came in and set new directions for the education work. She proposed a working party on 'Britain as a Multiracial Society', which led to the report *The New Black Presence in Britain*. She developed adult education work and started a regular bulletin. She generated an even greater network of other concerned organisations around the country, religious and secular. Her first report raised questions which are still apposite, 'Should the Churches seek to be a voice for the voiceless?', should they seek to 'speak the truth to those in power'? or should the work focus on the white community and its anxieties and fears? Cashmore's work pointed up the essential nature of education work in the Churches in this whole area.

EXTERNAL CONCERNS: NORTHERN IRELAND, CCME AND PCR

It is perhaps a surprise to learn that in 1972 CRRU set up a fund for community projects in Northern Ireland, which was administered jointly with the Roman Catholic Justice and Peace Commission. By autumn 1973 nearly £14,000 had been distributed to 19 projects, including the Shankill Youth and Community centre, Ballymurphy Enterprises and the Corrymeela Community. Subsequently the Irish Council of Churches launched its own 'Fund for Ireland', to support those working for reconciliation, fostering local community organisations and undertaking research. A leaflet urged the British Churches to retain an interest in what was happening in Ireland.

As has been indicated above, CRRU was interested from its earliest days in developments at the European level. It soon became the link agency for the Churches Committee for Migrant Workers in Europe, as it was then, now the Churches Commission for Migrants in Europe (CCME). CRRU participated in an early 1970s working party on clandestine and illegal migration. CCMWE also took up the issue of migrant women: Sybil Phoenix attended an Assembly on this theme in early 1974, and the report was sent out widely to European Churches' headquarters. CRRU also sought to raise money from the British Churches for the European work.

In March 1974 the Unit co-sponsored with the Catholics a conference on 'The EEC and Migrant Labour'. This heard of the misery of those who try to get into the wealthy European Community, to meet the need for cheap labour. It also heard of the importance of networking among migrant workers, trades unionists and left-wing political parties (and maybe the Churches) in trying to prevent exploitation. There was also discussion of how more balanced economic development in the world would reduce the pressure to migrate to Europe.

CRRU developed contacts on a global level also, setting up a Liaison Group to work with the World Council of Churches' Programme to Combat Racism (PCR). The Group's first chair was Stanley Booth-Clibborn, later to become a long-serving Bishop of Manchester. In 1973 the Unit produced a leaflet on South Africa, *Investment in Racism*, which gave information about church shareholdings in companies operating in South Africa and described WCC policy regarding companies and banks involved in supporting apartheid. It called for an active campaign against the inhumanity of apartheid and urged churches to be aware of 'the moral implications of their investments' and the Director of PCR, Baldwin Sjollema, visited London. CRRU produced a leaflet focusing on white racism, introducing the idea of 'institutional racism' and arguing for a 'redistribution of social, political, economic and cultural power'. The PCR set up the Special Fund and began to make grants to the southern African liberation movements.

The Methodist Church was the first to contribute directly to the Special Fund, then it stopped again when an individual member threatened legal action. The Church of England cut its support for the WCC because of its liberation movement grants. It is interesting to note in retrospect that almost all the movements funded by PCR subsequently became national governments (and not particularly revolutionary ones at that). Reaction to PCR and its Special Fund was another indicator of the level of racism in Church and society throughout this period.

Towards the end of this first period of CRRU's life Revd Dr Colin Morris had become the chair. He was succeeded at the end of 1975 by fellow Methodist Pauline Webb. About the same time Elliott Kendall became Director, and Roman Catholic Ultan Russell took over responsibility for the Projects Fund.

The Projects Fund

The Community and Race Relations Unit had inherited a system of funding multiracial projects from the Standing Committee on Migration, and one aspect of its terms of reference was to encourage local projects and evaluate them for grants with Christian Aid's support. The first substantial work in this field had been done by Michael Elliott, who was given the title 'Development Officer', signifying that he was to help projects develop as well as recommend them for funding. By the end of 1973 the Projects Fund was already supporting local initiatives in the London area, including the Harlesden Advice Centre (see p. 83), the Midlands, the north of England and Scotland.

During this period the priorities for grants were for community centres and workers, pre-school provision, youth work, welfare and advice services and language support. A selection made in March 1974 included support for community workers for the Brixton Neighbourhood Community Association (women's worker), St Silas Church, Sheffield, and the Moseley Road and Sparkhill Methodist Team Ministry, for youth hostels in Bristol and Leicester, and for the national Joint Council for the Welfare of Immigrants (JCWI).

One project which caused some controversy during this period was 'Towards Racial Justice' (TRJ), set up by – among others – Darcus Howe, now a TV presenter, and Rudi Narayan, a controversial black lawyer. TRJ, which received support in 1974 and 1975, operated from Brixton's 'front line' and aimed to set up a telephone legal advice line for anyone subjected to racial discrimination or attack. TRJ also published *Race Today*, which later received support from the PCR. *Race Today* was set up 'to respond to the growth of racism in Britain' and move beyond the 'community relations' approach to something 'more organically connected with the needs and hopes of black minorities themselves'. It was frequently critical of the police, the courts, Parliament, the Churches and others in authority. TRJ had a dozen black lawyers offering free advice, and produced a 'Rights on Arrest' card primarily for black youth.

The TRJ grants caused not only ongoing debate in CRRU but discussions with Christian Aid who were unsure if their money could be used for such bodies. Wilfred Wood, now Bishop of Croydon, stepped into the controversy, saying the Churches should concentrate on raising funds for the CRRU Projects Fund and leave the Unit to get on with distributing the money. These arguments symbolise the debate which continued to take place for the rest of CRRU's life – and beyond – about the rightness of support for 'militant' black organisations.

The style of the Projects Fund in this early period was to encourage projects to start, as well as to fund initiatives which were already going. This required what Elliott Kendall called an enormous amount of work from the staff, especially Ultan Russell and his successor Jeremy Hawthorn – who was well-known for carrying his bike on to trains and setting off around the projects in a particular city when he arrived. When Jeremy left in 1981 Ken Leech covered the work from his desk in Church House before Elizabeth Varley was appointed in January 1982. By this time the Fund had become widely known and many applications were having to be turned down.

Looking at later project listings, further interesting titles appear, both of continuing pieces of work and new initiatives which later became significant. For example, in 1980 the Aladura International Church in Wandsworth received £1,000 for pastoral expenses. That church was a founder member of the Council of African and Afro-Caribbean Churches (CAAC), which in turn became a founding member of CCBI. Its pastor, Father Olu Abiola, became the CCBI's first black President. The Asian Resource Centre and St James Advice Centre, both in Birmingham, the West Indian Counselling Service in Leeds, Wesley Hall (Leicester), South Riverside Community Project (Cardiff), St Paul's Project (Bristol) and the Scottish Churches Race Relations Group – all of which are still going in one form or another – received support in this period. The project listings are a unique and fascinating source from which to examine the history of community and race relations in Britain during the 1970s and 1980s.

The first church body to supplement Christian Aid's support for the Projects Fund was the Methodist Overseas Division, which in 1973 announced a gift of £10,000 per annum. By 1980 grants made had risen to £88,000 and had begun to receive quite wide publicity. The *Daily Telegraph* carried a heading 'Grant for Hindu Rugger', claiming that a Hindu Rugby Football Association and Notting Hill's annual Carnival were among 84 beneficiaries of 'grants for racial justice handed out by the British Council of Churches'. A subsequent 'short' in *Tribune* pointed out that the grant was to the Rugby Hindu Association, i.e. the town and not the sport. Disinformation has had a place in the history of CRRU, but it has also had its funny side.

At the beginning of the 1980s the Fund received a boost from the result of the debates in the Church of England about *The New Black Presence* (see p. 101). The Bishops of Liverpool and Ripon moved a 1979 General Synod resolution to the effect that Anglican Dioceses should aim to contribute £100,000 a year for seven years, starting in 1981. Donations reached about £65,000 in 1986, the high point, but subsequently fell and by the early 1990s were running at less than £10,000. In the meantime Christian Aid's support continued to rise, and grants were nearly £180,000 by 1989.

In 1990 the Church Urban Fund, one of the main outcomes of the Church of England's *Faith in the City* report, was asked to consider making good the original Anglican target of £100,000, and decided to give £80,000 to match a hoped-for £20,000 from the dioceses. This took the Projects Fund beyond the £250,000 mark, though arguably still proportionately lower in real terms than when it began with £40,000 in 1971. It was undoubtedly the long and committed support of Christian Aid which made for the success of the Projects Fund. The Methodist Church was the only Church to contribute consistently, while it also developed its own £100,000 Multiracial Projects Fund. This Fund has prompted the question of why Methodism was doing something separately which the Churches should be doing together, but this should not detract from its ongoing practical support for racial justice. Other Churches have given minor grants from time to time, but only on a 'one-off' basis.

The grant which caused the most controversy in the life of CRRU was a very modest one of £500, given to the Liverpool 8 Defence Committee in August 1981, in the aftermath of the Toxteth uprisings. The CRRU staff knew local church and community leaders well; two of them visited immediately after the disturbances. The grant's purpose was to help the Defence Committee provide legal assistance to local people, who in some cases had had members of their families detained for several days, with their whereabouts unknown. However, it drew forth a storm of reaction and it is probably worth rehearsing some of the arguments, which still continue in other forms in relation to Project Fund grants.

The story broke on 26 August 1981, with the main protagonists identified as the Merseyside Police Federation and the BCC. One reference point for press stories was a statement by Merseyside church leaders Archbishop Derek Warlock, Bishop David Sheppard and Methodist Chairman Revd Norwyn Denny. This condemned the violence and refused to participate in 'the continuing campaign against the police', but asked understanding for 'this gesture of help towards those who have felt alienated from the rest of the community'. For Liverpool 8 to stand up after years of massive deprivation, it said, support must be given to groups which are 'an authentic expression of some strongly held feelings'.

Press coverage ranged from Glasgow to Devon and Dublin to Colchester. A *Times* editorial commented that 'Racial consciousness and the liberation movements springing from it have aroused the Christian conscience', and felt that this has created debate about 'the political content of the Gospel'. It remarked that in the Churches 'activism is in the ascendant', but went on to attack the defence campaign and its 'refusal to speak with journalists, its political extremism and its campaign against the police'.

Peregrine Worsthorne in the *Sunday Telegraph* felt that questions must be asked.

> What Christian purpose is [the grant] intended to promote? How will it help to bring those charged or convicted to repentance or atonement?. . . Presumably the hope is that . . . this will open their hearts, and those of the deprived generally, to the Christian message.

Worsthorne went on to say that the rioters are more likely to believe they were justified in throwing petrol bombs at police and 'unless church leaders are just thick, it has to be supposed they are well aware' of this. (*Sunday Telegraph*, 30 August 1981).

The *Sunday Times* took a rather different view, in an article by John Whale, noting that Councils of Churches are partly about creating Christian unity, but partly about giving practical effect to that part of the Word which prescribes the care of 'all those who are in anyways afflicted or distressed'. They can do this by trying to persuade governments but also by putting 'their modest weight behind the activists'.

Looking back this was one of those baptisms of fire through which the shape and commitment of the Projects Fund was forged. It says much for the Merseyside church leaders that they stood by the grant, and for CRRU staff, who were under serious pressure. However, the event exposed the lack of understanding in much of rural and suburban Christianity about the realities of inner-city life. It demonstrated the need for 'education for repentance' which – for the most part – the Churches have still failed to undertake. This was a pity because the *New Black Presence* report had certainly laid the foundations.

The New Black Presence in Britain

When it was published in April 1976, the report *The New Black Presence in Britain* caused considerable discussion. It had been produced over a two-year period, after Gwen Cashmore's suggestion for a working party to the CRRU Board at the end of 1973. The terms of reference had been to assess the changing pattern of society with particular reference to immigration, to discover the forces which are at work, to articulate the principles revealed and to point towards the kind of society for which Britain should be aiming. It is informative to review the process by which it came to birth, as it was arguably a real watershed in the Churches' understanding of the realities of racism in British society.

Among the membership of the working party were Gus John, a black educationalist and former trainee Dominican, and latterly Director of Education for Hackney, Revd John Davies, later Bishop of Shrewsbury, David Bleakley, later General Secretary of the Irish Council of Churches, Colin Morris and Revd Theo Samuel, later the first Moderator of the Churches' Commission for Racial Justice.

The first paper to the group by Gus John posed some sharp questions about whether the Church itself was not 'an increasing paradox and a massive contradiction' and asked 'Is the Church not also the oppressor which contributes to the unjust order, suffocates Christ and stubs out the Spirit in God's people in the name of love, forgiveness and presumably human justice?'. It also raised questions about the Projects Fund, saying that the more important issue was to eradicate the conditions which give rise to inequity.

Gus John also pressed the group to do more thinking about the need for a historical analysis, 'multiracialism', radicalism and the relation of the Churches to black resistance. He believed that the conflict within British society would continue, that police repression would increase and that there might be attempts at repatriation. He then provided the basic analytical paper for the final report, pointing to the need for British society to understand the history of colonialism and post-colonialism, to accept the reality of institutional racism and to review what is meant by 'British identity'.

The New Black Presence recognised that it might be difficult for white people to understand the nature and the strength of the views of the black community.

> To these black people Church, School, Police and Social Services are seen to have linked arms against their entry into the benefits of white society. We realise that to many white people this will be an incomprehensible statement. Those who inherit the benefits of British society can perhaps look at its institutions with pride and satisfaction . . . their experience tells them that these institutions work to their advantage.

They cannot see how they exclude the less privileged.

The report also offered hope. It noted that 'assimilation' had been rejected as a solution; each sector of British society will need to work out its identity in the context of all other sectors, the Churches too. The report went on:

> We have great hope for what the black communities can contribute to a richer and more inclusive British life, when these communities have the freedom really to take responsibility for themselves. The Black Presence can offer a new awareness, out of its own rich understanding of man [sic] in society; it can bring insights and values that have long been eroded in the West. (p. 25)

The final draft of the report was discussed by the CRRU Board and by four meetings in different cities around the UK. It created a good deal of emotional response; there were those – black and white – who wanted it to go no further. Finally it was submitted to the BCC Assembly at Bangor in April 1976. The debate was opened by Rt Revd David Sheppard, Bishop of Liverpool. Observers recall that Gus John spoke vigorously and emotionally for the report, and that there was a good deal of opposition. A senior Baptist questioned Gus John's veracity in saying that 'white society does not give a damn' and 'the police simply follow the lead of the Government'. The Secretary of the Church of England's Board of Social Responsibility was more positive, saying it was a challenging testimony, and 'we need to comprehend the bitterness and pain out of which it is written'. Paul Oestreicher gave examples relating to the police from his own experience. Pauline Webb commented that this was all the beginning of a very long process, and so it has proved.

Finally the Assembly received the report (it did not adopt it), urged member churches to use it to encourage their committees and local churches to listen to the black experience, and accepted the challenge the report presents to our understanding of and obedience to the Christian faith.

Gwen Cashmore comments today that the most remarkable outcome of the publication of *The New Black Presence* was the way in which the mainstream Churches, including the Roman Catholics, took it into their system of debate and decision-making. The Methodists, the URC and the Church of England did this particularly thoroughly. In the latter the report was considered in most dioceses and many deaneries. It led to the 1979 General Synod resolution to contribute £100,000 a year to the Projects Fund. As far as CRRU's education work was concerned it was the exposure of local churches to the pain of the black experience that led to changes of mind and heart.

John Davies, the actual author of the report, later reflected, 'I have never known an issue with greater power to produce hostility between people who have previously seen each other as friends and allies. . ... But the more serious question was "Is it *true* what you are saying?". Davies said that in his experience the sentence in the report which caused the most difficulty was

> The basic issue is not a problem caused by black people; the basic issue concerns the nature of British society as a whole, and features of that society which have been there long before the recent phase of black immigration; the black communities are holding a mirror to British society.

He concluded that racism exists in order to shore up our 'vast discrepancies in the distribution of power'.

The turn of the decade and the 1981 Nationality Act

There was still much work to do in informing Christians on a range of community relations issues. About the same time as *The New Black Presence* received the go-ahead, CRRU published *Ethnic Minorities in Society* jointly with the Runnymede Trust. This was a reference guide on the numbers and distribution of minorities in the UK, current immigration controls, attitudes to black people and the place of the law. Next a more personal statement was published, *The Black Mirror* by Morris Stuart, giving white Christians one of their first clear insights into how Black Christians felt. Stuart wrote about issues such as 'Black Power', reminded his readers that 'Jesus is black', gave practical examples of racism that still ring bells today and offered guidance to would-be anti-racist white Christians.

About the same time a pamphlet on migrant communities in East London was published, with a foreword by the then Bishop of Stepney, Rt Revd Trevor Huddleston. The title was *They Sell Cheaper and They Live Very Odd*; it was written by Caroline Adams. The booklet reported some of the racist abuse the Bengali community in particular was having to face. Over the next two years CRRU published or distributed further materials on the National Front and related groups, including a leaflet *The Writing on the Wall* and a pamphlet by Malcolm Goldsmith, *A Christian Looks at the National Front*. In 1978 AFFOR (All Faiths for

One Race) and CRRU produced Tony Holden's *So What Are You Going to Do about the National Front?* Later an educational filmstrip *The Enemy Within* was produced, which sold well for over a decade.

In the meantime there had been a major development in the passing of the 1976 Race Relations Act. CRRU had been very supportive of the legislation, and had hoped for a much stronger Bill, but at least a law had been passed, racial discrimination in many forms was outlawed, and there were bodies in place to monitor such discrimination. In 1979 CRRU held a major conference at Loughborough University on the theme 'Racism and the World Church – Combating Racism in the 1980s'. The report was sharp and well-focused about what should be done in Britain. One of its key concerns was immigration and there were subsequent delegations to Home Office and Foreign Office ministers. It provided part of the platform for the Churches' position in the approach to the 1981 Immigration and Nationality Act.

The run-up to this Act was a particular time in which CRRU sought to build awareness in the Churches. It was from this Act that many of the problems of access and deportation referred to in chapter 1 flowed. This legislation has been one of the main headaches for CRRU and its successor body ever since. As it became clear that the new Conservative Government elected in 1979 was going to bring in major new legislation, the Roman Catholic Bishops' Conference of England and Wales produced a statement in mid-1979 'Concerning the Revision of the British Nationality Law', which was subsequently endorsed by the BCC.

The statement criticised the radical distinction made by the 1971 Act between 'patrials' and 'non-patrials', and the movement away from the spirit of the 1948 Nationality Act under which a citizen of a 'colony' was automatically a citizen of the UK. It called for any new law to state that Britain is now a multiracial society, that the principle of *ius soli* would be maintained (i.e. a baby born here would have British nationality), and that the rights and duties of all present UK and colonial citizens would be clearly set out. It also asserted that 'settled immigrants. . . who have not yet acquired British citizenship should have the same rights to freedom of movement in the EC as British citizens', a commitment for which the Churches and many other concerned bodies are still pressing even after the Single European Act has come into force.

As the content of the new legislation became clear, a number of Anglican Bishops, including David Sheppard of Liverpool and Robert Runcie, then of St Albans, made a strong statement referring to 'the cruel consequences of such unchristian and inhuman legislation' which 'degrades the society which requires and enacts it'. CRRU issued a strong press release, which created a certain degree of controversy, and produced its own pamphlet *A Tale of Two Citizenships*, written by Field Officer Jeremy Hawthorn.

In fact the BCC Assembly eventually endorsed the Unit's position and CRRU followed up the pamphlet by producing a study pack *So Who's British?* and organising a 48-hour vigil in June 1980 in St Margaret's Westminster. The vigil was sponsored by several other bodies and attended by the Archbishop of Canterbury and the Bishop of London. When the Bill was published CRRU issued further statements, pointing out that the Bill was about immigration control rather than citizenship, and supported a letter from Cardinal Hume on behalf of the Catholic Bishops expressing 'grave misgivings'. The Bishop of Truro met the Immigration Minister Timothy Raison and reiterated the Churches' concerns that the Bill was racially discriminatory. The Scottish Churches Race Relations Group also made representations. A critical resolution was passed at the BCC's April Assembly and the Anglican Bishops and Catholic peers kept up the opposition in the House of Lords, but the Bill was passed with only a few relatively insubstantial amendments.

As a follow-up to its work on the 1981 Act CRRU published a campaigning pack *As One Born Among Us*, which included case studies of what was happening to African, Caribbean and Asian communities as a result of the new law, and urged support for the non-racist immigration policies of AGIN, the newly-formed Action Group on Immigration and Nationality. However, the pack seemed to suffer from the same problem as much of CRRU's educational material, it was deemed only relevant to multiracial, inner-city churches, whereas it is in truth much more important for churches in the 'White Highlands' – who also have responsibility for our immigration laws – to take up such concerns.

The nature of these laws was admirably summarised in *The Closed Door*, written by CRRU Secretary Keith Jenkins in 1984, which described the way immigration controls had become increasingly restrictive since the 1940s. It was issued at a time of greater activity by the Churches, including a call by the General Synod to revise the Nationality Act, and a delegation to the Home Secretary led by the Archbishop of Canterbury. The booklet included a theological reflection, set out a more Christian approach, and reminded readers of the inhuman effects of current deportation practices. It urged an amnesty, to end the fears and uncertainties of many black residents. It also called attention to the plight of asylum-seekers, an issue which has taken up an increasing amount of time since, for both CRRU and CCRJ.

Finally *The Closed Door* urged prayer and protest:

> we must pray about and we must protest against injustices in immigration policy . . . executed in our name, for we cannot detach

ourselves from the society of which we are part . . . nor can we as Christians cut ourselves off from those who suffer the consequences.

The booklet received the full backing of the BCC and provided the basis for CRRU's continuing work on immigration and nationality issues through the rest of the 1980s.

The second decade (1981–92)

THE UPRISINGS OF 1981 AND INSTITUTIONAL RACISM

The Unit's work in the 1970s on immigration law, its causes and effects, was in a way a case-study on the reality of 'institutional racism'. This term had appeared as long ago as the statement of the WCC Central Committee when it met in 1969 and agreed to set up the Programme to Combat Racism. The statement said:

It is no longer sufficient to deal with the race problem at the level of person-to-person relationships. It is *institutional racism* as reflected in the economic and political power structures which must be challenged. Combatting racism must entail a *redistribution* of social, economic, political and cultural *power* from the powerful to the powerless.

It was the failure of British society to recognise this which led to uprisings in 1979 in Southall and in 1981 in Brixton, Toxteth, Handsworth and other places. After the 1979 demonstrations against the National Front in Southall, when teacher Blair Peach was killed, the Unit supported a public enquiry into the events. Its Chair was Professor Michael Dummett of Oxford University; other members were Pauline Webb, who chaired CRRU until 1979, and the Rt Revd Hewlett Thompson, then Bishop of Willesden, who became Chair of CRRU in 1981. The enquiry expressed its astonishment that a police investigation into the allegation that he had been killed by a police officer resulted in no proceedings, but neither was there a further investigation into who was responsible. Appeal Judge Lord Bridge said 'there is reason to suspect that Blair Peach died from a blow to the head struck by a police officer with an unauthorised and potentially lethal weapon'.

Following the disturbances in Brixton in April 1981 the Unit distributed a statement by the Brixton Council of Churches, which expressed the shame of the local churches as to the causes of the disturbances – 'bad housing, high unemployment, educational disadvantage, a racially-biassed Nationality Bill'. The statement also said that riot and public disorder was not an acceptable means of expression, but it was critical of the police. 'It seems as though the police force can never allow itself to be seen to be taking any advice, let alone the faintest hint of criticism'. There was 'repeated use of unreasonable force and demeaning treatment against individuals'. The local church leaders called for a new initiative in police–community liaison which eventually, via the Scarman Report, grew into the Police–Community Liaison Committees formed under some pressure from the Home Office. One local church leader, Revd Bob Nind, the Vicar of St Matthew's, was a member of the CRRU Board at the time, and an outspoken critic of police behaviour.

Revd Elliott Kendall, the Director, and Jeremy Hawthorn, the Field Officer, both left CRRU in August 1981. Kendall commented on how remarkable it was that so many were surprised at the Brixton uprisings, after there had been so many warnings about the police, unemployment, racist attacks and immigration legislation. He urged the Churches to listen to the victims, to help communicate their experiences to the Government and to press the authorities for a sustained effort towards justice and equality of opportunity. Hawthorn is more direct. He says 'State racism' is the real problem, the 'systematic racism pervading legislation on immigration, nationality, education and social welfare'. Opposing state racism is not 'respectable', and Hawthorn felt the Churches were unwilling to endure the pressure they might experience, and act together against racism.

Institutional racism was raised in another way for the BCC when a proposal from Bob Nind on 'affirmative action' was put forward, noting that the Council had not adopted an equal opportunities policy, nor were the Churches monitoring the practices of firms with which they did business. This was in the context of the 'contract compliance' initiatives of several Labour Councils, built on the US experience of coercive persuasion to get companies to employ more black workers. Affirmative action could include bringing black people on to committees, as well as employing more of them. The initiative eventually produced a BCC equal opportunities policy and regular monitoring of the workforce, which continued into the CCBI.

In the meantime Lord Scarman had concluded his report on the Brixton uprising and rejected the idea that institutional racism existed in British society. The CRRU Board responded that this was one conclusion of the report it could not accept, and noted that 'Considerable effort will have to be made in the coming months to find ways of overcoming this seemingly authoritative [view]'. The Board commented that the police and the criminal justice system are two 'institutions' in which racism has a serious and profound effect on the lives of black people. This position was vigorously advocated at the April 1982 BCC Assembly by Canon Ivor Smith Cameron, later to become Chair of CRRU from 1984 to 1990, and was given clear support.

The Unit then began to call together representatives from communities where violence had occurred, including Brixton, Toxteth, Handsworth, St Pauls (Bristol) and Southall. Three such meetings in 1982 led to a series of 'Inner City Consultations' between 1983 and 1985. Many stories were shared, and there was a comprehensive rebuttal of Scarman's position.

Later in 1982 CRRU published *Institutional Racism: A Reflection from Britain*, written by Sebastian Charles, a former Director of CRRU and the first black Canon of Westminster Abbey. Charles seeks to help the person in the pew understand the origins, nature and effects of this manifestation of racism. He also rejects Scarman's position and states that racial discrimination will only be eliminated by 'profound institutional change'. He notes the origins of racism in the colonial period, which helps us to understand why 'the great liberal institutions of parliament, the press, industrial organisations, the judiciary, institutions of education and research, administrative systems, the military, law enforcement agencies and the church were all infected by racism'.

Charles spells out a recipe for change with seven proposals related to the civil service, political institutions, the police and armed services, companies, the housing and education sectors, the Churches (especially in theological training) and Government, who all – by clear measurable steps – should begin to deal with their racism. These were of course themes which CRRU continued to raise over the next ten years. During its last year, 1992, CRRU published a survey on race equality in employment (showing that a few steps had been taken, but not many) and a survey of theological colleges (which showed that many still had not grasped the concept of institutional racism). Charles also raised the European context of institutional racism, something which CRRU was still addressing as it went out of existence.

THE CHURCHES AND CRIMINAL JUSTICE

One result of Scarman was that CRRU began to do more focused work on the processes of criminal justice. It criticised the police for issuing ethnic statistics on violent crime, while largely ignoring the statistics of racial attacks. At the beginning of 1983 the Unit began work on the Police and Criminal Evidence Bill (PACE) which followed up concerns over stop-and-search, increased powers of arrest and lack of accountability by police authorities – especially in London. The Unit was concerned that, at a time when there was already a gulf between the black community and the police, a Bill was being proposed which 'has the potential to drive a wedge between police and community'. A position paper was sent to the Home Secretary and other politicians, and a resolution calling for basic changes in the Bill passed by the BCC Spring Assembly.

The 1983 General Election caused PACE to fall, but it was reintroduced later in the year, with some modest amendments. The Unit continued to raise questions about stop-and-search powers, and this was expressed in a press release which quoted a Policy Studies Institute study showing that there was insufficient reason for one-third of police stops, many of which were on young blacks. 'Search and seizure' was another area of anxiety in which even confidential records could be taken from private offices. There was support for the setting out of new powers of arrest, but concern over the requirement for a 'satisfactory address', something which it was felt police might well use to detain young black people. The Unit also felt that the proposed 36 hours was unnecessarily long to keep someone without the check provided by reference to the courts, especially if people were also denied access to legal advice.

Another serious reservation with the proposed legislation was the permitted use of evidence, including confessions, obtained in breach of the code of practice on the treatment of prisoners. This had contemporary interest in the late 1980s and the 1990s because of a number of cases where 'uncorroborated confessional evidence' provided the main reason for a guilty verdict, and after which young men and women – usually black or Irish – were sent to prison for many years. The reservations were well-justified, as by 1992 CRRU had seen overturned the verdicts on the Tottenham Three, the Birmingham Six and the Guildford Four, and was supporting the campaigns of the Cardiff Three and the East Ham Two (the two Tamils jailed for the murder of other Tamils in a sectarian fire-bomb attack), all of whom were freed and whose cases are referred to elsewhere in this book (see p. 29). The Unit also assisted in funding a pamphlet from the Church of England Board of Social Responsibility on *Policing in a Democratic Society*. This dealt among other things with the relations between the police and the black community, where it noted that the issues central to the current debate focused on 'the contact between the police and black people on the streets'.

The only amendment proposed to PACE which succeeded was one making racial discrimination a police disciplinary offence. Unfortunately, despite many opportunities, this has very rarely been used, a fact which continues to generate cynicism in the black community over the seriousness with which the police tackle racism.

Criminal justice problems were highlighted in four 'Inner-City Consultations' organised by CRRU between 1982 and 1986 in London, Birmingham, Manchester and Leeds. All made reference to the problems of police–community relations. The Manchester meeting took place in the Moss Side/Hulme area and consideration of police issues was made inevitable by the award the previous day of substantial damages to three local young black people as the result of wrongful arrest and mistreatment.

The role of magistrates and their scarcity in inner cities was also discussed. This led to correspondence between CRRU and the Lord Chancellor's Department concerning the need for an increase in black magistrates. However, a 1992 Home Office report indicated that still only 2 per cent of magistrates were black. The Unit pressed for improved training to try to ensure an anti-racist approach by all magistrates. The 1986 Leeds Consultation felt police–black community problems began in the schools, where young blacks under-achieved, became frustrated and directed their anger at anyone in a position of authority. It believed that the potential for conflict was exacerbated by the lack of experience of many police officers of inner-city life.

One piece of CRRU's later work which developed from these consultations revolved around the numbers and situation of black people in prison. This led to a conference in Pentonville prison in March 1988 on 'The Needs of Black Christians in Prison'. Recommendations included more black chaplains, greater participation by black Christians in prison worship and increased support by chaplains to black prison staff. The Chaplain General agreed to look at the contribution of black people to the work of chaplains, to examine the special needs of 'immigration prisoners' and to continue to sensitise the Home Office to the importance of anti-racist perspectives in the prison service.

This led on to other work for CRRU on the criminal justice system, around the disproportionate numbers of black prisoners. The Unit produced a paper, *Return to Justice: Keeping Black People out of Prison.* Its recommendations included reducing unemployment, training and monitoring of police, magistrates, judges and prison officers, an enhanced role for the probation service and pursuit by Government of alternatives to custody.

One matter to which the Unit's attention was drawn during this exercise was the role of the police in determining the numbers of black people who come before the courts. A second paper on *Policing and the Black Community* was produced which listed a range of incidents where police racism was evident, including some in which large compensation sums had been paid. The biggest was £130,000 to Mrs Thora Rose for the death of her husband in police custody eight years earlier.

As a result of the two Papers a CRRU delegation met with John Patten MP and Lord Ferrers, the Home Office ministers for Prisons and Police respectively. It urged a clear commitment to eradicate racial discrimination in the criminal justice system.

However this did not appear in the 1991 Criminal Justice Act. One small amendment to Section 95 was gained in the Lords by Baroness Flather, giving the Minister power to report certain information on racial matters. When the new Churches' Commission for Racial Justice organised its first meeting with Home Office ministers in September 1992 it was presented with the first such report. Even last-minute lobbying in the passage of legislation can have a useful effect.

The full history of the BCC Community and Race Relations Unit in the 1970s and 1980s, along with the activities of the Churches more generally, remains to be written. CRRU was reasonably influential in its earlier years, possibly because the Churches themselves had more influence in society. Later in the 1980s the black communities became more informed, better resourced and more active, and rightly so. CRRU's contribution was not so vital, and it may have been diminished further by the apparent unwillingness of the Churches at both local and leadership level to give more vigorous support to its views. Revd Elliott Kendall, Director of the Unit between 1975 and 1981, commented in a personal conversation in mid-1992, not long before he died,

> It would be nice to think that CRRU was fully supported by the BCC. This is far from the truth. Especially after it gave support to the WCC Programme to Combat Racism CRRU received less than whole-hearted support from BCC Executive Committees and Assemblies.

As a Conservative administration consolidated its hold on power during the 1980s, rolled back many of the gains made in racial equality, and developed policies that were covertly if not overtly racist, the Churches as a body failed to make an effective impact. Activists felt that the analysis of the real causes and effects of racism was weak, and failed to draw on the crucial biblical teaching on righteousness and justice to which we shall refer later in chapter 6.

THE ECONOMIC DIMENSION

Although concern about the economic disadvantage of the black community had been around in one way or another since the Unit started, not to mention in Dr Harold Moody's appeal to the Churches back in 1940 (see pp. 60-61), it first appeared in a focused way in the inner-city consultations in 1985 and 1986. The 1985 gathering in Manchester pointed to the effects of unemployment which as usual were disproportionately felt at that time by black people. It noted that the Manpower Services Commission (MSC) was initiating some useful work through its Youth Training Schemes and Community Programmes but that such initiatives always had an uncertain future. It urged the development of a network of local resource centres which had advised people on a range of matters including financial possibilities. It also urged that if churches set up MSC projects there should be full participation in decision-making by the clients; that MSC funding should be secure and that local people should be more trusted in management. It is of course a matter of history that MSC fairly quickly gave way to new structures with economically more rigid criteria and eventually to Training and Enterprise Councils (TECs) which are private-sector-led and often have little accountability to local communities for the public money they control.

The Leeds meeting took place in the aftermath of the launch of the Archbishop of Canterbury's urban priority area (UPA) report *Faith in the City*, which was heavily attacked in Government circles for its so-called 'Marxism'. The meeting explored the employment question further. Working groups on 'Creating Employment' and 'Equal Opportunities' made a number of recommendations both to Church and Government. The first group reiterated criticism of the MSC, pressed for schemes such as earlier retirement, sabbaticals and job-sharing to create more jobs, and encouraged Church and Government to give more support to co-operatives and small businesses. The theological importance of the building of community was emphasised, as was demand for political action by the churches. The second group, while recognising that effective equal opportunities policies with proper monitoring would require resources, commended them to all employers, including the Churches. It also wanted to see the Churches encouraging self-help strategies among local black communities.

These themes were taken up in the Conference on 'Challenging Racism in Britain' held jointly with the World Council of Churches' Programme to Combat Racism (PCR) in November 1987. The Conference heard addresses by African-American and African speakers, including Paul Boateng MP, and was held at All Saints Pastoral Centre, St Albans. It concluded on All Saints' Day, and issued the 'All Saints Declaration' which called for a range of actions by both Churches and Government to combat racism. These included demands to allocate a significant percentage of church funds and make available church property to assist in creating black employment, and also to adopt equal opportunity policies to ensure 'adequate black representation at all levels in the churches'. The Government were asked to undertake substantial new investment schemes to create real jobs in partnership with local black communities, to undertake monitoring of their own employees and to extend the practice of contract compliance, by which public bodies letting contracts require their contractors to be equal opportunity employers and to take positive action towards black employment.

The importance attached to the economic dimension by the All Saints Conference led to a visit by two CRRU staff to the USA to see what the Churches there were doing. They met church and community leaders in five US cities, and looked at the whole range of strategies in use to try to achieve economic development in black communities. In San Francisco, churches and community groups had pressed local employers to maintain plants in ethnically-mixed areas. In Atlanta large banks had been criticised and in a few cases boycotted because of their refusal to invest in or support black businesses. In New York and San Francisco the black majority churches had evolved housing schemes which both gave employment and provided low-rent housing. In Chicago, under black Mayor Harold Washington, the city authorities had instituted an active programme of contract compliance by which the proportion of the city's contracts let to 'minority businesses' had increased to around 25 per cent, i.e. $600 million.

There were low-interest loan funds for black co-operatives and businesses, alternative investment (by which church funds allocated a small proportion of their portfolio to employment creating schemes), and the exposure of banks and finance houses for 'red-lining' minority communities, i.e. refusing to invest there. The latter work was done largely by the Interfaith Centre for Corporate Responsibility (ICCR), acting on behalf of church shareholders. ICCR had also developed strategies for persuading large employers to adopt equal opportunities policies for both women and minorities, and to monitor the results. This, along with pressure from the black communities, had brought about a steady increase in the numbers of black employees of major enterprises, and a 'trickle-up' of such employees into higher executive positions. At the same time, the majority of 'people of colour' in the USA remained poor, deprived and marginalised.

A group of US black church leaders then came to the UK in early 1990 to lead a conference on 'The Economic Empowerment of the Black Community' (EEBC). It heard addresses from Bernie Grant MP, Dr James Washington from the USA, and black people in the UK directly involved in the struggle for economic empowerment. The report, *Account of Hope*, was presented to the final Assembly of the British Council of Churches. Black representatives were cordially informed that 'they had started something'. The issue was referred on to the Council of Churches for Britain and Ireland (CCBI) which, in *Towards Economic Justice*, supported recommendations calling on Churches to adopt equal opportunities policies with monitoring, use the CRE's Code of Practice, explore setting up an ecumenical loan fund and press companies to adopt effective equal opportunity policies.

The EEBC initiative received little practical support from the Churches, perhaps because it touched ultimately on matters of finance, although 'corporate responsibility' as practised by the ICCR demands little in terms of actual finance or disinvestment. The Methodist Division of Finance, however, showed interest in the idea of corporate responsibility, and participated in the 'Race Equality in

Employment Project' (REEP), which grew out of the EEBC Consultation. This undertook the first detailed racial equality survey of many of the top UK employers, persuading 26 of them to reply to a detailed questionnaire.

A consultation chaired by Bishop Wilfred Wood discussed the results of the survey, and received input from Tim Smith, the Director of ICCR, REEP Chair Hyacinth Osborne and Roy Foulds of the Methodist Division of Finance. The resulting report *Buried Talents* (Race Equality in Employment Project, 1992) pointed to the wasted abilities of the black communities in the employment market, and urged both corporate investors like the Churches, and corporate employers such as major companies and banks, to take equal opportunities policies, monitoring and annual reporting much more seriously. This led on to the further work by the CCRJ referred to below.

Some other CRRU concerns

The sections above have summarised the major strands in the work of CRRU between 1971 and 1992, and at different periods different ones were the more prominent. There were many other minor strands which have been referred to in passing but which will have to wait until a fuller history is written before they are properly explored. The question of *relations with other faiths* has been one which has constantly been on CRRU's agenda, not least because successive Secretaries of the Committee for Relations with People of Other Faiths (CRPOF) were staff members of the CRRU Board. Their concerns were often tabled, if not discussed in detail, and over several years the CRRU/CRPOF Social Policy Group discussed matters which concerned both Committees, usually related to either immigration or education.

Education has been one of those strands which has not been fully explored here. CRRU did some work around the publication of the Swann Report in the mid-1980s, and sought to inform the Churches of its implications. Out of that discussion developed on the issue of 'separate schools', i.e. schools which would be organised and run by a non-Christian faith community. After much agonising the CRRU/CRPOF Social Policy Group came to a position that such schools would create even greater fragmentation in the education system of England and Wales than was there already. However if Muslims, for example, are to be denied the right to organise their schools, that has serious implications for those Churches which have done so for many years. The Social Policy Group asked the Boards of CRRU and CRPOF to request the Churches to reconsider their role in the education sector. Understandably representatives of those Churches with the greatest investment in the educational field felt this was not appropriate. Hence the Churches as a whole remain without a view on this important matter, although some denominations – in particular the Roman Catholics – have developed a position supportive of the rights of faith communities to their own schools.

Issues of *social welfare* also arose from time to time. In the early 1980s there was considerable discussion on the topics of adoption and fostering, and whether black children should always be fostered or adopted by black parents. This came about because some Labour-controlled local authorities were fairly insistent that black children should be placed only with black foster-parents, or only adopted by those of their own race. On the whole, the CRRU Board sympathised with this view, but did not wish to draw any hard and fast rules. In 1989 the Unit organised a seminar, in conjunction with the Church of England Board of Social Responsibility Race and Community Relations Committee, on *Mental Health and the Black Community.* This produced a useful report, which was circulated in church circles and to Diocesan Social Responsibility Officers. However the hoped-for take-up did not materialise, and there were insufficient staff resources to take the matter further effectively.

In 1986 *Faith in the City (FITC)* became an issue for the Board, partly in itself and partly arising from the Inner-City Consultations in 1985 and 1986. There was much support for its analysis, although comment was made that it did not effectively address the race issue. Its social and economic analysis was supposedly controversial but struck many chords with those actually involved in inner-city work. Very few if any of the criticisms came from this quarter; they came rather from that sector of the community who were themselves, or represented, the wealthy. Out of *Faith in the City*, despite its lack of specific race-related perspectives, came the suggestion that the Church of England should appoint at least two black officers, one to work on racism within the church structures and one to work on issues related to society as a whole. Another *FITC* recommendation was for the setting up of a 'Church Urban Fund' of some £15 million, the income from which would then be used to fund projects tackling urban deprivation around the country. Although the cost of the first proposal for the two officers was much lower, it had still not been fully achieved ten years after *FITC* reported, whereas the apparently more difficult task of urban fund-raising had been more or less completed by 1991. One conclusion that might be drawn from this is that the churches on the whole are much more interested in distributing largesse than in addressing the fundamental inequalities and injustices which exist both within themselves and in society as a whole. CRRU existed to address those injustices, either with or without the churches. Only history will tell whether or how much it succeeded.

The start of the CCRJ

At the 1987 ecumenical Swanwick Conference it was proposed by Church leaders that new structures should be considered, in order to take forward ecumenism in these islands. As a result in 1990 the British Council of Churches came to an end, and gave way to the Council of Churches for Britain and Ireland (CCBI). New forms of ecumenical relationships were set up, which included the Roman Catholic Church and more of the black-majority Churches. CRRU was given two extra years' life, until 1992, while the CCBI decided if it wished to continue work on race issues. There were some who thought a network among those in the Churches already working on race would be enough, but after much discussion and some pressure from the black-majority Churches it was decided to create a Churches' Commission for Racial Justice (CCRJ), which came into being in September 1992. It was inaugurated in a service led by Roman Catholic Bishop Vincent Nichols, Revd Esme Beswick and its first Moderator Revd Theo Samuel, who had been the CRRU Moderator for its final two years. It took up many of the concerns of CRRU, although in a different way, as it was now responsible to 25 Commissioners appointed by the Churches and the CCBI, and through them to the Churches. Here we give a brief account of three of the main issues which CRRU handed on to the CCRJ: immigration and asylum concerns, tackling the growing racial violence in British society, and the economic dimension referred to above (p. 111)

IMMIGRATION AND ASYLUM

As we have seen above there has been a long and consistent record on the part of some in the Churches in resisting both unnecessary restrictiveness and incipient racism in UK immigration law. They have sought actively to oppose certain changes in law and practice. Local churches have also been faced with very practical and pastoral problems. Occasionally churches at local and national level have felt constrained to support the 'last resort' of sanctuary, which although not breaking the law – because everyone knows where the person or family is – certainly confronts the law when it appears to have lost all compassion or humanity.

The first such sanctuaries to take place in recent times were in 1985 in two churches near Euston, one Anglican and one Catholic. In the first a Cypriot couple eventually gave up their struggle to stay in the UK, but in the second a Philippina and her child were successful. There followed 12-year-old Salema Begum in 1986 in Chorlton URC/Baptist church in Manchester, an African family with a father undergoing brain surgery who wished to remain anonymous in a Roman Catholic church in Fulham in 1988, an African nurse in a Glasgow Methodist Church and a Nigerian family with a child with sickle-cell anaemia in a Birmingham Methodist church (in addition to the Dansos) in 1989. In the longest sanctuary so far Sri Lankan student Viraj Mendis remained in the Church of the Ascension in Hulme, Manchester, from December 1986 until forcibly removed in January 1989. Sanctuaries also took place in the late 1980s in a Hindu mandir in Leicester, a Sikh gurdwara near Bradford and the Central Mosque in Birmingham.

Most of these cases involved threats to family life or health, although for Viraj Mendis the fear was for his personal safety. After he was forcibly returned to Sri Lanka he spent several months in hiding, armed men came looking for him and in the country generally thousands of young men were being killed in the war between the Tamil Tigers and the Government. After a few months friends including some Quakers assisted his escape to Germany, where he has lived since.

The inspiration for sanctuary had come from the Sanctuary Movement in the USA, where in the mid-1980s some five hundred congregations had declared themselves sanctuary churches, and some leaders of the movement had been sent to prison. The focus of the movement was the returning of asylum-seekers from the conflicts in El Salvador, Guatemala and Nicaragua to severe danger, and the US intelligence services tried every means to break it, including sending in spies with tape recorders to church meetings and worship services to record discussions and sermons. However, such was the movement's determination that by 1989 it had forced a substantial change in US policy and practice towards Central American refugees.

In late 1993 the CCRJ, recognising that there were quite a substantial number of families with children who had grown up in the UK, but were not entitled to stay here because of the removal of *ius soli* – citizenship by birth – in the 1981 Nationality Act, began to press for an amnesty. This was targeted at families who had been in the UK for more than five years, and had a child of at least two years of age born here, or who were self-sufficient in income and housing. The initiative was triggered by the death of Joy Gardner in August 1993, in front of her 6-year-old son, while police and immigration officers were attempting to remove her with handcuffs, a body-belt and a gag. Joy Gardner, like the Dansos and the Ogunwobis, was not an 'illegal immigrant' but an overstayer. People overstay for many reasons: they fail courses and have to keep trying as they cannot afford to go home without a qualification, or they run out of money – when their country's currency fails or parents become ill. They fall in love, get married and have children, or conditions worsen at home and there is no hope of work to support their family, or there is danger from ethnic conflicts. In November 1994

117

the CCRJ presented a Petition for 'Amnesty' of over 30,000 signatures to the Home Office, but the Government remained unmoved. This is an issue which is unlikely to go away over the second half of the decade.

With regard to issues affecting refugees the Churches have sought in particular to oppose refusals and removals to countries where there is serious conflict, and therefore danger – even when asylum-seekers cannot prove to the satisfaction of the Home Office that they personally face persecution and are therefore a refugee under the narrowest interpretation of the 1951 Geneva Convention. In the first half of the 1990s that certainly included Zaire, and in response to a CCRJ request the Bishop of Ripon undertook detailed correspondence with Home Office ministers in 1993 and 1994, urging that because of the dangers in Zaire no-one should be sent back there. One case in particular angered church bodies: that of Anthony Lemba, who was deported in August 1994, after several appeals for clemency by Rt Revd Roger Sainsbury, the Bishop of Barking and a CCRJ Commissioner. Nothing was then heard for several months from Mr Lemba, and by the end of 1994 his supporters presumed he had been killed.

A brief outline of the kind of things happening to refugees from Zaire during 1993 and 1994 may be illustrative, as it has been of considerable concern to some in the Churches, including the CCRJ. Zairean asylum-seekers appear to have been particularly unpopular with the Home Office. It is true that a few were caught in the early 1990s making multiple applications, and getting involved in social security fraud, but the Home Office claimed that would be eradicated particularly by the finger-printing measures introduced by the 1993 Act. Another reason for Government antipathy to the Zaireans may have been a desire to retain a positive relationship with President Mobutu. Few would disagree, however, that Zaire is a dangerous country, particularly for those associated with opposition to Mobutu.

A disproportionate number of Zairean refugees seem always to have been kept in British prisons and in the new Detention Centres, opened by the Home Office after the 1993 Act. Some of them clearly suffered maltreatment amounting to torture before they left for Britain. Others, having arrived here, were trying to hold together families who had suffered grave traumas. The refusal rate for Zaireans rose to over 99 per cent by the end of 1994. Despite all the efforts of concerned agencies and church leaders during 1993/4, it seems that a number of detainees were deported and either detained or killed. Several who made specific commitments to keep in touch with supporters in the UK have not done so. A report issued by Asylum Aid in early 1995, *Adding Insult to Injury*, sponsored by the CCRJ, recounts the experiences of Zairean refugees and some of the extraordinary reasons given by the Home Office in rejecting their claims.

The CCRJ, apart from supporting the bishops in their interventions, has co-ordinated an active church response to the continuing use of detention by the authorities to enable them to deport asylum seekers more easily. A conference in September 1992, which included input from Lord Clinton-Davies of the Refugee Council, the Anglican Bishop of Woolwich and the Director of the Catholic Fund for Overseas Development, strongly urged an end to detention, unless there was specific evidence suggesting a threat to national security. The Commission supported the setting up of a Churches Refugee Network, which was to bring together all those in the churches with concern for refugees, and to co-ordinate action in areas where it needed to be taken.

The Conference of European Churches and the World Council of Churches have also become actively involved in refugee issues, as indicated above. They and the CCME are involved in the European Churches Working Group on Asylum and Refugees (ECWGAR) which co-ordinates the refugee work of the Churches across Europe. Recent developments in this field, and vital questions about root causes of refugeeism, are discussed in detail in a book published in 1993 by the World Council of Churches, *Beyond Borders: Refugees, Migrants and Human Rights in the Post-Cold War Era* by Elizabeth Ferris. This is an overview of the issues of refugees and international migration, an area which is beyond the scope of this book, but is crucial to address for a global understanding of the effects of racism and racial discrimination in the world as a whole.

TACKLING RACIAL VIOLENCE

The CCRJ, on behalf of the Churches, has continued to raise matters of racial justice in the criminal justice system. Specific attempts have been made to ensure that the performance of the police was being monitored. The visits co-ordinated by CRRU to Government ministers in 1990 regarding the behaviour of the police were followed up by CCRJ in September 1992 urging a European Community approach to issues of racial violence. The Minister concerned, Peter Lloyd, stated the Conservative Government view that inter-governmental consultation would be more effective than European Community law, but agreed to consider reconvening the Government's Racial Attacks Group, which brought together senior officials from different Government departments to report on and monitor progress in this field.

In its final year CRRU had given support to amendments to the 1991 Criminal Justice Act, and although only Baroness Flather's Section 95 amendment to provide regular reporting on potential discrimination was successful, this has been useful. After the first such report in 1992, the CCRJ offered a number of criticisms and suggestions, and pressed for an annual analysis. The second report appeared only in 1994, although it was an improvement. More important for the field of racial violence, however, is the work of the Racial Attacks Group (RAG). It produced reports in 1990 and 1991 but was then apparently disbanded. CCRJ, with others, argued for its re-establishment. This occurred in 1995 and RAG is to provide further reports.

In 1994 the CCRJ pressed with others for a strengthening of the law against racial violence. The Government responded with only a minor amendment creating an offence of 'intentional harassment', but also consulted the judiciary who began to evolve a policy of 'weighted sentencing' where racial motivation was an aggravating feature of a particular offence. The first evidence of this came in heavier sentences meted out to those responsible for attacks on black men who were going out with white women, in Birmingham and in Ilford. In the latter case the perpetrators' sentences were lengthened on appeal.

During its first years the CCRJ became particularly concerned about the spread of extreme right-wing groups, in areas such as east London, south Wales, and the West and East Midlands. When a British National Party (BNP) Councillor was elected in the Isle of Dogs in September 1993 the CCRJ gave support to local churches and community organisations as they helped to get him defeated at the subsequent elections, although he did increase his vote. Voting was, however, only the tip of the iceberg of BNP activity, and racial attacks became an everyday feature of life in Tower Hamlets and Newham. The CCRJ made the link between such violence and urban deprivation at a meeting in December 1994 with Baroness Blatch, then the Home Office Minister for community relations, and urged more effective economic policies for inner-city areas as an essential step to remove some of the causative factors in racial violence.

Since 1990 CRRU and CCRJ have also had meetings and correspondence with the Metropolitan Police as the force most involved with these concerns, and the area where most – though not by any means all – attacks have taken place. Such conversations have been difficult. The police do not want to acknowledge that as society is racist so are its institutions; the church side seemed to find it much easier to admit to racism than did the police. Church representatives urged a proper structure for reporting racial incidents in all the Metropolitan Police Divisions, incorporating Divisional racial harassment units, even those where there were fewer black people. They also urged that training in dealing with racial attacks become mandatory, instead of optional, and that support be given to middle-ranking officers having to take responsibility for investigating or taking disciplinary action with regard to any allegations of racial discrimination, or lack of action on racial violence, by junior officers.

The Churches' delegation was encouraged to hear in October 1993 that the Metropolitan Police had set up an Equal Opportunities Board but less happy to discover it was only to meet once a year. Rt Revd Roger Sainsbury, Bishop of Barking and a CCRJ Commissioner, said in a letter to the Metropolitan Commissioner in early 1994 that the Churches remained concerned about reports from local parishes about the racially discriminatory behaviour of some police officers, and this was a matter of particular importance.

A further contribution CRRU and the CCRJ have made is by contributing grants either themselves or by recommendations to the World Council of Churches' Programme to Combat Racism, to local projects supporting victims of racial attacks. These have included Newham and Southall/Hounslow Monitoring Projects and Greenwich Action Committee Against Racial Attacks. Hence by continually raising the issue of racial violence with the authorities, and supporting local action, it is hoped the Churches may be having an effect, although it would help if both local and national church leaders were more outspoken.

ECONOMIC EMPOWERMENT

In 1991, as mentioned above, out of the Economic Empowerment of the Black Community (EEBC) initiative, CRRU had helped to fund a survey of some of the country's top employers which produced the *Buried Talents* report (p. 114). This had urged regular ethnic monitoring and reporting of employees. The Council of Churches itself undertakes such monitoring, reporting the results annually, and in 1994 was able to demonstrate that some 20 per cent of its executive staff and over 50 per cent of its administrative staff were black or minority ethnic. In 1993, to follow up *Buried Talents,* REEP and the CCRJ between them evolved the ten Wood–Sheppard Principles on Race Equality in Employment, named after the first black Church of England Bishop, Wilfred Wood, and David Sheppard, the Bishop of Liverpool.

From 1994 these Principles were put to church employers and to major companies, asking them to endorse the Principles, undertake the positive action and ethnic monitoring they propose, and produce an annual report of their employee profile from year to year in order to demonstrate the results. This was done partly by individual shareholders and partly by one or two church investors, particularly the Methodist Church. In the end racist – and anti-racist – activity is best measured by results. It is vital for us in the Churches to endorse and practise the Wood–Sheppard Principles, with the discipline of annual reporting. Only then will we be able to ascertain that, while attempting rightly to be the physicians of society, we are at least in the process of healing ourselves.

Suggestions made to the Churches as a result of the EEBC initiative by CRRU and the *Towards Economic Justice* paper referred to above (p. 113) have not so far been taken up. Ideas of 'positive action' such as employing 1 per cent of the Churches' capital funds for black community enterprise, either directly or in the form of an Ecumenical Loan Fund, have been ignored. From EEBC the Church Commissioners were asked to invest up to £1 million in a Greater London Enterprise fund set up to assist small minority businesses – among others. Although a previous similar fund had been a success both in returns and in the businesses assisted the Commissioners said they were unable to be involved in the initiative as they could only invest a small proportion of funds in this way, due to the legal obligation to maximise returns. Subsequently the value of the Commissioners' assets fell by over £800 million due to investment on the property market.

Alongside the 'moral approach' to black economic empowerment, the riots in Los Angeles, like those in Toxteth, Handsworth and Brixton before them, helped to remind comfortable, wealthy, white society that its economic security is built on too narrow a base, and if it wants to develop relatively smoothly it needs to distribute its fruits rather more widely, both to black and minority employees and indeed to the black communities as a whole. CRRU's whole economic empowerment initiative was built on the premise that inequalities in opportunity for wealth creation and in its distribution are both theologically and socially unhealthy, and lead to waste, instability and, if stark enough, to violence. The CCRJ and the Churches will need to concentrate on such matters more vigorously in the future.

Much of the activity of individual denominations has been only hinted at in the above. Initiatives were undertaken by particular Churches which are still on-going. These include the Catholic Association for Racial Justice (CARJ), formed when the Catholic Commission for Racial Justice split into the Catholic Bishops Committee on Community Relations and the more independent CARJ. There is also MELRAW, originally Methodist Leadership Racism Awareness Workshops, evolved under the leadership of Sybil Phoenix and Revd Vic Watson, and now including 'Ecumenical' in its title. The Church of England took the lead in developing the Simon of Cyrene Theological Institute, aimed at providing access courses for those from the black and minority communities who wished to enter ministry or priesthood, or simply learn theology. The black-majority Churches were active in pressing for the formation of the Centre for Black and White Christian Partnership, but were always disappointed in the extent of majority-church support. The richness of these initiatives is seen currently in the Christian Network for Racial Justice, facilitated by the CCRJ. Both the Network and the Commission will have much to do to address the agenda outlined in the final chapter and to bring about the Jubilee to which it points.

5

Perspectives from the USA

There are clearly considerable differences in history, culture, geography and sociology between experiences of race in Britain and those in the USA. However, there are also many things in common, and a good deal to learn. Among the differences is that large numbers of people originating from Africa have been in the USA much longer than in the case in the UK, even though they arrived in the latter first. Also, they came there directly rather than, in most cases, via several generations in the Caribbean. They entered the Churches even before the 'United States' was formed. They were directly involved in the struggle for emancipation from slavery, and their labour has helped America grow rich. This has undoubtedly given them the feeling of a more explicit stake in the country and its resources than is the case for many black people in the UK – though the latter remind us rightly that they too contributed greatly to the prosperity of Britain through the system of slavery and the exploitation of the colonies, and indeed their labour within the UK.

Again, in the USA, native Americans were present long before the white man came, with his bartering, his greed for land and the power of his gun (being deliberately gender-specific). Since the invasion of the Americas the indigenous peoples of the continent have been decimated by disease and hunger, confined to increasingly small areas and 'reservations', and forced to struggle to hold on to some identity, some dignity and some control of their ancestral lands.

The USA being far larger than the UK, its minorities are widely spread, although many are concentrated in the inner cities, as in the UK. Britain, however, does not have the equivalent of the poor black farmers of the south, the old 'share-croppers', who are now fast being pushed off the land, nor the migrant rural labourers of California or Texas. Hence there is a difference in consciousness in relation to the land. Again, in the USA black people have made more progress up the social (and economic) scale; there are more 'role-models' of the stature of Martin Luther King, Jesse Jackson, Ella Fitzgerald, Alice Walker, Carl Lewis, Toni Morrison or Spike Lee. Such progress has now begun in Britain, and will doubtless expand.

The original migrants to North America were European; they included Germans, Greeks, Italians, English and Irish. However, there is some evidence that Africans crossed the Atlantic first, at least to Central America. Then there are 'Asians', originating from the 'Pacific rim' – Taiwan, Japan, China, Vietnam and Korea. Other more recent immigration has come either from the south (Latino people from Mexico and the countries of Central America where there has been so much US-sponsored violence in the past fifty years), from the Caribbean or from Eastern Europe. There is therefore an enormous diversity of language and culture, although in the USA – perhaps due to its own origins – there seems to be a greater ability to accept and absorb diversity. In both the USA and the UK it is most often the relationship between those of European and of African origin which tends to be the touchstone by which justice, equality and good 'community relations' are measured. Certainly in both countries it is mostly those of African background who are likely to offer a theological analysis of the challenges that face the wider society, although in the USA such analysis is more developed and comes from Latinos and Latinas (men and women of South America origin) and from native Americans as well. In both countries Asians of different faith communities also have perspectives to contribute.

Then there are the US Churches where black and white Christians have been confronting one another and arguing, learning and celebrating together for many years. The separatism of the 1960s and 1970s in the USA seems to have evolved into a greater understanding and degree of respect, although black Christians are still very wary of whites who claim to have overcome their racism, and 11 o'clock on a Sunday morning is still the most segregated hour in North America. The Black Caucuses in the white-majority churches still meet, and the Black Churches maintain a vigorous and active identity over against what were often their parent denominations of long ago.

There is therefore much for British anti-racists, especially Christian ones, to learn from the USA. The psychological, economic and theological workings of racism, the depth of disadvantage which white society inflicts on black peoples, the internalised inferiority which is imprinted by constant use of negative images, the observation and documentation of white behaviour – individually and in larger groups, all these have been analysed, monitored and reported in the USA. Again the positive images of black people there, the progress made when opportunities are available, the contribution of black and minority people to the culture and economy of the wider society, the efforts of white people to recognise their own racism and try to change, are all US realities which help demonstrate what can be done. Not all the answers for the UK will be found but much insight and experience will be gained, which will be invaluable in the struggle to eliminate racism, wherever it appears.

I shall take a quick look now at the history of black people in the USA, especially in relation to the part played by Christians in opposition to slavery, and then review the era of Martin Luther King and the Civil Rights struggle. I shall then refer to some of the significant developments in Black Nationalism, take note of the US debate on 'Race or Class?' and look briefly at the dynamic behind Black Theology, a very important development which is now evolving in Britain.

History
SLAVERY AND THE STRUGGLE FOR EMANCIPATION

African people arrived in the USA in increasing numbers on slave ships during the seventeenth, eighteenth and early nineteenth centuries, along with their kin who were shipped to the islands of the Caribbean and the eastern coasts of South America. They were transported to work the land – sugar, tobacco, but perhaps most of all 'King Cotton'. Over these centuries hundreds of thousands of black slaves were spread across the southern half of the then-British colony of America, as far west as what is now Texas. As the argument about slavery gathered momentum in the newly-independent United States, the slaves became one of the foci of the differences between the northerners who had discerned there was no real social and economic future in slavery and the Confederate southerners who were more in need of its exploitative structures.

The black historian Vincent Harding, a close associate of Martin Luther King, has explored the history of this period in detail in his seminal work *There is a River* (1981). He chronicles the earliest reactions of the captive Africans to their slavery, and their constant resistance and struggle against their fate. From the seventeenth century Africans were beginning to organise, burning white property, escaping to deprive the planters of their labour and – from time to time – joining together in desperation and in sizeable groups, to attack white communities.

Many of them were killed, committed suicide or underwent severe torture. Harding reports how in 1740 a considerable number of Africans got together in the Charleston area and were reported to be obtaining weapons to take over the city. They were ambushed and 50 were captured. These were hanged at the rate of ten a day, to intimidate other negroes. There are later accounts of black rebels being mutilated and left to hang on gibbets, and others receiving 200 lashes in public. Harding describes the whole movement towards freedom and identity as a river, hence his book's title, and remarks that – when such punishments were commonplace in the struggle for freedom – it was amazing that 'the forward movement of the river' was not stopped.

So the struggle continued. Slaves who left their masters and hid in the country-side or swamps became known as 'outlyers', and caused constant problems for the authorities. Resistance spread to the north also, and in 1793 three black people were executed for starting a destructive fire in the city of Albany, in New York State. In the next three years there were major fires in Newark (New Jersey) and in New York City itself, as well as Charleston and Baltimore. So, according to Harding, by the end of the century there had developed three levels of black response. The first was survival, the 'maintenance of black life and spirit', and of 'sanity, strength and dignity'. The second was a black radicalism which by slaves withdrawing labour or by their more direct destruction ate away at the bits of the economic system 'based on their own submissive bodies'. The third level was those who organised and participated in actions which undermined white power and wealth.

Resistance also grew with regard to the white-controlled Churches. In some of them blacks were accepted as long as they knew their place. However it was as early as the eighteenth century that independent black Churches came into being. The white Churches, like many other institutions in North America's white society, had justified slavery and practised white supremacy. The Churches therefore became a battleground, for – says Harding – Africans have an innate spirituality and while they wished to practice their new-found faith they wished to do so on an equal footing, as that was the very basis of the faith.

Black Baptist churches sprang up in Georgia, and then in 1787 Richard Allen and some black colleagues walked out of the Philadelphia Methodist Church in which they worshipped, and formed the Free Africa Society. The Philadelphia church had been the one in which Allen was converted, and to which he had brought many others through evangelistic activity, but in which he could no longer accept an inferior status. This departure led eventually to the formation of the African Methodist Episcopal Church, now one of the largest black American denominations. This Church was given a further boost when in 1818 nearly 5,000 black Methodists in Charleston withdrew from the white-led Methodist Church. Their gatherings were harassed and broken up, their leaders arrested and in 1821 the white authorities closed one of their largest churches. Such stories help us to understand the development of the large independent black Churches in the USA, and also have echoes in the processes by which independent churches were initiated by African and African-Caribbean Christians in the UK some 150 years later.

Harding goes on to describe North America's major slave revolts, often led by those inspired by Christian faith such as David Walker and Nat Turner. Turner gathered a small force together in Virginia in 1831 and laid his plans, sincerely believing that the God he had learned about from the Christian churches was with him. Inevitably Turner's ill-equipped followers were defeated, and most killed. Turner himself was hanged in November 1831. Despite white intention that Turner's death should be a lesson to others, he became a legend within the African community. The same happened to David Walker, a staunch black Methodist and writer for *Freedom's Journal*, the first black US newspaper, who was apparently poisoned by white plotters. Harding reports that the State of Mississippi became so anxious about the power of black religion that it passed the following statute: 'It is unlawful for any slave, free Negro, or mulatto to preach the Gospel upon pain of receiving 39 lashes upon the naked back.'

One whom Nat Turner inspired was Frederick Douglass, who was born around 1818 on the east coast of Maryland. Like Equiano and Cugoano in England, Douglass wrote down his own story which was published in 1845 as *Narrative of the Life of Frederick Douglass, An American Slave, Written by Himself*. He recounts how through ignorance the wife of his master began to teach him to read, using her son's school books. She was soon prevented by her husband who said, 'if you teach that nigger (speaking of myself) how to read there would be no keeping him. It would forever unfit him to be a slave'. Douglass persevered however, and was able to read some of the published arguments against slavery. He learned to write by copying the son's school work. Douglass offers uncomfortable insights into the effect of 'religion' upon slave-owners – some even used their beliefs to justify their cruelty – but himself appears to have retained a genuine faith. He recounts the behaviour of, among others, the Reverends Weedon and Hopkin of the 'Reformed Methodist Church' who frequently whipped their slaves whether they behaved well or ill, 'to remind them of their master's authority'. One of Douglass' responses was to start his own Sunday School class to teach a few fellow slaves how to read. The class was broken up by the Reformed Methodist class leaders who 'rushed in upon us with sticks and stones. . . all calling themselves Christians, humble followers of the Lord Jesus Christ!' They warned Douglass that if he persisted, he would end up like Nat Turner!

The nature of Douglass' own faith frequently appears in his story. When he was transferred to Baltimore he comments:

> I may be deemed superstitious, and even egotistical, in regarding this event as a special interposition by divine Providence in my favour. But I should be false to the earliest sentiments of my soul if I suppressed the opinion. . . .. This good spirit was from God, and to him I offer thanksgiving and praise.

Slaves in the USA had to wait longer for emancipation than those under British rule. However, Douglass was a member of a black congregation in Boston on 31

December 1862, one of hundreds meeting in US cities that night, which gathered to celebrate joyously the proclamation of emancipation. President Lincoln, however, grabbed centre stage, and out of this event, remarks Vincent Harding, instead of black slave resistance being credited, the myth of Abraham Lincoln as the great emancipator was born.

Emancipation or not, black people still had to struggle to make manifest the reality that slavery was ended. Their Christian faith often strengthened them. One such believer was Sojourner Truth. Harding describes one incident in which she put into practice the new-found freedom. In early 1865 in Arlington, Virginia, a law was passed to desegregate the horse-car public transport system. When the cars refused to stop for her Truth created such a disturbance that a crowd gathered making it impossible for the next car to get through. Truth promptly got on board, to be told by the conductor to get out and ride on the front by the horses. She refused, alighted even beyond her original stop with the words 'Bless God, I have had a ride!', and had the conductor arrested and dismissed.

According to Harding, and black theologians like James Cone, it is here that 'Black Theology' has its roots, in the Bible message, in the teaching of Christianity to the slaves, and in the 'Negro Spirituals'. Cone, for many the originator of Black Theology with his book *Black Theology and Black Power* (1969), frequently quotes supposedly-innocuous spirituals to make this point, for example:

> When Israel was in Egypt's land,
> Let my people go!
> Oppressed so hard they could not stand,
> Let my people go!
> Go down, Moses, way down in Egypt's land,
> Tell old Pharoah, to let my people go!

Another example is 'Steal Away to Jesus', which when sung usually meant a slave would be slipping away by night on the 'underground railroad' to the north and freedom. 'Swing Low, Sweet Chariot' has the same theme. Harding in *There is a River* offers numerous examples of the power and meaning of the spirituals.

MARTIN LUTHER KING AND THE CIVIL RIGHTS MOVEMENT

Even when slavery was ended, in 1863, things did not change overmuch for the majority of black people. Alex Haley's *Roots* in book and TV film form, while not particularly reliable historically, helped to get across to many people – black and white – for the first time the immensity of the evil of slavery and how its aftermath still fundamentally affects social and economic life in North America.

Years before *Roots*, however, the conscience of many white people and the spirits of many black people had been awakened by the freedom campaigns of Martin Luther King and his colleagues, beginning with the Montgomery bus boycott in 1955. It was to a large extent through King's prayer meetings, sermons and writings, but above all through his action campaigns, that black America began to stand up against white oppression and white racism, and take its 'strides towards freedom'.

Eventually what King later called 'America's third revolution – the Negro Revolution' broke out in the early 1960s, which he wrote about in *Why We Can't Wait*, pointing out that for the first time 'almost one thousand cities were engulfed in civil turmoil'. It was reminiscent of the French Revolution. The streets had become a battleground, as in the 1830s of England's tumultuous Chartist movement. 'As in these two revolutions', wrote King,

> a submerged social group, propelled by a burning need for justice, lifting itself with sudden swiftness, moving with determination and majestic scorn for risk and danger, created an uprising so powerful that it shook a huge society from its comfortable base.

King went on to point to the 'two concentric circles of segregation' of US blacks, the circle of colour and the circle of poverty. He compared the growing independence movement in Africa with the neo-slavery still extant in North America. He wrote and preached of how the campaigns, the opposition, the threats and the jailings only served to build black people's determination to win equal treatment in prejudiced American society, and he marched himself, into danger, to demonstrate this in practice. Going to jail for black people became a 'badge of honour', and all the activities gave people a 'sense of somebodiness', and made them eager for freedom. What is more it was all to be achieved by the morally-superior and Christian-based method of militant non-violence, incorporating 'soul force'. King was convinced that forcing guilty whites to punish innocent blacks would shame and defeat the white racists. King is almost endlessly quotable and his writings with their flowing prose but very direct messages coming out of firm Christian conviction are inspirational in any context of the struggle for racial justice. But it was his willingness to act that above anything else led to his achievements.

King has been already the subject of at least three mighty biographies, *Let the Trumpet Sound* (1982) by Stephen Oates, *Bearing the Cross* by David Garrow (1986) and the two volumes of *Parting the Waters* by Taylor Branch (1988). Another vital resource in *A Testament of Hope*, a summary of King's writings edited in 1986 by Dr James Washington. Oates' book is the most focused on the person of King himself. It is to a degree sycophantic, concentrating on King's achievements and avoiding reference to some of his shortcomings. The 500-page volume details King's birth, his childhood and his student days, firstly at Atlanta's black Morehouse College where he graduated in sociology, then at Crozer Seminary in Pennsylvania, and finally at the University of Boston (a wide-ranging PhD in the philosophy of religion). He chronicles the way King was practically dragged in to lead the Montgomery bus boycott, the challenges to Selma and Birmingham, the 'I have a Dream' series of speeches culminating at the Washington Memorial and the award of the Nobel Peace Prize. Oates reports on King's journey to the north of the USA, to oppose racism in Chicago, on the continuing debates and differences in the Civil Rights Movement, on King's courageous criticism of the Vietnam war, on his awakening to the integral relationship between racism, poverty and militarism and finally on the reactions to his shooting in Memphis on 4 April 1968.

By that time, despite all the efforts of the US intelligence services, King had become a figure of international renown. Newspapers around the world deplored his murder, the Pope poured out his 'profound sadness', the Japanese foreign minister said his country was 'gravely concerned', South African newspapers printed special editions, Nigerian government officials bemoaned this 'sad and inhumane killing' and both major parties in the British House of Commons tabled resolutions expressing their horror. There was comment around the world at the racism that bedevilled the world's greatest 'free power'.

Garrow's even more detailed work is subtitled *Martin Luther King and the Southern Christian Leadership Conference*, and seeks to set King's work more in the context of the movement he helped to found and lead. The very title is a reminder that King could not have done what he did without being part of an organisation, of a movement. Garrow analyses again the bus boycott in Montgomery, which first catapulted King to national recognition, the beginnings of the SCLC, the death threats to King's family and his exchanges with Robert and John F. Kennedy over the voter registration drives, with a freshness of detail clearly arising from painstaking research. He exposes the disagreements within the SCLC leadership, the disenchantment with its old and more cautious leadership among the younger activists on the Student Non-violent Co-ordinating Committee (SNCC), conflicts with other black church leaders such as Joseph H. Jackson, King's difficulties in breaking through in Chicago and also his sexual involvements, some of which were taped by the FBI.

It is in Garrow's two final chapters, however, that there may be lessons to be learned for the British scene. The first is entitled 'Economic Justice and Vietnam' and covers the period from mid-1966 to the summer of 1967. It describes how King's increasing concentration on issues of poverty, employment and poor housing among the black community dovetailed with his growing antipathy towards the Vietnam war. His concern over economic inequality was intensified by his experiences in Chicago in the summer of 1966 when seeking more job opportunities and open housing for the black communities. He returned to this theme repeatedly in his speeches, telling a Texas audience that there were few things 'more thoroughly sinful than economic injustice' and stating in Alabama that white Americans had never intended to 'integrate housing, integrate schools, or be fair with Negroes about jobs'.

An agreement forged with the Chicago city administration did little to change the deprivation of blacks in the northern city and King complained vigorously to Mayor Daley. He promoted Jesse Jackson whose 'Operation Breadbasket' had won job gains for blacks from soft-drink and supermarket chains. Such progress gradually continued and another supermarket firm agreed to purchase from black manufacturers and open accounts at black banks. Some of these strategies were beginning to be used in Britain by black people in the 1980s, although a 'whitelash' against affirmative action for race equality began developing in the USA in the early 1990s and by 1995 was making itself heard.

King recognised, however, that such achievements were minor compared to what needed to be done. Alongside these crumbs he saw enormous funds being squandered on space probes and military activities. The two were brought together, according to Garrow, in an experience at Atlanta airport, en route for a month's writing in Jamaica. King picked up a magazine with an article on 'The Children of Vietnam', and Garrow quotes King's friend Bernard Lee who was sharing a meal with him before they travelled together:

> He froze as he looked at the pictures from Vietnam. He saw a picture of a Vietnamese mother holding her dead baby, a baby killed by our military. Then Martin just pushed the plate of food away from him. I looked up and said 'Doesn't it taste any good?' And he answered 'Nothing will ever taste any good until I do everything I can to end that war'. Looking back Lee explained, 'That's when the decision was made. Martin had known about the war before then, of course, and had spoken out against it. But it was then he decided to commit himself to oppose it. (p. 543)

King then came out in open opposition to his country's national policy. In early 1967 he spoke out three times in major speeches against the Vietnam war, and was quite heavily attacked, both by the major white 'liberal' newspapers and by some colleagues in the Civil Rights Movement. However, he linked directly the need to end wasteful and destructive military expenditure in Vietnam with the necessity for investment in homes and jobs for black Americans. At this time he was supporting campaigns for housing and work in Louisville in the south and Cleveland in the north, but still found time for a speech in California in which he said that the movement's new phase would be a 'struggle for genuine equality' which would involve a 'radical redistribution of economic and political power'. In talking to his own staff he began to emphasise the inter-relatedness of racism, economic exploitation and political power, and later told Operation Breadbasket that their movement had to seek the restructuring of American society. King was, during this period, developing the analysis which the white establishment quickly identified as an even more serious threat than any he had presented thus far, and which most probably led to his assassination.

Garrow's final chapter leading up to King's death, 'The Poor People's Campaign and Memphis', refers for the first time to King's movement towards socialist beliefs and his rejection of the American capitalist system. This went as far as questioning the direction that Jesse Jackson's 'Operation Breadbasket' had now taken. One of King's colleagues queried the wisdom of replacing white-led profit-oriented capitalism with blacks doing the same thing, and King agreed. It was later in 1967 that King conceived of the 'Poor People's March', and began to build toward what amounted to a 'March for Jobs' on Washington, DC, eventually planned for April 1968. The overall goal was a $30 billion anti-poverty effort, including full employment, a guaranteed annual income and funds to construct half a million units of low-income housing per year. There were disagreements within King's own supporters as to the efficacy of the enterprise, but it received a boost when President Johnson's 'National Advisory Committee on Civil Disorders' concluded that the major cause of the 1967 summer riots was white racism. Similar investigations by church bodies into the riots in Los Angeles 25 years later, over the beating of Rodney King, came to similar conclusions, as have reports on the uprisings in Britain since the late 1970s. It was racism too in the policies of the Memphis city authorities that took Martin King on his last fateful journey. Perhaps it was an appropriate epitaph that in the end King died because of his solidarity with low-paid, discriminated-against dustmen, and his determination to march in Memphis against the twin evils of poverty and racism.

Branch's later analysis was subtitled *America in the King Years 1954–63*. It attempts a history of the USA rather than a biography, its thesis being that King's life was the 'best and most important metaphor' for the history of postwar America. It offers a deeper analysis of the role of Hoover's FBI in monitoring, undermining and rumouring about King and his colleagues in a way which both limited his positive influence, especially with President Kennedy and his Attorney-General brother Bobby, and enabled certain organs of the State to rubbish King both privately and later in public. Hoover was obsessed with communism, and was convinced that one of King's closest advisers, white lawyer Stanley Levison, was a Kremlin agent. It was claims such as these which prepared the climate for King's assassination. The FBI files from bugging Levison's phones have provided rich material for King's biographers.

King was certainly a prophet. Today he is often described as a saint by people who have not troubled to read in depth what he said and did, especially in his last two years, with its implications for the USA, Britain and human society as a whole. King's message and actions were non-violent, but they were also militant. They struck at the selfish, racist, capitalist roots of US society, and the majority of North Americans – most whites and even some blacks – resented him. White students at the University of Texas cheered when they heard he had been killed. James Cone was sure that it was the weak and negative response to King's ministry by whites which led to his murder, writing

'I am convinced that King's death was due to an ethos created by the white Church, which permits whites to kill blacks at will without any fear of reprisal'. With the subsequent benefit of the work of Garrow and Branch it might be added that the State also seems to have played its part.

Cone, writing shortly after Martin Luther King's death, states his belief at that time that King really gained greater popularity among church people, especially whites, only as he came to be seen as the lesser of two evils, the 'peaceful alternative' to the presence of Black Nationalism and the rise of Black Power. More of that soon, but it appears that King was moving towards a rapprochement with the advocates of Black Power when he was killed. Those who now see him as a saint should not do so without taking on board the challenge he had begun to represent not only to white racism but also to the whole manner in which the world's 'people of colour' are exploited, including through the international trading and financial system.

Alongside the last two years of King's ministry, perhaps influenced by Black Nationalism, more militant streams had emerged among black church leaders, although their action component was still smaller than that of King's campaigns. This thinking did however lead to a degree of separatism of black Christians from white ones. Again there is no direct parallel to the UK situation, but there is enough food for thought to make it worth our while pursuing US history just a little further. These streams converged in the National Committee of Black Churchmen (later amended to 'Black Christians'). The NCBC placed full-page advertisements in the *New York Times* in July and November 1966, addressing the issues of white racism and black power. The differences between black and white church leaders became acute and in one of his articles in the mammoth and fascinating *Black Theology: A Documentary History 1966–79*

(1979) Gayraud Wilmore describes how fundamental and painful these disparities had become:

> When on September 27th, 1967, a national conference on urban
> problems sponsored by the National Council of Churches exploded
> into two caucuses, one Black and one White, it was apparent that
> the differences were acute and a new era of polarisation had begun.
> (p. 19)

At one point the White group sent a delegation to the Black meeting but were
refused admission. The two caucuses then produced their own statements as
part of a common document. Wilmore regards this as one of the most important
documents in the *Documentary History* he edited with James Cone, because it
shows the development in black leaders' thinking a year after the challenge of
Black Power first came to the National Council of Churches. Some of the white
leaders were shocked and offended by the demand for black separatism, but
reluctantly they accepted it.

This incident is recorded here in some detail as it illustrates the anger particularly among the younger black clergy, and the determination that the structural
racism in the mainstream US denominations should be tackled head on. It was
out of the debates, struggles and confrontations that followed that the Black
Theology movement was finally born. Another vital factor which led to its birth
was the Black Nationalism which also influenced Martin Luther King. So let us
now obtain at least a glimpse into the thinking particularly of Malcolm X,
arguably the foremost Black Nationalist in the USA in the last thirty years,
whose contribution was brought back to prominence in the film of his life produced by Spike Lee in 1993.

Black nationalism and Black power

One of the original exponents of the need for black people to withdraw from
white contact in order to develop themselves separately was Marcus Mosiah
Garvey, born in Jamaica in 1887. He learned his separatist approach young,
from the white side, and from a Methodist family. Adolph Edwards, who in 1979
published the booklet *Marcus Garvey 1887-1940*, tells of a 'most traumatic
experience which . . . coloured his subsequent philosophy'. As a youngster in
Jamaica he had played with local children, white as well as black.

> Joining in the childish fun was a white girl – the daughter of a
> Methodist minister. At the appropriate time she was packed off to
> school in Scotland, with a firm admonition from her parents that

she should never write or get in touch with him for he was a 'nigger'. In [Garvey's] own words, 'It was then that I found for the first time that there was some difference in humanity and that there were different races, each having its own separate and distinct social life'. (p. 6)

He did not think of playing with white girls any more 'even if they might be next door neighbours'.

Garvey visited Central America, Venezuela and Britain before returning to Jamaica in 1914 to form his Universal Negro Improvement Association (UNIA). He went to the USA in 1916 and within months, through his remarkable oratory, UNIA was well-established. By 1919 it claimed branches in thirty cities, with two million members, and had started a weekly paper, *The Negro World*. Garvey manifested his separatism by purchasing a large auditorium in Harlem, establishing a steamship line and a chain of factories, and designing a flag of red, black and green – representing spilt negro blood, racial pride and new life in Africa. It was Garvey's vision that he would lead a returning pilgrimage of the descendants of slaves. Such visions, however, did not detract from black rights within the USA. He said that the redemption of Africa 'does not mean that we must give up our domestic rights' and that black people could be loyal citizens of the USA or Britain while fighting for Africa and 'the emancipation of the Race'. Garvey was a master of public relations, he got to know African leaders such as Kenyatta and Nkrumah. He gave many black people both hope and pride, and pricked the consciences of white and black middle classes. Edwards chooses one sentence to encapsulate Garvey's philosophy, 'I shall teach the black man to see beauty in himself'.

Manning Marable, a black American professor of sociology, identifies black nationalism as dating from the 1850s, when emancipated slaves first began to express support for separate black development. *In Race, Reform and Rebellion: The Second Reconstruction in Black America, 1945–1982* (1984) he defines the ideals of black nationalism as

> rejection of racial integration; a desire to develop all-black socio-economic institutions; an affinity for the cultural and political heritage of black Africa; a commitment to create all-black political structures to fight against white racism; a deep reluctance to participate in coalitions which involve a white majority; the advocacy of armed self-defence of the black community; and, in religion and culture, an ethos and a spirituality which consciously rejected the imposition of white western dogmas. (p. 59)

Marable notes that by the 1950s Garveyism had almost disappeared; this was partly due to accusations of financial improprieties. It was then that the Nation of Islam, or the 'Black Muslims', sprang to prominence. The movement began in 1930s Detroit, but did not make much impact until a new leader styling himself 'Elijah Muhammed' came on the scene. According to Marable, Muhammed realised that no other movement, including the Black Churches and the Civil Rights Movement, had an effective programme to recruit and transform the convicts, drug addicts and other delinquents who were over-represented in the black community at that time. Muhammed began to organise them and by 1960 the membership of the 'Nation of Islam' was between 65,000 and 100,000, with Temples in many major cities.

Professor Essien-Udom, a Nigerian sociologist, spent several years studying the development of the Black Muslims. He states that people joined for identity, with a desire for self-improvement, and because of their dissatisfaction with the status of 'blackness' in America. He cites a number of case-studies where it is clear that self-respect and self-organisation were key motivations; there was also desire for a strong leader. People had rejected the Churches because of their 'otherworldly' concerns, and lack of encouragement to members to improve themselves here and now. Some referred back to Marcus Garvey as someone they wanted to emulate.

Both Essien-Udom and Marable stress the important role played by Malcolm X in the development of the Muslims during the 1950s. Malcolm, born in 1925, the son of a travelling Baptist preacher, had seen his father killed – quite possibly by racists – and his family destroyed by the white social welfare establishment. As a boy he was placed with a white foster-family, and tried to fit in, but despite their kindness they seemed also thoroughly prejudiced. He writes in *The Autobiography of Malcolm X* (1968):

> They would even talk about me, or about 'niggers', as if I wasn't there, as if I wouldn't understand what the word meant. . .. What I am trying to say is that it just never dawned on them that I would understand, that I wasn't a pet, but a human being. (p. 107)

By his late teens Malcolm had become a hustler, drug-dealer and pimp in the Boston and New York City ghettoes. He was imprisoned more than once. However, his father had been a Garvey supporter and this may have finally surfaced in Malcolm's consciousness. His older brother became a Muslim and other Muslims influenced him while he was serving a prison sentence in his mid-twenties. When he came out in 1952 he joined the Muslims, gave his whole allegiance to Elijah Muhammed and was named Malcolm X, the 'X' signifying the African name he would never know. By 1954 Malcolm had become Minister of the Muslims' prestigious Temple 7 in Harlem. Although the Muslims' critics – black and white – accused them of race hatred against whites, Malcolm always denied this, saying that what the Muslims wanted was 'freedom, justice and equality'. If the white man did not actively support this he was evil, a 'blonde-haired, blue-eyed devil'. But, said Malcolm, this did not mean Muslims hated particular individual whites.

Malcolm's outspokenness began to affect the younger leaders of the Civil Rights Movement as they struggled through the 1950s and early 1960s to combat white racism, first in the south and then in the north. It caused a vigorous debate in the Student Nonviolent Co-ordinating Committee (SNCC), which had been set up by King's Southern Leadership Christian Conference and the Congress on Racial Equality (CORE). Malcolm was able to attract the poor and disadvantaged blacks of the ghettoes in a way the more sedate and middle-class groups could not. In fact some civil rights leaders, although more cautious in their public statements, agreed with what Malcolm was saying. His sharp, clear, articulate analysis made him much quoted in the white media, which at the same time attacked him for his ideals. Marable summarises his impact thus:

> It is difficult for historians to capture the vibrant essence of Malcolm X, his earthy and human character, his position as a revolutionary teacher for a generation of young militants, his total love for the dispossessed. . . . Malcolm rose from being a pimp, drug dealer and ghetto hustler into the most forceful proponent of nationalism since Garvey. His rhetoric, more so even than King's, was almost hypnotic on black audiences . . . he preached a militant message which changed the lives of thousands of poor and oppressed blacks. (p. 96)

The constant theme of Malcolm's speeches was the mixed racial character of the US black community, whose grandmothers and great-grandmothers had suffered the attacks of the white rapists. Marable describes what Malcolm wanted from whites:

> Every white man in America, when he looks into a black man's eyes, should fall to his knees and say 'I'm sorry, I'm sorry – my kind has committed history's greatest crime against your kind; will you give me the chance to atone? But do you brothers and sisters expect any white man to do that? No, you know better! (p. 97)

Essien-Udom says, however, that despite Malcolm's rhetoric, and all the activities of the Muslims, it was difficult to identify their political programme. Malcolm found this frustrating, and himself increasingly spoke out on political issues, something which caused growing tension in his relationship with Elijah Muhammed, a disagreement which was ultimately to prove fatal.

It was undoubtedly Malcolm's influence which led to the first use of the slogan 'Black Power' by SNCC spokesperson Stokely Carmichael, on the Memphis-to-Jackson Freedom March in June 1966. Martin King was troubled by the phrase, which he felt sounded like a demand for black domination or even black supremacy. He sought to persuade others not to use it. Meanwhile more conservative black leaders, seeing their carefully cultivated bridges to the white establishment being swept away, vigorously attacked the 'Black Power' slogan. James Cone however, in his 1991 volume *Martin and Malcolm and America*, says that King was positively influenced by the Black Power advocates. He says they forced King to use more black role-models in his speeches, to quote more black authors and to revise his image of Jesus as a white man. King refused to accept the implicit condemnation of black power drawn up by some civil rights leaders. He published his own view in a *New York Times* advertisement:

> The caption read 'IT IS NOT ENOUGH TO CONDEMN BLACK POWER'. While commenting that 'the slogan was an unwise choice', because of its 'violent connotations', he urges whites to examine its meaning at a deeper level. 'Negroes have to acquire a share of power so that they can act in their own interests and as an independent social force.' (p. 270)

As Cone goes on to comment, with the emergence of the white backlash King soon realised that to share power with blacks was 'not an item on the white agenda'.

The reaction to the 'Black Power' slogan was one of those influences which began to radicalise Martin Luther King. He began to lose his optimism that if only white people could be shown the effects of racism they would amend their behaviour and change society; but although whites were outraged by the actions of Bull Connor of Birmingham and Jim Clark of Selma, and their police forces, they never seemed really to believe in equality. When King went north and sought to use civil disobedience to place the issue of black poverty in the national spotlight he got little white support. Cone says that this was when disillusion with the white community began to take hold.

> It was in this context that Martin's views about whites began to change radically, moving closer to Malcolm's. Since only a few whites supported economic equality and the majority were passionately against it, Martin said regretfully, as he spoke to Louisville blacks, 'I am sorry to have to say to you that the vast

majority of white Americans are racist, either consciously or unconsciously'. To his staff he said, as they prepared for the Second March on Washington, 'We live in a confused . . . sick, neurotic nation'. (p. 290)

It is Cone's view that in the last year of Malcolm's life, after he had broken with Elijah Muhammed and the Black Muslims, and started to develop a more far-reaching programme, Martin and Malcolm began to approach one another. Malcolm had formed the 'Organisation for Afro-American Unity' (OAAU) in the summer of 1964, after expulsion from the Muslims for his description of President Kennedy's assassination as 'the chickens coming home to roost'. According to Marable, 'the actual programme of the OAAU was reformist' and looked little different from the radical arm of the Civil Rights Movement. However, Malcolm could still catch the media with comments about what he wanted from white people. In a rally of the OAAU soon after the passage of the 1964 Civil Rights Act he is sharply dismissive about it, saying (rightly) that it would never stop discrimination in housing, education, jobs or policing in New York. He goes on to call for white allies as committed as John Brown, who 'went to war against white people to free slaves'. John Brown is the hero of the old Civil War song which says that 'John Brown's body lies a-mouldering in the grave, but his Truth goes marching on'. He was executed for his temerity and Malcolm wanted more whites with his kind of commitment.

The supporters of Black Power, like the Muslims, failed to come up with a viable political programme. Some black radicals pictured 'Black Power' as a revolutionary force, bringing about socialist transformation of the USA. According to Manning Marable, many black youths adopted it as an ideological concept; however, it was soon taken over by more conservative groupings. The national Black Power conferences of 1967 and 1968 were held in white hotels, with white company sponsorship, and even President Nixon endorsed the theme. 'Black Power' had been hurriedly hijacked to become almost synonymous with 'Black capitalism', an approach geared to obtaining more material benefits for black people, or at least for their children. Marable states that both radicals and conservatives 'laid claim to the mantle of Malcolm' and the forms in which the idea of Black Power was communicated were therefore contradictory.

Perhaps if Malcolm had survived it would have been different. He had shown little sign of developing a serious economic alternative to US capitalism, even after breaking from the Muslims, but he became deeply critical of capitalism during his last years, and a few months before his death in 1965 stated, in lurid terms, that it had no future. He says in *By Any Means Necessary* (1970),

> It is impossible for capitalism to survive, primarily because the system of capitalism needs some blood to suck. Capitalism used to be like an eagle but now it's more like a vulture. It used to be strong enough to go and suck anybody's blood whether they were strong or not. But now it has become cowardly, like the vulture, and it can only suck the blood of the helpless. (p. 165)

Malcolm and Martin had therefore come to a common conclusion, if by different paths and with different perspectives, as to the need for a radical restructuring of both the USA and the world economy, if racism was to be overcome and justice to unfold. They were both assassinated almost as soon as they began to put forward this view. James Cone believes that both their perspectives are needed. He writes of their 'two roads to freedom', from their different worlds of the south, with its post-slavery black Christianity, and the north, with its post-Christian blacks living in poverty under the shadow of affluence. Martin came to understand the alienation and the anger of the northern black, post-Watts, and Malcolm came to see how effective King was in facing down and undermining the racism that had such a stranglehold on every part of southern black life. Also, Malcolm helped Martin to see how you could sit down with white politicians and business leaders in the north in a way that was difficult if not impossible in the south – but that the results would be no different. He also corrected Martin in his understanding of black pride and independence. Martin, however, was always pointing out that in the end there was no other place for the black person – or the white one – to go, and that if black people resorted to violence they would be the losers, and when it was over things would be no different.

Malcolm's role has been adopted to some degree by Nation of Islam leader Minister Louis Farrakhan in the mid-1990s. He has caused much heart-searching among both black and white anti-racists, because of his anti-Semitic statements, particularly in the aftermath of the 'Million Man March' in October 1995. In *Race Matters* (1994) black intellectual Cornel West contributes an important analysis of Black-Jewish relations, in the context of the Nation's teaching, but the issue remains quite seriously divisive among progressive US movements. In the same book Professor West has an essay on Malcolm X which is both supportive and critical. He writes that Malcolm 'sharply crystallised the relation of black affirmation of self, black desire for freedom, black rage against American society and the likelihood of early black death'. Malcolm was the 'first real black spokesperson who looked ferocious white racism in the eye, didn't blink, and lived long enough to tell America the truth'.

It is understandable, according to West, that contemporary black youth focus on Malcolm X as the embodiment of black rage at the effects of racism. Young blacks 'are up against the forces of death, destruction and disease unprecedented in the everyday life of black urban people'. West wants to build on the best of Malcolm, ensuring that his concept of psychic conversion takes root. He conceives the idea of a 'jazz freedom fighter', who will 'galvanize and energize world-weary people into forms of organization with accountable leadership that promotes critical exchange and broad reflection'. Jazz needs both the soloist and the group, and the individual player sustains and increases the creative tension within the band. It is an inspiring metaphor.

Martin and Malcolm gave a new and positive dimension to the idea of 'Black Power', in relation to the ability black people have to put their finger on the shameful inequalities of our world, their economic and political causes, and the kind of commitment and compassion needed to get them changed. Their legacies are as important for peace-with-justice in Britain and the rest of Europe as they are for the USA. Racism is as vicious, demeaning and destructive a factor on this side of the Atlantic as on theirs. Both Martin and Malcolm were 39 when killed, some six years older – according to tradition – than a man from Galilee who was also a disturber of the (unjust) peace. Often human beings get too cautious when they leave their thirties, or lose the edge of an active hope which can threaten undeserving and sometimes corrupt establishments. That *might* have happened to Malcolm and Martin; sadly we shall never know.

Race or class?

The Civil Rights Movement has been one stream of consciousness and activity by which blacks and white supporters have challenged racism since the 1960s. Another stream of thinking which has travelled alongside this has been a class analysis, inspired by Marxism and the Russian Revolution of the first decades of the twentieth century. Some black leaders have found it essential to incorporate a class perspective into their thinking. The former Detroit autoworker James Boggs, in *Racism and the Class Struggle* (1970), made a vigorous attack on black capitalism as simply replacing white exploiters with black ones, and offered a distinctive Marxist analysis of the 'American Revolution', in which militant blacks would be the vanguard. He put forward a cogent perspective on the desperate plight and potentially challenging role of black youth, the importance of blacks being educated for 'the jobs of the future' and the need for social ownership rather than private enterprise. The black community could only satisfactorily be developed, he said, through 'community control of the public institutions, public funds and other community resources, including land inside the black community'.

Manning Marable describes the 'Great Debate' between the black Marxist-Leninists and the narrower cultural nationalists in the 1970s as something of a disaster. After President Nixon had espoused Black Power as Black Capitalism, thereby draining the term of almost all its original meaning, black radicals dropped it, adopting 'Pan-Africanism' instead. However, arguments and splits developed in the Marxist and Africanist movements. Some argued that race was the defining factor in oppression, that blacks could survive in a capitalist society, and should seek to make the best of it. Others argued from a more classical Marxist view that class had the most powerful effect, and therefore that blacks should join with white radicals to change fundamentally the class structure of American society. Some who argued for both perspectives to be kept on board thought that the real enemy were the 'middle-class Black strivers' whose personal selfishness was the best fodder for the Marxists.

As a Black Christian intellectual, Cornel West argued for both a class and a race analysis, and in the early 1980s he was one of the few black Christians who did urge dialogue with the Marxists. He rarely failed in his speeches or writings to point to the outrageous maldistribution of wealth in US society. In *Prophesy Deliverance!* (1982) he noted that black theologians rarely drew attention to the facts that in 'liberal capitalist America' only 1 per cent own 33 per cent of the wealth and the bottom 45 per cent own only 2 per cent of the wealth, and that racist interpretations of the Gospel also support the capitalist system and its gross inequalities. West goes on, 'This . . . raises the age-old question as to whether class position or racial status is the major determinant of black oppression in America . . . [or rather] contributes most to the fundamental form of powerlessness in America'. West's view was that middle-class white people have little more power than middle-class black people, hence 'class position contributes more than racial status to the basic form of powerlessness in America'. The most powerful group in US society are 'those multiple corporate owners who dictate crucial corporate policies over a variety of production flows', and they ensure powerlessness both among the US poor and the poor of the 'Third World'.

One form in which this debate developed further in the 1980s was around the question of a black underclass, whether it exists, and what acceptance of the concept implies. One of the works which helped to stimulate the controversy was *The Declining Significance of Race* by William Julius Wilson (1978). Its thesis was that the application of 'affirmative action' policies, which encouraged more employment of minorities and more trade with minority businesses, was resulting in the creation of a larger black middle class, while leaving the majority of the black community in much the same conditions of poverty as before. This was taken by some critics to be an attack on affirmative action policies. Wilson therefore followed up his first work with *The Truly Disadvantaged* (1987), subtitled *The*

Inner City, the Underclass and Public Policy. This gave a more comprehensive analysis of the 'ghetto underclass', largely created by the economic policies of the white State over the previous decades, and outlined some of the policies necessary to reverse the trend.

Wilson believes that neither race-specific policies nor job-training and employment programmes will resolve a desperate situation, and that new programmes on their own need to be constructed which can be viewed positively by the more-advantaged social groups. He identifies himself with the early 1960s plan by King's lieutenant Bayard Rustin, which proposed that blacks press for fundamental economic reform, including national economic planning containing training and public works programmes. Hence Wilson picks up in a new way on King's pragmatism and on his belief that all Americans, black and white, have to find a way of living together. He wants to identify the vital economic dimension of racism, but to seek solutions to inequality by including the white poor with the black poor as beneficiaries, and thus perhaps circumventing the white racism which would deny all improvement to black communities. Economic initiatives should be linked, according to Wilson, with child-care and support programmes, and a proper system of family allowances. Civil rights organisations should urge such policies on Government for *all* disadvantaged communities, not just minority ethnic groups.

Cornel West, in *Race Matters*, takes a similar view but also has some sharp criticism of the market. He points to the 1992 Los Angeles disturbances as an expression of 'social rage' which needs to be taken extremely seriously. He says that what was witnessed in Los Angeles was the results of 'a lethal linkage of economic decline, cultural decay and political lethargy . . . race was the visible catalyst, not the underlying cause'. West points to the departure of secure jobs to low-wage areas within the USA or outside, housing polices that are creating 'chocolate cities and vanilla suburbs', and increasing concentration of wealth ownership, all of which create division by both race and class. West argues that 'saturation of market forces and market moralities' is shattering black society, and a paucity of black leadership is entrenching the problem. The market seduces with its offers of pleasure and comfort; it dehumanises and undermines 'non-market values' such as love, care and service to others.

Some urban churches are continuing to make modest attempts to feed, clothe, house and employ a few hundred, or even a few thousand people – many of them black. The State, however, must take the main responsibility for providing a minimum income, and decent housing for every citizen, as Martin Luther King used to demand, and for distributing with a degree of fairness the wealth of the richest society the world has ever known. Currently the USA is failing to live up either to the hopes of its founding parents, the sentiments of its own Declàration of Independence or the modest expectations of its black and minority citizens. Violence is endemic and will remain so while inequalities continue so high. Neither a frightening level of black imprisonment nor a rising rate of capital punishment will stop it. Differences of class are exacerbated by those of race, and a fundamental economic and political restructuring is essential if the USA is ever to approach a society which would reflect its professed faith that all are created equal.

Black Theology

Black Theology emerged at the end of the 1960s, in the context of the climax of the Civil Rights Movement, the murder of Martin Luther King and the rebellions across the USA. Some of its influence has been felt in Britain, but few white people, even those working in multiracial areas, have engaged with it. Its ideas and dynamic can be extremely informative and spirit-changing; the hope is that those who are stimulated here will pursue the original sources. The language is sometimes harsh, and the truth painful to hear, but it brings a broadening of theological perspective. It better equips God's ministers and teachers to interpret the Gospel in the context of today's world.

Black Theology has also developed in South Africa, and different forms of Caribbean, Latin American and Asian theology have also evolved in the last two decades. Debate among these different theologies has gone on throughout the 1970s and 1980s in EATWOT, the Ecumenical Association of Third World Theologians. The following section draws mainly on Black Theology from the USA, as it provides the best parallels with the British situation. It should always be remembered however that Black Theology in the USA arose out of the context of Black Nationalism, which was an essential element in its formulation.

It is unclear as to when the term 'Black Theology' first came to be used. In *Black Theology: A Documentary History*, Gayraud Wilmore says it could have been in Cone's *Black Theology and Black Power*. However it may have been used previously by the National Council of Black Churchmen (as it was then), to describe 'an understanding of the relevance of the gospel for Black liberation conceived mainly by Black pastors and church executives who were struggling to define their faith vis-à-vis a White religious establishment which had betrayed them'. Black Theology was 'the intellectual spark that flew from the anvil of oppression upon which the Black religious groups were hammered into existence', says Wilmore, and

Black people have done theology out of their guts, out of individual and collective experiences of struggle. The message of the Bible did not come to us in monasteries, in theological libraries . . . but under the lash of plantation overseers and in the dilapidated, impoverished ghettoes of a hundred cities. (p. 3)

In the same volume Cone recounts the birth of *Black Theology and Black Power* amidst his white-hot anger in the shadow of the assassination of Martin Luther King. In it he argues for a theology whose sole purpose is to apply the liberating power of the Christian Gospel to black people under white oppression, and which aims to destroy racism. For Cone, 'Christianity needs remaking in the light of black oppression'. He goes on,

The task of Black Theology then is to analyze the black man's condition in the light of God's revelation in Jesus Christ with the purpose of creating a new understanding of black dignity among black people, and providing the necessary soul in that people, to destroy white racism . . . to analyze the nature of the Christian faith in such a way that black people can say Yes to blackness and No to whiteness and mean it. (p. 117)

Cone finishes ferociously. Black Theology 'confronts white society as the racist Antichrist, warning the oppressor that nothing will be spared in the fight for freedom'.

As with all the newer non-white-male-European theologies the *context* from which Black Theology arises is seen by its proponents as vital. We have heard above something of the context in which Black Theology evolved in the USA; Cone reminds us of the place of parts of the Church in that context:

During the most fervent period of lynching, the Church scarcely said a word against it . . . until 1929 most churches scarcely uttered a word about white inhumanity towards blacks . . . Myrdal pointed out 'Methodist and Baptist preachers were active in reviving the Ku Klux Klan after the First World War'. There is little doubt the Church has been and is a racist institution, and there is little sign that she even cares about it. (p. 78)

There are worrying signs that in the current revival of the Klan, and similar bodies like the 'White Aryan Nation' and 'Posse Comitatus', right-wing 'Christians' are again playing a leading part.

Let us step outside the USA, to South Africa and Britain, in considering what Black theologians say about God, the Spirit, the Bible, and the Church. Again these can only be glimpses, but should encourage readers to seek the primary sources. We begin with the theology of Allan Boesak, a former President of the 'coloured' Dutch Reformed Church in South Africa, but latterly more active in the African National Congress. Boesak has fallen from grace in both his religious and political careers, but his earlier writings remain clear and full of insight. He believes that, despite the prominence of people like Archbishop Tutu, Beyers Naude, Barney Pityana, Stanley Mogoba and Cedric Mayson in the anti-apartheid struggle, the Churches by and large failed. In *Farewell to Innocence* (1976) he states that the 'appalling silence and indifference' with regard to the treatment of black people, are in themselves 'judgement and condemnation'. On *God*, Boesak declares:

> Black theology seeks the God of the Bible, who is totally and com-pletely different from the God whites have for so long preached to blacks. The God of the Bible is the God of liberation rather than oppression; a God of justice rather than injustice; a God of freedom and humanity rather than enslavement and subservience; a God of love, righteousness and community rather than hatred, self-inter-est and exploitation. (p. 10)

Cone – in 'politically-incorrect' language he would never use now – sees God as actively involved in the people's struggle in a way white people seem unable to appreciate:

> Black rebellion is a manifestation of God himself actively involved in the present-day affairs of men for the purpose of liberating a peo-ple. Through his work, black people now know there is something more important than life itself. (p. 38)

In looking at the person of *Christ* black theology cannot accept the picture it receives of the 'white Jesus'. Boesak quotes Vincent Harding:

> We first met this [white] Christ on slave ships. We heard his name sung in praise while we died in our thousands, chained in stinking holds beneath the decks, locked in with terror and disease, and sad memories of our families and homes. When we leaped from the decks to be seized by sharks we saw his name carved in the ship's solid sides. When our women were raped in the cabins they must have noted the great and holy books on the shelves. Our introduc-tion to this Christ was not propitious, and the horrors continued on America's soil.

Boesak remarks that this same white Christ in the South African context was always on the side of the powerful; he 'blessed the whites' weapons and assured them of victory'. Boesak affirms with Cone the centrality of the Black Messiah. Cone sees that Messiah continuing the way of the Cross through the black struggle, 'If Christ is present today, actively risking all for the freedom of man, he must be acting through the most radical elements of Black Power'.

To Black theologians the *Spirit* is active in human life, 'accomplishing the work of salvation begun in the election of Israel and continued in Christ'. Cone also sees the power of the Spirit as an inspiration to those who are committed to change:

> To be possessed by God's Spirit means that the believer is willing to be obedient unto death, becoming the means through whom God makes his will known, and the vehicle of the activity of God himself. (p. 59)

The Spirit, according to Boesak, is present in the movements for Black Power and Black Theology, and he quotes radical US pastor Albert Cleage:-

> The Holy Spirit is the revolutionary power which comes to an exploited people as they struggle to escape from powerlessness and to end the institutional oppression forced upon them by an enemy . . . the language of the Holy Spirit cannot but be the language of revolt. (quoted on p. 72)

Black theologians take the *Bible* very seriously. They point to the Exodus experience of the Hebrew people and frequently refer to the great themes which grow from the Old Testament into the New – creation, salvation and redemption. The righteousness of God is a key concept for Cone. He says white theologians have been no help in seeking to *apply* this notion:

> They fail to give proper emphasis . . . to the biblical idea of God's righteousness as the divine decision to vindicate the poor, the needy and the helpless in society. Much of this abstract theological disputation and speculation – the favourite pastime for many theological societies – serves as a substitute for relevant involvement in a world where men die for lack of political justice. (p. 43)

Boesak also criticises white theology for 'pietising' the message of the Bible:

> The tendency to spiritualise the biblical message is still dominant. We are in full agreement with Gutiérrez . . . when he warns that this excessive spiritualisation is something we should profoundly mistrust. It stems from a Western, dualistic pattern of thought foreign to Biblical mentality. (p. 22)

147

The *Church* is seen as a vehicle for white perceptions and aspirations. Boesak notes that while slavery flourished, black civilisations were destroyed, human dignity was annihilated and genocide reigned. The white churches 'became part of an especially aggressive, intolerant power, using everything from missionaries to gunboats, from development aid to napalm, to become Lords of the rest of the planet'.

James Cone goes further, seeing not merely the miserable failure of the white churches to manifest to the world 'God's intention for humanity' but their racism as a denial of the Incarnation. He quotes Loescher, 'Long before the little signs "Whites Only" and "Coloureds" appeared in public utilities, they had appeared in the Church'. Could the white Churches be called Christian at all?

In an essay in *Theology in the City* (ed. Harvey, 1989) Nyameko Barney Pityana, colleague of Steve Biko, Anglican priest and ex-Director of the World Council of Churches' Programme to Combat Racism, raises questions about the *Faith in the City* report (Archbishop of Canterbury's Commission on Urban Priority Areas) and its theological approach. Out of his English parish experience he says the theology of the report articulates 'Christendom values', and that there needs to be a change in 'the theological outlook which has so long undergirded British church and social life. . . .. Black people need to own the Church and exercise their freedom within it'.

One of the results of the tendency towards enforced separation, both theological and ecclesiastical, in the USA, Africa and Europe, has been the evolution of the 'Black Churches' or 'Black-majority Churches', from one of which James Cone himself comes. He is not uncritical of these churches, but sees them as inevitable. Black people must say 'no' to 'assimilation', 'no' to 'integration'. They need to organise themselves, take power over their own lives, 'until whites . . . are able to accept the beauty of blackness . . . black people must withdraw and form their own culture, their own way of life'.

Pityana identifies the unifying theme for blacks as '*Pilgrim*':

> British blacks share together the *pilgrim* experience. It must have taken the faith of Abraham for many to travel to unknown lands. They all come from places far away to claim a sense of belonging in this land where God will help them to take root (Genesis 12. 1–3), and they bring blessings to their adopted country. Black people have a right to claim Abraham the wandering Aramaean as their ancestor. (p. 109)

Most black theologians are critical of 'white liberals' who want to find the easy way to reconciliation. Boesak feels the role of the liberal has to be re-evaluated, saying the question is 'whether whites are willing to identify with what the oppressed are doing to secure their liberation, and aid that liberation in their own communities'.

This applies in the USA, South Africa and between the rich 'first' and poor 'third' world. Cone writes:

> The liberal then is one who sees 'both sides' of the issue, and shies away from 'extremism' in any form. He wants to change the heart of the racist without ceasing to be his friend; he wants progress without conflict. Therefore when he sees blacks engaging in civil disobedience and demanding 'Freedom Now' he is disturbed. . .. The liberal . . . wants change without risk, victory without blood. (p. 27)

The message of Black Theology is sharp, clear and uncomfortable. For many white congregations and clergy, the fiery language of writers like Cone may seem drastic, but in a wide-ranging survey of British theological colleges carried out by Raj Patel for the BCC Community and Race Relations Unit, and published as *Equal Partners?* (1992), it was clear few had taken on board even the gentlest insights of black theology. This was true in terms of content of courses, books in libraries, or ethnic origins of staff and students.

Cornel West in *Prophesy Deliverance!* (1982) classifies various periods in the development of Black Theology. He identifies as key a paper by Cone which says it is time for black people to move beyond simply surviving in a racist, capitalist society and take seriously 'our dreams about a new heaven and a new earth'. Can such a dream include capitalism, asks Cone, or is it more radically attuned to the socialism of, say, Tanzania's Arusha Declaration? In his later writings Cone develops this theme further. In *Speaking the Truth* (1986), he points out that while we say we are concerned for the poor 'we do not analyze and fight against the socio-economic structures responsible for their poverty'. There are food programmes, and hospital and jail ministries, but 'such projects are not designed to challenge the capitalist system that creates human misery. Churches are often incapable of attacking the root causes of oppression because they are beneficiaries of the system responsible for it' (p. 112). West also believes it is important for Black Theology to critique capitalism. He wants more dialogue between black Christians and Marxists, because both focus on the plight of 'the exploited, oppressed and degraded peoples of the world'.

A recent development in Black Theology in the USA is '*womanist theology*', which has grown to some extent from the writings of novelist Alice Walker, the first to use the term 'womanist'. According to its proponents it arises from the 'richness, complexity, uniqueness and struggle' which are an integral part of being black and female in a hostile society. It is also linked with 'Afrocentricity', a concept evolved partly from US black nationalist perspectives by Molefi Kete Asante. It is theology which may only be written by black women. In a book of essays, *Living the Intersection: Womanism and Afrocentrism in Theology* (1995), the editor, Cheryl Sanders, describes the womanist perspective as 'mining the culture and history of African American women' in a way which will foster 'life and wholeness for the African American community'.

Living the Intersection explores a theological response to the particular situation of black women. Most of the essays are critical of the propagators of Afrocentrism, suggesting they are still shackled with the culture of patriarchy, but argue that the perspectives of Afrocentrism and Womanism together have 'something special to say to the world'. The key essay by Sanders refers to the histories of black women like Jarena Lee (born 1783), Zilpha Elaw (1790) and Amanda Berry Smith (1837). Zilpha Elaw was an itinerant Methodist preacher on the east US coast who had her autobiography published in London in 1846. Sanders describes how Elaw and the others are rooted in the tradition of black women in the Bible, with their special struggle for affirmation of their faith. Sanders writes, 'Upon closer scrutiny of its accounts of black women's lives, the Scriptures reveal God's sustenance of the single mother, the faithful wife, the devout poor and the virtuous privileged' (p. 142). Pointing to the women who were drawn into 'intimate though sometimes exploitative relationships' with Abraham, Moses and Solomon, Sanders argues that women are 'key players in salvation history'. Womanist theology, like other dimensions of black theology, offers creative insights for an understanding of the nature of God in our contemporary society.

There have been some British responses to the phenomenon of Black Theology. Garnet Parris has an essay in *A Time to Speak: Perspectives of Black Christians in Britain*, edited by Paul Grant and Raj Patel (1990). He says 'our understanding of Black Theology goes beyond the Church as an ecclesiastical institution to embrace aspects of Black life and culture which white scholars have regarded as secular, non-Christian and even anti-Christian'. It is a comprehensive term describing

> the quasi-religious, quasi-secular yearning of an oppressed Black people. It has to do with our expressed thoughts and feelings about the meaning of that oppression. It has to do with everything black people have felt, believed and practised, from slavery to the present, which expressed in some way our ultimate interest in throwing off the yoke of white bondage and affirming ourselves as autonomous, self-determining human beings.

Parris believes Black Theology incorporates relevant truth where it is to be found, therefore people believe that, although Malcolm X was not a Christian,

> he knew and spoke the truth about what it means to be Black in White America . . . [and] it is impossible for Black Christians not to believe that the God of Jesus Christ was revealed in the life and ministry of Malcolm X.

Can there then be reconciliation between White and Black? Parris believes that

> Reconciliation . . . can only follow liberation. Black theology must confront the white churches with the judgement of God, with the demand for repentance and reparation, before true reconciliation between Black and white can take place.

Black theologians, including those developing their ideas in a British setting, frequently place Jesus firmly among the disadvantaged, oppressed and crucified – and in the European context that means the migrant worker, the imprisoned asylum-seeker, the black teenager, *'le clandestine'* (French terminology for an illegal immigrant) – all seeking a ledge of survival to which to cling. The Incarnation takes place among these communities, says Black Theology. That is where God is made flesh, and dwells among us. From there come atonement, redemption and salvation, rather than from fine robes and incense, loud choruses or individualistic, success-affirming sermons. If Cone and other black theologians are right, and 'Christ is Black, baby', he will be hard to find in the churches of the wealthy European Union. Let us then explore a theology for Europe, a theology of struggle, which may help us as white people to discover a way of being Christian in a world of continuing racial inequality and injustice and – too frequently – of hatred.

6

A theological reflection – the necessity of struggle

'Struggle' is not a common theological category. Nor does it make frequent appearances in the biblical texts. The only mention of it in my slightly elderly Concordance relates to Genesis 25. 22 where Esau and Jacob 'struggled together' in the womb – not perhaps an inappropriate reference, as they continued to struggle together outside it and Jacob eventually cheated Esau of his inheritance in a way not too far removed from the way white people have often treated blacks.

Struggle, however, contains vital elements for Christian thinking about racial justice. It suggests effort, it implies reaction or resistance against that effort, but it also carries the connotation of movement, of progress that is likely eventually to achieve. It describes too, with some accuracy, the dynamic in biblical times most analogous to our striving for racial justice in the world today. To be properly biblical and theological we should probably talk about 'struggle for justice' or 'struggle for righteousness', but as that might become rather repetitive we will content ourselves with 'struggle', with the aim of justice being understood. The struggle we are dealing with here is an opportunity offered to white people as they have a choice whether or not to engage in it. Black people, however, have little choice: like Simon of Cyrene they have no escape.

Let us then first examine briefly some biblical material, as it provides a backdrop for more contemporary concerns.

Racism in the Bible?

Some would say that racism and racial justice are relatively modern concepts, and that there is no real history of or reference to such things in the Bible. However, examining the thinking of the Hebrews as they developed their self-awareness as the 'chosen people' is instructive. Much of the historical part of the

Old Testament was of course written down centuries after it was supposed to have occurred, and interpreted with hindsight by those who believed that Yahweh had chosen them as his 'most favoured nation'.

There are clearly both positives and negatives about the 'chosen people' syndrome. The perception of the Hebrew people about the nature of God and Creation has made an enormous contribution to religious thought and practice. They brought together ideas, experiences and myths, from their own history and that of others, and produced an understanding of the world, within a religious framework, which no other nation was able to match. The negative side was a growth in pride and even arrogance. The prophets frequently warned their political and military leaders of selfishness, greed and irreligious practices, and often rightly predicted their downfalls. 'Chosen people' of whatever religion can be difficult to influence or dissuade.

The Old Testament is written out of a conviction that Yahweh was guiding and controlling the people's destiny. The sense of a strong and even interventionist hand is communicated, ensuring the success of the Hebrew enterprise. We pass over perhaps too easily the appalling behaviour of Joseph's brothers, the mass deaths of the Egyptians by plague or drowning, and the slaughter that seems often to have accompanied the Hebrew takeover of Canaan. There is a general assumption that death and destruction is permissible, if not blessed, when carried out in Yahweh's name. This seems to be concretised in the triumphalism surrounding the kingship of David, whose political and military genius finally bound the twelve tribes together sufficiently for the Israelites to become one of the strongest nations of the time.

There does not seem to have been anything particularly uplifting about David's rule. It was established among some pretty unsavoury incidents, the arm's-length murder of Uriah the Hittite, husband of Bathsheba, being the best known. The second book of Samuel is overall a tale of violence, lust and intrigue which, were it written up in contemporary language and supplied with a sufficiently garish cover, would doubtless become a best-seller on many a station bookstall. This period, however, was seen as the epitome of Hebrew achievement, and is looked back to even today as Israel's 'golden age'. The Messiah himself was to come of David's line. If indeed Jesus did so his character was fortunately radically different from that of his illustrious ancestor.

The kings of both Israel and Judah apparently followed David's example to a greater or lesser degree, depending on their abilities and competence. When Solomon died about 930 BCE, instead of his son Rehoboam adopting a conciliatory line with those of the northern areas who followed Jeroboam, he determined to exert his authority over them (1 Kings 12). An internecine civil war was prevented only by the intervention of the prophet Shemaiah, who managed to persuade the would-be combatants that Yahweh was not in favour of the inevitable slaughter. So Rehoboam became king in the south, and Jeroboam in the north, but both strayed from the worship of Yahweh. Jeroboam made idols; Rehoboam built false altars and introduced male cult prostitutes. Finally the northern kingdom was besieged and destroyed by the Assyrians in 721 BCE. In the south Judah struggled on for another hundred years, but Manasseh built altars to Baal and Amon continued much the same, followed by other kings who 'did evil in the sight of the Lord'. Eventually Judah was captured by the Babylonians and the leadership taken into exile. Jerusalem lay in ruins for many years, until Nehemiah and Ezra struggled to rebuild both the city and the sense of identity of the Israelites.

That extremely telescoped history may serve to remind us that the only group who came out of these several centuries maintaining much dignity was the prophets. They persistently tried to recall the people, and their leaders, to the true nature of the worship of Yahweh, and the kind of society Yahweh wants. It is their writings which affect us most as we reflect on them in worship and Bible study. They battled against greed, pride, syncretism and the lust for power which characterises so much of Hebrew history through Samuel, Kings and Chronicles, and in which of course Hebrew history is not alone. This struggle between exclusivity with arrogance, and tolerance with justice, crystallises in the debate around the restoration of Jerusalem between the followers of Ezra and – to some degree – Nehemiah, and the writers of Jonah and Ruth. The latter two tracts were almost certainly written during this period, between 450 and 350 BCE, as were the books of Ezra and Nehemiah.

The motivation of Ezra/Nehemiah is the restoration of Jerusalem as political and religious capital, requiring the fairly brutal exclusion of whatever might prevent that. There were reasons why this was important, and we should not totally condemn Ezra and Nehemiah, but their methods were drastic. Nehemiah returns to rebuild Jerusalem (Nehemiah 2) in the face of mockery and opposition from the leaders of the Samaritans and other local peoples, but then turns upon those Jews who had married women from the other ethnic communities, and whose children could not speak Hebrew. 'I argued with them and reviled them, I beat them and tore out their hair', and he made them swear in Yahweh's name not to allow their sons and daughters to marry out of the race again (Nehemiah 13. 25). Ezra was even more vigorous in his version of what we might now call 'ethnic cleansing'. He bemoans the failures of the past and the fact that the Hebrews have become slaves (Ezra 9), and makes reference to the defiled land which has been 'polluted by the foreign population with their abominable practices'. Then the people confess that they have 'committed an offence in marrying foreign wives', and all who have foreign wives must 'present themselves at appointed times . . . until God's anger against us on this account is averted' (Ezra 9. 10–14). So they begin their enquiry (inquisition?), and the named families have to 'dismiss' their wives and children, presumably to fend for themselves in the surrounding desert.

There is however another stream of tradition, developing through the prophets, which looked outwards beyond the chosen people and increasingly saw Yahweh as the God of all. Amos, writing in the middle of the eighth century BCE, has a vigorous commitment to justice, abhors empty religious ritual and suggests that Yahweh will use other peoples to punish Israel if she does not hear Him. First Isaiah castigates the children of Israel for their worship of idols, their false rituals and their personal ornaments and fine clothing. At the same time, he says, the poor are cheated, and the widow and orphan ignored. He announces that Yahweh will act through a far-off nation, Assyria, to destroy his faithless people, and issues prophecies relating to Assyria, Moab, Damascus, Egypt and others, suggesting that he believed Yahweh was in fact God of all the nations. Second Isaiah (i.e. the author of Isaiah chapters 40-55), writing in the time of the Exile in the sixth century, understands Yahweh as the creator of the whole world, and the God of all. In a well-known example the prophet has Yahweh recognising Cyrus, king of the Persians, as 'His anointed', i.e. Messiah, and saying he will level the way before Cyrus, break down gates of bronze before him and give him treasures, so he will know who is God (Isaiah 45. 1–5). Yahweh gives his blessing to Cyrus, who is to grant Yahweh's people a degree of freedom, 'so that men from the rising and setting sun may know that there is none but I' (Isaiah 45. 6).

It is the authors of Ruth and Jonah, however, who really take on the nationalist and supremacist strain in the Israelite tradition. These two books are of importance beyond their size. Both carry messages of the breadth of vision, the depth of acceptance, the length of tolerance of the true people of Yahweh. Ruth, the woman of Moab, is willing to accompany her mother-in-law to the foreign land of Israel, to leave her culture, customs and language, and support Naomi in her declining years. Boaz, perhaps rather seduced by Naomi and Ruth's tactics, is willing to go beyond what is required of him by the all-important 'Law', both in regard to the gleaning of his fields and the marriage he offers. From their 'mixed marriage' comes Obed, a 'mixed-race' son, and the women say to Naomi, 'Blessed be the Lord . . . the child will give you new life, and cherish you in your old age; for your daughter-in-law who loves you, who has proved better to you than seven Israelite sons, has borne him' (Ruth 4. 14–15). And Obed became the father of Jesse, the father of David, of whose mixed line the Messiah himself was reputedly born. David may not have been the ideal monarch, but the followers of Ezra could not have been happy at the idea that the chosen people's greatest king was tainted with foreign blood.

The story of Jonah – dissimilar to the books of the other 'minor prophets', more a kind of parable – makes a similar point from a different perspective. Firstly the sailors, foreigners all, did their best to save Jonah, and only threw him overboard as a very last resort (Jonah 1). Then came the journey to 'Nineveh', long destroyed by the time Jonah was written, but according to the tale a vast, violent and wicked city. Yet the Ninevites are said to have believed Jonah when he threatened them with Yahweh's destruction, and they repent, fast, pray and dress in sackcloth. When he sees what has happened Yahweh himself repents and does not 'bring upon them the disaster he had threatened' (Jonah 3.10). Jonah is thoroughly put out. He is well aware of Yahweh's qualities, he knows him to be 'a God generous and compassionate, long-suffering and ever-constant, and always willing to repent of disaster' (4. 2). But he is so dismayed with Yahweh's sensitivity he wants to die.

Yahweh tries to teach Jonah a lesson, with the withering gourd: 'You are sorry for the gourd, though you did not go to the trouble of growing it. . .. And should I not be sorry for the great city of Nineveh, with all its 120,000 who cannot tell their right hand from their left, and cattle without number?' (Jonah 4. 10–11). Ruth and Jonah are a vital part of the struggle to combat the exclusivist and nationalist stream of Hebrew thought, and to present a more tolerant and 'ecumenical' view.

It was out of this period of the attempted recreation of a new identity for Israel that the negative approach towards the people of Samaria arose. The attitude of the Jews towards the Samaritans appears to have some of the same dynamics as that which today we call racism – the Samaritans were mistrusted, regarded as inferior, viewed as having little proper culture or history, not expected to use the same vessels, despised and excluded. No doubt there would have been some saying, 'Why are they here? They have taken our land and our jobs, and are undermining our culture.'

How does Jesus confront the prejudice – the racism, if it is such – of his day? In fact he relates so well to these foreigners, and gets up the noses of the Jewish authorities to such an extent, that they actually accuse of him of *being* a Samaritan, the ultimate insult. In rage at Jesus' accusations that they are children of the devil the leaders react, 'Are we not right in saying that you are a Samaritan and that you are possessed?' (John 8. 48). Jesus responds that he is not possessed, but (deliberately?) does not deny that he is a Samaritan. Let us then look briefly at four occasions where the issue of the detested Samaritans arises in the Gospels.

First there is the story of the Samaritan woman at the well, in John 4; the initial surprise is Jesus' request for a drink, and on two counts. The woman responds

'What! You a Jew, ask a drink of me a Samaritan woman!' (4. 9), raising questions not just of race but gender as well. There then follows the almost flirtatious conversation about 'living water', but matters become serious again when Jesus makes reference to the woman's previous husbands. This in turn becomes an exchange over the relative merits of Gerizim (on Mount Samaria) and Jerusalem as centres of worship, but the implication of what Jesus says is that he is the one in whom the different traditions are drawn together, and that the time has come when both Samaritans and Jews might worship together 'in spirit and in truth'(4. 24). The woman then emerges as one of the first Christian missionaries, going to call the townspeople: 'Come and see a man who has told me everything I ever did. Could this be the Messiah?' (4. 29). The message is clearly that Jesus is Messiah for Samaritans as well as Jews.

In Luke 9 we find the first of a number of incidents relating to Samaritans in the third Gospel. As in John 4, Jesus takes what is the less common road between Galilee and Judaea, passing through Samaria instead of Perea on the east side of Jordan. He seeks accommodation in a Samaritan village but, because the party was en route for Jerusalem (and therefore Jews), the villagers would not have them. James and John urge Jesus to burn up the village, but 'Jesus turned and rebuked them', and they went elsewhere (Luke 9. 56). Jesus was not prepared to indulge the bigotry of even his closest disciples.

Chapter 10 of Luke contains the story of the Good Samaritan, probably the most effective piece of anti-racist pedagogy in the Bible. Although the care of those left to die by the roadside is obviously important, the fundamental point of the story is that the true 'neighbour' was a member of the Jews' favourite hate-group, the contemptible Samaritans. Such was the adversarial lawyer's discomfiture that he could not bring himself to name the benefactor's ethnic origin, responding, perhaps through partly-clenched teeth, 'The one who showed him kindness' (Luke 10. 37). By touching the corpse the priest or Levite would have become ritually unclean. Jesus is again demonstrating his opposition both to empty ritual and to prejudice, which doubtless further inflamed the anger of the ethnic and legal purists towards him.

Finally in Luke 17 we find the story of the cleansing of the ten lepers, in the 'borderlands of Samaria and Galilee'. The men call out to Jesus to have pity on them; he tells them to show themselves to the priests. On the way they find themselves healed, but only one returns and thanks Jesus. He is a Samaritan. The passage does not comment on the ethnic origin of the other nine, but the presumption must be that they were Jews. Jesus asks, eyebrows perhaps a little raised, 'Could none be found to come back and give praise to God except this foreigner?' (Luke

17. 18). The Greek word translated by the NEB as 'foreigner', *'allogenais'*, is also the word used for a person 'of another race'.

Thus Jesus commits himself to the tradition represented by Second Isaiah and the writers of Ruth and Jonah, and to the struggle against racial intolerance and religious supremacy, manifested in the thought and practice of the Jewish leadership. His approach to the Samaritan issue requires an anti-racist commitment to a degree which is not yet fully recognised by Christians or the Church.

There is other material in the New Testament which can be explored to undergird the Christian view that the God of the Bible is the God of all, in whose sight all are of equal worth. The make-up of the earliest Christian community in Acts, Peter's vision in Acts 10 and the subsequent conversion of Cornelius' household are important parts of this. Paul's insistence in preaching to the Gentiles, against the more conservative views of the 'establishment' of the original apostles, is a further example (Galatians 2). Paul follows this with his clarion message in Galatians 3. 28 that 'there is no such thing as Jew and Greek, slave and freeman, male and female; for you are all one person in Christ Jesus'. For Paul, Christ is available to all, of whatever ethnic or economic origin, though there must be a response from the hearer, in terms of faith, for that offer to be effective. It is interesting to speculate whether there was any ethnic or class basis in the competing Christian 'parties' in 1 Corinthians 1. Apollos was an Alexandrian Jew, from a different tradition to more 'working-class' Peter from Galilee (despite his boat-ownership), and from the high-born Roman citizen Paul of Tarsus. Space prevents us from pursuing that possibility further.

It is our argument that there were forms of behaviour and social structures in biblical times which approximate to a contemporary understanding of racism. However, let us leave the New Testament with the vision of Revelation 21 before us, the vision of the City of God, with no Temple, by whose light walk *all* the peoples, and to which shall be brought 'the wealth and splendour of the nations' (Revelation 21. 26) – hopefully not gained by the exploitation of others. Through the spiritual City flows 'the river of the water of life', on each side of which stands the 'tree of life . . . the leaves of the tree serve for the healing of the nations' (22. 2). Should the broad-based, tolerant, multicultural Christian tradition be understood as the river of life, the Church as the Tree and the true followers of Jesus as the leaves, offering justice and reconciliation among all races, and all nations? They should, but it will not come to pass without struggle.

THE STRUGGLE FOR JUSTICE AND RECONCILIATION

When things are difficult, in racial justice terms, there is always a cry for recon-ciliation. It almost always comes from those in power, anxious to ameliorate or minimise any threatened anger or violence. This has been true repeatedly of South Africa, of the USA, and of Britain too. To some degree it is an enlightened reaction; there are other forces which immediately want to clamp down hard on any signs of black dissent. 'We have to keep them in their place', is the message; 'if they get even a taste of power we could lose everything we fought for'.

Fighting is unfortunately something that white supremacists have been good at, for several centuries, and it has benefited them with a satisfactorily high stan-dard of living in many cases. Where that high standard has not been universal, richer whites have tended to use the inequalities to divide poor whites from poor blacks, and set them to scrap with each other for the crumbs.

Reconciliation is an important concept, and a necessary aim. It must not be diminished to refer only to the peace which those with wealth and power seek when their position is threatened. It contains within its meaning the sense of a return to the way things were, or should be, not 'conciliation' but 're-concilia-tion'. The prerequisites for this are repentance and justice; without them there can be no genuine reconciliation. The situation can be summed up in the (nor-mally black) activists' cry 'No Justice, No Peace!'.

How indeed can we expect to be reconciled with our sisters and our brothers without some equalising of the conditions from which we approach a peace-making occasion or process? That is why the struggle for justice needs to come first. Only when it is actively engaged in can discussions about reconciliation begin legitimately to surface. The grace and patience manifested by many black people in many places, and their propensity to compromise, to forgive injustice past and present, should not be allowed to mask either the amount of hurt cre-ated or the rightness of some kind of reparation.

First, however, let us explore the meaning of 'struggle for justice', with help from some of the theologians of liberation who have opened so many eyes to the true nature of the Christian Gospel in contemporary times. Liberation theology may be derided by some in the West as passé. They see it as declining alongside the apparent weakening of socialism. However, liberation theology is rooted in the Bible and Christian tradition, and will only become irrelevant when oppression is ended. The analysis by liberation theologians of what has been going on eco-nomically in the world, and their focus on the 'responsibility' of the 'Christian' nations for this, cannot be avoided by anybody with a serious claim to faith in the final years of the twentieth century. We take brief glimpses into the work of

Peruvian Catholic Gustavo Gutiérrez, Argentinian Methodist José Míguez Bonino and Sri Lankan priest Tissa Balasuriya.

We shall then examine the dimensions of understanding, repentance and 'justice-making', drawing on thinking by white and black Christians from Britain, South Africa and North America. Finally let us ask the question 'What makes for genuine reconciliation in a racially-divided society and world?'.

THE MEANING OF STRUGGLE

One of the fundamental things theological students learn regarding Jesus' teaching about the Kingdom of God is that it is 'already but not yet'; that the Kingdom, or kingly rule, of God is made manifest in the ministry of Jesus but that it will be completed at some time in the future. The theological debate about the Kingdom is a fascinating one, and this is not the place to explore it in detail. Perhaps two important ideas come out of that debate, for our purposes: the fact that there is a tension between the already-but-not-yet, which implies some kind of dynamic in which the followers of Jesus should be engaged, and the lack of clarity as to what exactly the end-time will be, and how it will come about.

Whatever else God may want, and however this may be brought about, the challenge of the Gospel is for its believers to work towards the fulfilment of the Kingdom – a place or state where all are fit and able to experience God's presence and activity. We need to be in peace and charity with our neighbour. Hence all disciples of Jesus must be engaged in the struggle for peace-with-justice in this world, in a movement towards the fair and equal distribution of the resources of the earth for all God's people. However, we live in the tension between what is – with all its disparities, its hatred, its racial divisions – and what ought to be – equality, love-for-all, justice among all the variety of the human race. Part of the meaning of struggle is that we cannot always see the end-point, but we know in what direction we must go. It is like climbing a mountain in the mist. The higher reaches occasionally appear, the top rarely, but we know we have to go further. Direction and encouragement is given us, in the form of the Scriptures and the tradition and history of the People of God.

The New Testament concludes, aptly, with the visionary chapters of Revelation 21 and 22. Who can fail to be moved by that vision to which we referred at the end of the last section? It is not meant as a description, of course, as to how it will be in the year 5000, or whatever, but it gives us a sense of the kind of community, the sort of 'heaven', the vision towards which we must struggle.

The way in which liberation theologians originally used struggle was in the form of 'class struggle', writing as they were in the late 1960s and 1970s, and using a 'Christian-Marxist' analysis of their social context. However, there is a shift in the emphasis of liberation theology from a relation to revolutionary struggle, when it inspired the Sandinistas of Nicaragua, as well as other movements for fundamental change. It has now assumed the task of unmasking the effects of the 'victorious' capitalist system and persuading – or even 'seducing' as the Leonardo Boff puts it – the privileged. They need to see solidarity with the 'disposable masses' and recognition of a common humanity as crucial for the survival of our planet. My use of struggle seeks to take account of that shift. Reflection on what those theologians said continues, however, to offer important pointers to a whole understanding of struggle. Frederick Douglass, Olaudah Equiano, Mary Seacole, Malcolm X and many others also offer essential insights.

Gustavo Gutiérrez, in his ground-breaking *Theology of Liberation* (1973) begins by defining a new understanding of theology as 'critical reflection on praxis'. By praxis he means actions or deeds, which have not normally come within the purview of Western 'head-centred' theology. He acknowledges the place of Marxism in getting Christians to realise afresh that the relationship between thought and activity is important, and that Marx has acted as a catalyst, stimulating theological thought to 'reflect on the meaning of the transformation of this world and the action of man in history'.

The purpose of this reflection is 'to balance and even to reject the primacy and almost exclusiveness which doctrine has enjoyed in Christian life . . . the intention is to recognise the . . . importance of concrete behaviour, of deeds, of action, of praxis in the Christian life'. Or, to put it another way, 'you will recognise them [the bad and the good] by their fruits' (Matthew 7. 20).

Hence Christians must be engaged in the struggle for the Kingdom, the struggle for better things. For Gutiérrez that must, at least partly, be expressed in social and economic terms, and the aim is liberation – both for the oppressed and the oppressor. But there are various levels to the liberation struggle. Firstly, 'liberation expresses the aspirations of oppressed peoples and social classes', including racially oppressed peoples. Secondly, it is an understanding of history in which 'the unfolding of all man's dimensions is demanded . . . [and which] leads to the creation of a new man [sic] and a qualitatively different society'. In 1973 inclusive language had not yet become part of the 'qualitatively different society'! Finally, says Gutiérrez, liberation reveals new things in the Bible: Christ is the one who liberates us from sin, the root of all injustice and oppression, and enables human beings to live in communion with him, in the new humanity.

This, however, will not be achieved without pain, without struggle, without the Cross. It will not be achieved without love of the neighbour, in whom Christ resides; 'We find the Lord in our encounters with men, especially the poor, marginated and exploited ones. An act of love towards them is an act of love towards God'. But such love means in practice involvement in 'class struggle', using the Marxist categories of ruling, middle and working classes. These terms may have become to a degree outdated; we may want now simply to refer to the 'rich' and the 'poor'. That may not matter as long as those of us reading this are aware that the great majority of us reside in the 'rich' category. What Gutiérrez says about the class struggle is vital, however.

> The class struggle is a fact, and neutrality in this matter is impossible. The class struggle is part of our economic, social, political, cultural and religious reality. . ... Recognition of the existence of the class struggle does not depend on our religious or ethical options. . . oppression and exploitation . . . are endured and perceived first of all by those who have been marginated by [our] civilisation and do not have their own voice in the Church. (p. 274)

He goes on to comment that liberation cannot be achieved except by resolutely opting for the oppressed – economically, culturally, racially or whatever – and therefore combating the oppressors. It is perhaps not surprising that liberation theology has not been greatly welcomed in the West, nor that it is now being quietly ignored.

Míguez Bonino also recognises the class struggle as a reality. In a chapter 'Love, Reconciliation and Class Struggle' from his book *Revolutionary Theology Comes of Age* (1975) he summarises the Marxist view that 'It is a process through which the oppressed discover their identity and strength, and consciously assume the struggle. . ... The outcome of the struggle, and its intended aim, is . . . the suppression of oppression and the elimination of the struggle' (p. 107). Míguez Bonino then comments on 'class', noting that Marxism focuses on humanity as workers, while Christianity understands us more in intellectual and spiritual terms, and in our relation to self, to neighbour and to God. Míguez Bonino finds the two related rather than contradictory, and refuses to accept that 'class struggle' can be labelled as unchristian, per se. He actually reverts to the sixteenth century, to call John Calvin as a witness:

> Even Calvin, with keen realism, describes the economic and social realms, under the sway of sin, as a battlefield in which greed and self-seeking have destroyed an original community of justice and introduced exploitation, injustice and disorder. (p. 119)

If, then, struggle between rich and poor, powerful and powerless, white and black, exists, and can be identified in one form as class struggle, then can God avoid taking sides? Bonino focuses sharply on the Church's failure to acknowledge reality:

Why is it that ecclesiastical pronouncements, after recognizing the intolerable injustice of the situation and even singling out the economic and social structures responsible for it, issue an appeal to the beneficiaries of the situation and a condemnation of the struggle of the oppressed to change it? Why is it that they can't see that the . . . result of such unreality . . . is a reinforcement of those very structures and powers recognized as oppressive and unjust, a weakening of the struggle through which change can effectively come about in *history*? (p. 120)

He sees it as a willingness by the Church, at bottom, to accept the status quo, to seek conciliation at any price, which is then not *re*conciliation but a 'sacralising' of the present order, however unjust, racist, sexist or classist it may be. This idea of conciliation has nothing to do, says Míguez Bonino, with the reconciliation taught in the Scriptures:

Reconciliation means in the Bible not the ignoring or explaining away of the contradiction but its effective removal. . . Reconciliation is not achieved by some sort of compromise between the new and the old but through the defeat of the old and the victory of the new age. The ideological appropriation of the Christian doctrine of reconciliation by the liberal capitalist system in order to conceal the brutal fact of class and imperialist exploitation and conflict is one – if not the – major heresy of our time. (p. 121)

Tough words, but written from a context in which poverty and oppression was, and is, endemic. Even if totalitarian socialism as the major alternative to market capitalism has collapsed in its previous Eastern European form this does not mean it has gone for good. Nor does it mean that liberal capitalism is more blessed by God. It means we have to try again to understand the nature of the Kingdom, at least in its earthly dimension, and that needs further effort. The Gospels make it clear that Jesus eschewed the way of violence to achieve the freedom of the Jewish people. He took the role of servant, and 'identified himself with the impotence of the oppressed'. But this does not mean, according to Míguez Bonino, that there is any 'specifically Christian struggle'. He goes on,

Christians assume, and participate in, human struggles by identifying with the oppressed. But they have no particularly divine or religious power to contribute. There is no room for crusades, for sacred wars. Secondly it means that Christians are called to use for this struggle the same rational tools that are at the disposal of all human beings . . . analysis, ideology, strategy, tactics. There is no divine substitute for the painful and long processes of history. (p. 124)

Christians have usually confused the ways of *their* nation with the divine way, says Míguez Bonino. This is certainly the case in the ways in which conciliation, development and reformism are preferred over against the class struggle and fundamental change to which we have referred.

Christianity offers no easy way, and when Christians seek to avoid analysis, and engagement with the oppressed, they are avoiding the strategy and the methodology of the Kingdom. The way of struggle always involves cost, whether violence is involved or not, but it is essential for the wellbeing of the neighbour, 'for it is not our life or comfort as Christians which is at stake – at this point the Christian community can only follow the road of the Cross – but the life and humanity of our neighbour'. The Cross, and the reconciliation it can bring, are the basis and the motivation for the struggle for freedom for all, in which we are together engaged.

In his later volume, *Towards a Christian Political Ethics* (1983), Míguez Bonino explores the relationship between justice and order. He notes that, centuries ago, Augustine of Hippo saw justice and love as the two foundations of the eternal city, which impinges on the earthly one. Justice relates to the structures of the city, love to the motivation which points the way to individual activity. The justice which Christians talk about is God's justice, and 'God's justice stands critically over against the status quo. There is a tension between the eschatological kingdom and the earthly "arrangements"'. And, Míguez Bonino believes – contrary to Augustine – when justice cannot be achieved without disrupting order, then justice predominates, for it is Míguez Bonino's view that 'Justice is the foundation of order'.

Writing from the perspective of south Asia in the early 1980s Father Tissa Balasuriya in his *Planetary Theology* takes a global view. He describes the world system, particularly as it affects Asia, and points to the necessity of a new world order, if things are ever to change for the poor. He describes the place of racism in the system of obtaining and retaining privilege for white people:

> Politically the world system has been built up by white expansionism. There have been large scale exterminations of people due to racial intolerance, as in the advance of white people into the Americas, Australia and New Zealand. The violence of more powerful racial groups has been a major driving force in history. . ..
> Marginalised racial groups have to struggle to maintain their identity, to affirm their rights, or even simply to survive. (p. 48)

Balasuriya goes on to delineate strategies for 'Worldwide Transformations' which he believes are essential for a Christian approach to the world. He states that 'structural selfishness' is the real enemy, and the task is twofold, 'transformation of persons and radical change of structures'. To bring this about he describes levels, stages and means of struggle.

> I use the word 'struggle' here because I take it as axiomatic that some form of conflict of interests is necessarily involved in this process. If we want justice at any level against organised injustice, some type of active combat . . . is required. For no-one gives up power unless persuaded or compelled to do so. (p. 97)

There are local, national and international levels of struggle, according to Balasuriya. Action has to be taken at local level on issues such as housing, but with national and international perspectives. Coalitions between different oppressed groups are useful. The national level is the primary practical area for liberation struggles to take place. Poor countries need to try to free themselves from the domination of world capitalism: 'in most Third World Countries the struggle for justice is a struggle for national self-determination and liberation from foreign exploitation'. Such national struggles can also be necessary in the 'socialist bloc'. Balasuriya points, too, to the importance of international alliances such as the Organisation of African Unity, the Group of 77 and to some degree the United Nations.

Methods and means of struggle are important: the wrong ones may enmesh us in non-essentials. Social welfare is not harmful, says Balasuriya, but does little to bring about the redistribution of wealth or power. Violence cannot be the preferred means of struggle for anyone, but because of the violence of the existing order, it may be inevitable. We should always remember that 'violence is first imposed by the powerful in their defence of the status quo'. In our society that seems to be as true of the policing of Handsworth or Brixton as it is of the behaviour of ruling elites in the 'Third World' or of the dominant Western capitalist powers in their global economic and military policies.

Balasuriya sets out a range of options for the non-violent struggle against capitalism. These include changing personal lifestyle, the continual questioning of the standard of living in Western countries, the challenging of exploitation by transnational corporations and banks, and the contesting of military threats and 'pacification' by Western Governments. Swiss banks and the international financial institutions should be a particular target.

> Today we have a system of worldwide robbery. Humanity can be truly human only by taking part in the struggle to eliminate

exploitation of person by person, and country by country, through the system of global domination. (p. 108)

Hence, says Balasuriya, struggle and contestation will be a feature of the lives of many (he might have said all). It must not be left only to oppressed peoples in poor countries. 'We have a situation . . . in which the struggle against the unjust world system has to take place everywhere simultaneously.'

The theologians of liberation assist us in exploring the meaning of, and the need for, struggle. Their own understanding, however, has developed and changed. In a conversation in late 1994 Leonardo Boff, who has worked and written in Brazil for many years, remarked that while theories were fine and important the Christian could not wait while people were dying. There had to be some development which retained criticism of exploitative systems while using any means available to offer people practical hope. The struggle is therefore to analyse and challenge the system, while wresting from it what one can to give life. There is then a collective dimension to struggle, with implications at local, national and international levels, and a personal dimension also. In this book's context the collective is about tackling structural racism, and striving for a more equitable sharing of power and resources. I shall look in the following sections at the personal struggle, but it is essential to hold together these two dimensions. It is impossible to battle effectively with personal racism without involvement in the broader struggle; those who aim to challenge racist injustice in the wider society, without constantly re-examining themselves, will find they lack the sustenance and vision to be effective.

THE STRUGGLE FOR UNDERSTANDING

At a recent 'forum' on racial justice in a white, middle-class church a young man got up and asked passionately why it was that when he passed a group of black youths on a street corner he felt suspicion, fear and anger. What was the *root* of his fear and mistrust, he wanted to know. The answers were varied – history, psychological conditioning, the human anxiety about the different, the 'out-group'. Suggestions of what to do about it included reading black authors and black newspapers, seeking black friendships, trying to see the world more as black people see it, overcoming fear with familiarity.

There is of course an ongoing debate as to how possible it is for white people really to understand the black experience, to see the world through the eyes of black and minority people. It is, however, the experience of most white people who are struggling against their own and society's racism that they benefit from at least trying to understand how things look to black people.

166

That may not always be a comfortable search. There is a well-known story of the young white woman who hastened up to Malcolm X after a Harlem rally, to ask what she could do. 'Nothing', came the answer, 'there is nothing white people can do for us'. The young woman left in tears. Malcolm later commented that he wished he had not said that, and he went on to say in an interview recorded only a month before his death and published posthumously in *By Any Means Necessary*, 'Whites who are sincere should organise among themselves and figure out some strategy to break down the prejudice that exists in white communities. This is where they can function . . . more effectively . . . and this has never been done'.

White people need to work in white communities, and in our own minds. We need to accept our racism and continue to struggle with it. I believe there are three stages through which white people need to go before true reconciliation can occur – *listening* to black people; *repenting* of white sin; and *responding* in committed, sacrificial action to the inequalities and injustices to which black people are subject. And this does not happen in a single Damascus Road experience. As Revd Joseph Agne, a white Methodist Minister who served the Office for Racial Justice of the US National Council of Churches between 1992 and 1995, says in one of his addresses,

> Racism impacts all of us who are white and we need to admit we have no power over racism by ourselves and we need to admit its power over us. Then we can behave in new ways. We are never *former racists*, only *recovering racists*, and we need to be daily vigilant about our addiction . . . those of us who are white, let's be honest with ourselves. Let's bring down our defences and let go of the energy it takes to pretend we are not racist.

Agne also emphasises the necessity to *listen*, to 'believe the experience of racial ethnic persons'. He speaks of telling white committees and congregations about what is happening to black people and feeling that he is not being heard, even feeling disbelieved.

Agne goes on in his address to speak of an experience where – as he puts it – after he had made a 'short but beautiful speech' on some anti-racist concern a black Methodist minister took him for a walk, and explained how racist his speech had been. Says Agne, 'I denied, and denied and denied – at least three times like Peter'. He then spent most of the night awake, wrestling with what he had been told, until finally God's grace took effect, and he saw that his friend was right.

James Cone in *Black Theology and Black Power* aims to break through the barrier of white ignorance and disinterest. He was writing out of the black outrage at the assassination of Martin Luther King and he says with brutal frankness that the time has come for white Americans to be silent and *listen* to black people. Why do white people think they have 'the intellectual ability or the moral sensitivity to know what blacks feel, or ease the pain, to smooth the hurt, to eradicate the resentment?' If they know so much they should know blacks need to stop listening to whites in order to be free.

Patrick Kalilombe is a Roman Catholic bishop from Malawi in central southern Africa, but has since 1985 been director of the Centre for Black and White Christian Partnership, based in Birmingham. He is characteristically gentle in this sensitive area of persuading whites to listen. He says that in tackling racism white Christians will be helped by two things:

> By drawing *outsiders* into their discussions so that fresh insights are forthcoming all the time, and by listening attentively to the voice of the *victims* of racism so that those who are on the receiving end are not just the topic but also integral partners in the reflection and planning.

In *Church in Black and White* (1994) John Wilkinson, an Anglican priest who has worked in Birmingham for many years, has written that in many churches black people are still 'invisible people'. The suppression of their voices and experience began under slavery and continued through colonial times. In 1985 Wilkinson conducted a survey among black Anglicans to try to discover something of their views, experiences and spirituality. He found it a deeply informative and rewarding process. He describes how black people's religious and cultural needs and insights have been largely ignored. Most of those he questioned were of African Caribbean origin, though a few were from Africa and Asia. The response of more than a few black Christians was to leave and join the 'black-led' or 'black majority' churches – or at least to attend a 'traditional' church on Sunday morning, while going to a 'spiritually black' church later in the day.

Revd Novette Thompson is a black Methodist minister serving in a multiracial community not far from the Harlesden of chapter 3. She is a member of the Archbishop of Canterbury's Urban Theology Group, and in an essay in the Group's book *God in the City* (1995), published to celebrate the tenth anniversary of *Faith in the City*, she writes of how 'black and white are having to struggle with the issue of racism in society'. It is not easy for either, and Thompson invokes the analogy of the striving for birth. She says, 'The labour for new birth has to take place both within the white community as well as within the black community. It is necessarily painful for both'.

White British Christians continue to find it extraordinarily difficult to listen to black Christians, whether in the field of worship, liturgy, spirituality or social concerns, and whether in ordinary church meetings or in academic discourse. However, listening, in order to understand, is an essential part of the preparation if repentance is to be genuine and reconciliation possible.

THE STRUGGLE FOR REPENTANCE

It may be preferable that repentance is not a struggle, but inevitably it is. As in the story of Joseph Agne's sleepless night, realisation of our need to change does not come easily. It was not easy for Nicodemus, it seemed even more difficult for the rich young ruler, it appears to have been impossible for the Pharisees. James Cone quotes the rich young ruler in asking 'Is there any hope for the white Church?', in terms of its own conversion, and says this will depend on whether the white church will ask 'What must I do to be saved?'. Cone believes that the one who seriously asks that question is able to receive forgiveness, and that it is time for the white church to ask it.

Allan Boesak links repentance with suffering as well as struggle. He believes that blacks look 'beyond the limitations of oppression and inhumanity to see the open possibilities of reconciliation and genuine community'. This represents 'a process of real metanoia, of *conversion*'. What then are the fruits of the conversion of which both Cone and Boesak speak? The first is the communication of the Black experience to the white community, then comes the call to radical discipleship, challenging the power structures both in the Church and beyond. 'It is', says Cone, 'the job of the Church to become Black with him and accept the shame which white society places on blacks'.

The need for the Church to face the suffering of the poor, and the victims of white economic power in the world, is also stressed by Tissa Balasuriya. In his reflection on the meaning of Holy Communion and how it has been manipulated, *The Eucharist and Human Liberation*, he asks very direct questions. One example is, 'Why is it that, in spite of hundreds and thousands of Eucharistic celebrations, Christians continue as selfish as before?' Another is, 'Why is it that people who claim Eucharistic love and sharing deprive the poor people of the world of food, capital, employment, even land?' (p. xi). He points out that we go to Church on Sunday, and say 'Give us this day our daily bread', but 'our social and economic options deprive the hungry of food, the multitudes of remunerative work'. In this desperate situation the Eucharist should draw us together. It is a sacrament for the nourishment of the baptised and 'it is also a sacrament of repentance and conversion'. The Eucharist and, by extension, the whole worship and activity of the Church, should lead us even in the midst of disunity and discrimination to conversion and action for the renewal of society.

Wilkinson cites the importance of black people coming together and making their voice heard, not only for themselves but for the sake of white Christians. He describes a 'survival theology' by which black people manage to get by in the white-dominated theological institutions, but says this leads to 'ghettoisation' rather than liberation.

> Survival and liberation together, however, imply a community which is willing to bring its gifts and heritage to white people as a call to repentance and an offering of forgiveness, which is willing to struggle for the transformation of church and society . . . the Black liberation programme is not simply a list of activities to be undertaken zealously over a period of time; it is a much deeper call to the white-dominated church to repent, receive forgiveness and be remade. (p. 263)

Joseph Agne warns against white people saying 'I am not racist'. Sometimes black people may feel able to say to whites, 'You seem to be overcoming your ancestral racism'. In an unpublished sermon Agne makes an analogy with the way we remember our favourite records or tapes. We can often remember the first notes and words of the next song on the tape, he says.

> That's the way it is with our racist tapes. They play even when we don't expect them to. These racist tapes say some strange things -
>
> ● Our tapes say African American men are violent. . .
>
> ● Our tapes say that Asian Americans are cunning and inscrutable. They don't look us in the eye. . .
>
> ● Our tapes say Latin Americans are lazy, that Indians are savages and alcoholics. . .
>
> ● Our tapes say that Black men are interested sexually in white women, never mind that most interracial sex involved and involves white men.
>
> These tapes and many more soothe stereotypes into our ears and blast stereotypes into our minds.

Agne goes on to describe how we act on these tapes, consciously and unconsciously, how they come from 'family, church, teachers, friends, advertisements, movies, TV, pastors, music, textbooks and newspapers'. He concludes that anti-racism is a positive term and asks, 'Do we believe getting rid of racism is a loss for us? Is giving up racism something we do and pay a big price? Or is getting rid of racism facing up to our own addiction to power and control?'

Hence the need for repentance, for *metanoia* – turning away from, for conversion. We turn away as followers of Jesus from racism, we repent, we turn towards anti-racism – but we are never entirely free. As Agne says, we need to become 'anti-racist racists', or 'recovering racists' – recalling that the term 'racist' refers to something partly inbred within us, partly institutionalised in our societies, a poison ensconced within us, not something we have actively espoused. White people are no more free from racism than free from sin.

Wilkinson describes the 'conversion process' white people need to go through. He says the grace of God begins to work when the 'cry of the oppressed' is really heard, when the white Church really encounters 'the *cry* of "God's Black Slave" from the Cross'. It is the cry for relief, for justice, the cry of the righteous, of the suffering servant, of desertion. The cry is one of judgement, against white people, it sets God apart from them. But to hear and accept judgement, says Wilkinson, does not mean white people should 'wallow in guilt'. They should not simply assume that white is bad, black is good; this would reverse oppression rather than transcend it. The cry is also one for repentance, a cry to white people, that they might make a 'quantum leap', to understand something of what the victims have suffered.

Wilkinson recalls the words of a white priest after watching the old BCC Community and Race Relations Unit filmstrip *The Enemy Within* (see p. 104). 'To think', he said, 'that this is what we have done to them'. Such repentance, says Wilkinson, 'is the gateway to new life'. The struggle to be an effective recovering racist is difficult, but essential for the white Christian.

THE STRUGGLE FOR JUSTICE

The obverse of the struggle for repentance, which is primarily but not only an individual struggle, is the struggle for justice, which is primarily but not only collective and structural. It is first of all the individual who must come to an acceptance of failure and of sin, even if a good deal of that sin has roots which are historical, economic and political. Without that personal conviction the grace of God cannot work. When, however, it does work, it creates new opportunities and challenges. White people have to take on what James Cone calls 'the awesome political responsibility which follows from justification by faith'. Cone continues,

> To be made righteous through Christ places a man in a situation where he too, like Christ, must be for the poor, for God and against

171

> the world . . . no Christian can evade this responsibility . . . whoever fights for the poor fights for God. (p. 47)

The thrust of Cone's argument is echoed by Black and Liberation theologians of all backgrounds, and acknowledged in more enlightened areas of the white community, for example by Bishop David Sheppard in *Bias to the Poor*, by the Archbishop of Canterbury's Commission on Urban Priority Areas report *Faith in the City* and by radical observers such as Revd Kenneth Leech.

Writing in 1983 David Sheppard describes the reality of multiracial inner-city life as seen from what he admits is the privileged position of an Anglican Bishop. He describes the problems of urban housing estates in Liverpool, of unemployment particularly among young blacks in both Liverpool and London, and of black communities with the police in both cities. The book is a good advocate for racial justice. Perhaps it could have argued for a greater depth of repentance, degree of struggle and shift in power. It is important to undertake what Cone calls the 'awesome responsibility' arising from our redemption and salvation.

Bias to the Poor was in a way a forerunner for *Faith in the City* (FITC), which appeared in late 1985. FITC criticised the status quo and suggested radical solutions, and was duly rubbished by sources close to the Conservative Government, and certain sections of the media. It did suggest that 'some degree of economic restructuring of society might be appropriate', though it did not go as far as Martin Luther King had done in challenging the powers in the USA. Ken Leech rightly describes FITC's strengths as its descriptive and analytic approach, its focus on the persistence and growth of urban poverty and deprivation, and its role as 'the first semi-official response' to issues of structural racism within the Church of England.

FITC does raise issues of equality and justice. It states that a market economy 'does not *necessarily* lead to inequality', though some might question that statement. It comments that 'poverty reflects the structural inequality of the nation'. It remarks that fewer members of the Church of England are willing to rectify injustices in society, over against the 'ambulance work' of helping the unfortunate individual. In its section on 'Theology', FITC points to 'the prophetic call for justice', with its concern for 'the rights of the weak and the poor'. It resists, however, the application of liberation theology to the British scene, with the explanation that it has grown out of 'political and economic conditions radically different from our own'. Keen observers of liberation theology disagree with that, but FITC does acknowledge that 'Liberation theology opens up the possibility that new priorities, as well as new methods, can restore to us a theology that is truly relevant to the needs and aspirations of people today'.

In practical matters *FITC* pressed for a higher Rate Support Grant (which, in the early 1990s, was still being reduced), urged an increase of the Urban Programme (which was savagely cut again in late 1992, prior to being eliminated altogether), argued for partnership with voluntary organisations in lowering unemployment (which continues to rise), and encouraged a rising public housing programme (which continues to fall). *FITC* was certainly pushing for a greater degree of social and economic justice, though its pleas and policy suggestions fell largely on deaf ears. Its approach to racial justice was weak. There is a section on 'The Church and Minority Ethnic Groups', about some of the things the Church must do in the field of racial justice. It does not however say much to Government on matters of concern to the black communities, except in terms of their place in UPAs as a whole. The only time it mentions affirmative action, it seems more concerned about affirmation by gender than race – both of course being important.

The successor to *FITC*, *Staying in the City* (Bishops' Advisory Group for Urban Priority Areas, 1995), fails to address the economic policies of Government and City as a major cause of the problems it identifies. These include the widening gap between rich and poor, the shift of taxation to lower- and middle-income groups and increasing dependency on benefit. *SITC* repeats the findings of damning research already done, but does not allocate blame as – as the Bishop of Leicester announced at the launch – 'we *all* have a responsibility'. Many may feel that some have a lot more responsibility than others, and a lot more money as a result.

In *Struggle in Babylon* (1988) Kenneth Leech is particularly sharp on this kind of weakness. He notes that *FITC* 'has nothing to say about racism as a structural reality in church and nation'. He believes the report fails to recognise 'the degree to which racism is part of our culture – of the sense of "Britishness" – and the role of the Church of England in reinforcing this cultural nationalism'. The report reads as if 'racism could be removed without too much disturbance of the body politic', but if racism is endemic, 'to threaten racism is to threaten the stability of that unjust order of which it is a central part'. Leech feels that, at bottom, *FITC* fails to recognise, or to tackle, the class and cultural role of the Church of England, the Church–State alliance which lies at the heart of the British Establishment.

Pityana is also unhappy with this dimension of *FITC*. He comments:

> Significantly . . . the Report fails to address the question of nationality, nor does it face up to the essential or structural inequality in British society. . . .. The Report is Eurocentric in its mould. No effort is made to examine the history and culture of the black communi-

> ties. . ... It appeals to the conscience of the wealthy and powerful to
> give due regard to the needs of the poor, the implication being that
> *they* hold the key to change towards a more just and caring society.
> (p. 105)

It is unlikely that Leech or Pityana would be any happier with *Staying in the City*.

Hence there are weaknesses, some of them very serious ones, in some of the British Christian attempts to challenge racial injustice, and to 'make things right'. Both the Prophets and Jesus were actively and in some cases painfully aware of the nature of the struggle for justice. The message is repeated in different ways in the Magnificat, Jesus' first sermon in Luke 4, his attitude to the Samaritans which we referred to earlier, his teaching about the rich, his devastating attacks upon the spiritually arrogant, and in Paul's understanding of what it really means for human beings to be 'in Christ'.

It was not the parables of Jesus that led to his crucifixion, nor his healings, nor even his championing of women, children and foreigners. It was his challenge to those in power – spiritual power as much as temporal power – because they had ceased to try to 'make things right', to struggle for justice, even within the confines of the Roman occupation.

For white people to be taken seriously by black people we must be actively, determinedly and consistently involved in the struggle for racial justice. Hence it is essential for white Christians to be engaged in the kinds of struggle outlined in our last chapter – battles for affirmative action in employment and investment, quality education for all, a fair criminal justice system, a non-racist immigration policy, anti-deportation campaigns, opposition to racial violence, and the hundreds of other opportunities and challenges which confront the 'anti-racist racist', as Agne calls those white Christians who like him struggle with this issue.

But the style in which this is done must be cautious. It must accept black wisdom and black leadership. As Agne puts it, white people must learn to live without always being in control. White efforts should be aimed at the white-dominated power structures. They must not always expect the black community to provide resources or personnel; it has its own priorities and its own struggles. White people should never forget that racism is not a black problem, it is a white problem, and it is white people who must deal with it, in themselves and their communities, but with help and direction from black people if they have the time, the energy and the emotional resilience.

Paul Grant and Raj Patel, in their introduction to *A Time to Speak* (1990), issue a particularly strong warning against paternalism and colonization. They point out that 'many have made their reputations and careers from "interpreting" Black faith to indifferent intellectuals and earnest clerics. We the victims of this "spiritual colonization" have been observed and pronounced upon'. This reinforces the vital point that this book should encourage those who have not yet read black authors to do so.

And if white people are not seeking to 'make things right' by changing that situation, we are not serious about any stated commitment to racial justice. If we are, then new possibilities arise.

RECONCILIATION?

If the three stages of *listening, repenting* and *responding* (see p. 167) have been faithfully followed through then the opportunity for reconciliation arises. Cone believes the New Testament doctrine of reconciliation in this context means 'freeing the racist of racism by making him confront blacks' as people. Reconciliation says, 'Look man, the revolution is on, whose side are you on?' Anti-racists need to demonstrate the side we belong to by both our self-examination and our activity. We need to be vigorously engaged in campaigns and activities which strike at the structural racism in our societies.

The importance of not misusing the term 'reconciliation' is highlighted by Paul Grant in his *A Time to Speak* essay. He points out that 'reconciliation' can be used simply to sanctify the actions of white Christians 'setting the ground rules for what Black people can legitimately do for themselves'. He also makes reference to the way the term has been used in the South African context to actually criticise blacks who refuse to renounce self-defence as a pre-condition for negotiations (something whites never contemplated, of course).

Grant is particularly critical of Christians who seem to use a conservative interpretation of the doctrine of the atonement, that Christ paid with his blood for all our sin, to argue that blacks should bear their sufferings with fortitude. Blacks have been exhorted to 'turn the other cheek', and to 'accept responsibility for the salvation of those who have no concern for us'. He goes on:

> Here, and only here, have white Christians in Britain been willing to allow Black people to adopt the role of Christ: 'The sin of racism has to be stopped at any cost, so if you just pick up that cross over there . . .' (p. 54)

Grant criticises sharply white people who deny blacks their right to self-organisation and self-defence, and suggests that in the Bible there is plenty to argue that God does not want the poor to go on allowing their oppressors to exploit them. It is for the oppressors to recognise what they are doing, and change. Blacks have every right to resist. Grant goes on to point out that 'the biblical principle is there can be no reconciliation without repentance and justice' (p. 56).

Like '*metanoia*', reconciliation is not a passive but an active word. In the Greek it means 'exchange', e.g. of money, and among people the radical exchange of enmity for friendship. Reconciliation requires action, it needs movement, and it also implies cost. In the case of reconciliation between God and humanity, Christ has come to supply the stimulation, the movement, to bridge the gap, to pay the price. But who is suffering to generate the dynamic for the reconciliation of white with black? And, to quote Jesse Jackson, 'Who is bearing the pain? How is it being redistributed?'.

The kind of struggles in which white anti-racist racists must be involved to prepare the ground for reconciliation, and bear some of the pain, have been referred to in the previous section. Practical examples follow in the next chapter. It is essential for our spiritual health that we are so engaged. We are 'entrusted with the message of reconciliation, we come therefore as Christ's ambassadors' (2 Corinthians 5. 19). It is the purpose of our existence as Church.

The struggle against racism is both external and internal. It is both present and continuing, like the Kingdom of God. But if white people are prepared to take on the struggle, to bear some of the pain, we shall not be lonely. The Grace of God, most often manifested through the Black communities, will be with us, and we shall discover the painful and the joyful realities of reconciliation, and salvation, along the way.

7

Agenda for the twenty-first century

A vision for Europe

Looking forward into a new century has to be a mixture of hopefulness, anxiety and realism. There must be realism because there can be no false hopes that the mere ticking of a clock at midnight on the 31st of December 1999 is by itself going to change the hearts and minds of humanity. There will also be anxiety because given what humankind has done in the present century, and given the onward march of science and technology, it is uncomfortable to speculate what might happen in the next.

However, hopefulness also has its place, and for Christians we could do worse than resurrect the Old Testament concept of the Jubilee, where in the fiftieth year land or housing which has been bought, taken or won should be returned to those who have lost it, in order that they might regain their birthright. This was intended to prevent the creation of a permanently dispossessed class who would rapidly become reliant on the rest of the community, with the accompanying dependency, alienation, anger and sense of injustice. We shall outline at the end of this chapter, having explored the problems, what such a Jubilee might mean in the context of racial justice. Pope John Paul has already outlined a rather cautious Christian agenda for the millennium in his Apostolic Letter *Tertio Millennio Adveniente*. We hope to offer something more radical.

In the meantime, to create an agenda we must have a vision, and we must remind ourselves that whatever we envision for our community, local or national, it must now be in the context of the European Union. We shall therefore outline briefly a vision for that Union of fifteen countries. Then we need to consider what we can do, as individuals, as part of a church, as citizens of Europe and as a tiny part of the world community. We may not be able to do a great deal to bring about global racial justice, so let us make sure that what we do undertake is as productive as possible.

The European Community began from the vision of relatively few political leaders, who were primarily concerned to ensure that after 1945 the countries of Western Europe – especially Germany and France – never went to war with one another again. They were also looking to strengthen a particular economic system, market capitalism, over against the perceived 'threat' of communism which had demonstrated its potential during the war years. It is possible that both the political and economic history of Europe would have been rather different if a less suspicious and confrontational attitude had been adopted towards the Soviet Union and its related states. We shall never know.

The growth of the European Community, and its gradual transformation into the European Union, have been rooted in a capitalist economy. There have been some differences as to the vigour with which that capitalism should be encouraged. Some countries, such as Sweden, the Netherlands and even Christian Democratic Germany, have emphasised the 'social market', where the welfare state is regarded as a vital aspect of the whole system. Others, such as Thatcher's (and Major's) Britain and Berlusconi's Italy, have sought to downgrade the importance of a social safety net.

Any vision for Europe – or rather the European Union – which is going to make sense will have to see it in a global context. It is tempting to introduce everything into a vision, and include the totally unlikely along with the just-about-possible. The two paragraphs below seek to set out a realistic vision for the EU as we move towards the millennium, not asking for anything which appears completely impossible, but giving the activist visionary plenty for which to aim and to struggle.

The European Union will begin to contribute to a world where the gap between the rich largely white nations and the poor largely black nations will begin to *narrow*, where greater authority will be given to a revivified United Nations and its agencies, where trade and investment will actually *favour the poor* rather than simply be promised, where hunger will decline, and where the debt *will be cancelled* for the poorest and most sympathetically restructured for the rest.

Within the EU those who have been resident for more than five years will all be recognised as equal citizens, racial discrimination and racial attacks will be outlawed and eradicated, the cultures of all EU residents from wherever they originate will be celebrated, people from other continents – especially those with family here – will be able to come, go or stay with ease and frequency, and Europe will be a place of respite and sanctuary for all who feel forced to leave their homeland due to persecution, conflict or famine.

In economic terms, which are often the single most important controlling factor of what actually happens in human society, it is difficult to envisage even this limited vision coming to pass without a move away from market capitalism and towards people-centred economic and social structures, i.e. some contemporary form of socialism. It would be essential to maintain the democratic elements of Western European society. It was the lack of democracy, of the people being unable to influence those who ruled them, which contributed to the collapse of the totalitarian 'socialist' regimes of Eastern Europe. The values of socialism, in terms of each contributing according to ability, each receiving according to need, the basics of life provided to all, full employment, equality of condition and not merely opportunity, are far more likely to lead to the above vision than the values of capitalism, based as they are on the importance of the individual, the survival of the fittest and the harnessing of the more selfish aspects of human nature.

The four circles

The four circles in which Christians need to act, on a vision of racial justice or any other vision, are the personal, the church or local community, the 'national' and the global. These circles do inter-relate, and it is helpful to feel that even if we are only doing something in our own personal or church circles, it is part of the wider circles of national and global activity. The word 'national' is in inverted commas partly because it is something of a suspect word in itself (see chapter 1), but also because in any of the 'nations' of the British Isles today we also have to see ourselves in a wider context. As the English, Scots, Welsh and Northern Irish have for some time been part of 'Britain' or 'the United Kingdom', so now we belong, with the African-British and Asian-British and so on, in the larger European Union.

In each of the four circles the concept of struggle, the struggle for justice, will be essential in our thinking. That is not to say there will be no celebration, and no joy, but a vital dimension will be that of pressing forward, often against resistance – and sometimes very vigorous resistance – in order to move towards our goal. There will also be a sense of participation, of co-operation, in a wider movement of which – either as individuals or groups – we are simply a modest part. The circles that follow are, inevitably from this author, 'white circles', for white people. Black people may be interested to read through them, but the contents of 'black circles' might well be different, and they would be for black people to construct.

The individual circle

The circle for the individual will include seeking information and experience, financial commitment and a form of spiritual discipline. One of the most important things in today's highly communicative world is the source of our information. In Western countries newspapers and television tend to be owned by individuals or groups committed to the status quo or to an even more vigorous form of market capitalism. Even public service broadcasting has to be cautious, especially when more conservative Governments are in power. It is therefore vital firstly to obtain news information from the least biassed 'official media' sources, secondly to supplement that from publications produced by minority groups and thirdly to learn from the experiences of those most directly affected.

In terms of race it is very useful to read the minority press regularly. The weekly newspapers *The Voice*, *Caribbean Times* and *Asian Times* are the most accessible: they should be available through any newsagent. These give a rather different view of the world from even the liberal national press. Their home news often has stories of race attacks, police harassment and institutional discrimination which only occasionally appear even in the most sympathetic organs of the 'mainstream media'. Their foreign news looks at the experience of minorities in Western countries, or takes the perspective of the poor rather than the rich in international relationships. Features are about issues affecting the black communities, which are sometimes the same as those affecting whites, but are approached differently. Interviews are with black people in positions of authority or achievement. After a few months the world begins to look different. Minority magazines such as *Impact*, *Ebony*, *Kaleidoscope* or *West Africa* also help.

As far as gathering useful information is concerned there are many organisations, voluntary or semi-statutory, which produce newsletters, bulletins, reports or magazines. The Commission for Racial Equality has its own bulletin, publishes reports on particular issues from time to time and promotes a Journal three times a year which looks in more depth at the various sectors in the field. The Runnymede Trust also produces a useful monthly publication which covers a wide range of issues. On immigration and refugee concerns the Joint Council for the Welfare of Immigrants has a quarterly newsletter and the Refugee Council has a monthly bulletin. On more explicit racism and racial attacks *Searchlight* is a vital monthly and *CARF*, the Campaign Against Racism and Fascism, puts out its publication every two months. *CARF* also covers Europe and the USA. Other excellent sources on racism in Europe are the Institute for Race Relations' *European Race Audit* and the *Migration Newssheet*, which summarises the press from around the continent each month.

If it is possible to make direct contact with people personally affected by racial injustice, such as race attack victims, asylum seekers, those experiencing discrimination from the criminal justice system and so on, this gives a more immediate perspective. It is often easier than people think to make such contacts, through the network of the churches. In early 1994 one church member invited a refugee, who had experienced arrest, detention in a maximum security prison and threats from police and prison officers, to speak in a Sunday morning church service. Even the black people in the congregation were moved to say they had not realised such things were going on, and the church began to sign petitions and make collections. Black organisations, including church bodies, are often very willing to assist with requests for contacts, as long as they know they are genuine and may lead to some kind of response.

If newspapers and broadcasters write about racial justice concerns, without apparently seeking the view of those most affected, it is important to write or ring up and tell them so. The objections that 'people won't understand their accent', or 'we couldn't find anyone to talk to', have to be gently but firmly taken apart. On the other hand vulnerable people who are already experiencing discrimination have to be protected from more of the same at the hands of certain unsympathetic, unscrupulous and not infrequently racist journalists.

It is essential to scan upcoming television and radio programmes and make special attempts to catch those about or made by black or minority communities. There are not many, and the video recorder enables many of us to record TV programmes we might otherwise miss. We can then keep them as a record, and use them for educating our friends or our church. It is important to write and commend broadcasters when a good programme is shown on racial justice issues, especially if it is produced by people from the minority communities.

Another source of widening one's perspectives, and overcoming decades of conditioning, is to read the work of writers from different ethnic and cultural origins. This can include novels, such as those of Alice Walker, Ben Okri, Toni Morrison, Ralph Ellison or V. S. Naipaul. It can also include biography, autobiography, history, social studies and – especially for Christians – theology. As indicated earlier, 'Black Theology' gives a very different perspective on the world from theology written by white theologians, and is often easier to understand. Reading one book a quarter in this field is a reasonable target.

There are reference books to obtain such as the two volumes of *The World's Great Men of Color*, written by J. A. Rogers before the gender revolution took place in the USA, and containing information on men (and women) who pre-dated Christ, and come from four continents. The subjects include Hannibal, Cleopatra, Abraha (Emperor of Ethiopia, 'whose adoption of Christianity changed the world'), St Benedict, Pushkin, Alexandre Dumas *père* and Alexandre Dumas *fils*, English composer Samuel Coleridge-Taylor, violinist George Bridgetower (accompanist to Beethoven, who is also said to have been a man of colour), Mary Seacole (the 'black Florence Nightingale' – see chapter 2) and the poet Robert Browning.

Financial commitment is also essential in this work. Individuals need to decide which racial justice body or bodies they want to support, and at what level this can be done. At a time when charities and campaigning bodies are finding it increasingly difficult to attract income, sacrificial giving by Christians is crucial. Bodies chosen can include aid agencies like Christian Aid and the World Development Movement (WDM), who are engaged in trying to change the balance of power in the world, and should also include if possible organisations of the black communities themselves. After-tax tithing remains an appropriate target for giving, except perhaps for those on lower incomes, and has Biblical support. Two per cent of income for racial justice, including global economic justice, should be a *minimum* financial target for any Christian.

Finally the need for spiritual preparation and discipline should not be forgotten. This includes (for white people) inculcating a deep sense of repentance for all the racism of past and present. Such a stance does not require constant guilt, rather the development of a profound awareness or consciousness, along with a growth towards greater sensitivity and willingness to act. This approach will help us, for example, when reading a magazine or watching TV advertising, to spot overtones or assumptions which are racist, and to decide how to make our protest. It will also help us in our public prayers to pray for radical change: for example, in praying for asylum-seekers detained in prisons, to pray also for urgent change in the system which puts them there and eventual change in whatever situation has caused them to flee. As individuals, even after years of effort, we often still swing between facing backwards towards the old racism and forwards towards embracing racial justice. The latter position means we should be continually assessing our responses to events and situations, and constantly seeking to make these more positive.

The local church

In the context of our discussion of the second 'circle', denominations are fairly irrelevant and there are basically two types of churches to which white people go, the multiracial and the 'almost white'. The multiracial church might be described as one where at least 10 per cent of the congregation are from minority ethnic groups. This includes churches where 90 per cent or more of the congregation are from such communities, which is now the case in more than a few inner-city churches. The almost white church encompasses those whose membership may be of entirely white English (or Scottish or Welsh) stock, but where there may be minority families in the community whose children, for example, may come to a youth group, or where at holiday time the occasional black family may pay a visit.

Superficially many multiracial churches are splendidly happy families. Black people often bring the kind of outgoing warmth and friendliness into a congregation that is sometimes lacking in almost white congregations. However it is important for such a church also to look below the surface to check that all is as it seems. The kind of questions which may be asked are 'Who greets those who arrive for Sunday morning worship?'; 'What proportion of the preachers, worship leaders and Junior Church teachers are black?'; 'Are there "black images" around the church – pictures or posters?'; and perhaps most importantly 'Who holds the power, in terms of the key offices in the church?'.

When one raises questions like this in a multiracial church the responses can often be hurt and angry, from black people as well as white. However, we cannot be criticising Government and big business for not doing enough to end discrimination and create equality of condition as well as equality of opportunity, if we are not willing to take this on even at the local level of the church. There are methods by which local churches can address this whole area in structured and comparatively non-threatening ways. 'Evangelical Christians for Racial Justice' has produced an excellent booklet which assists with a kind of audit for a local church, entitled *Better Will Come* by Maurice Hobb *et al*. Any multiracial church could work through this with great profit.

The USA also has something to offer in this particular circle. One of its contemporary mission beacons is the 'Rock of Our Salvation' Church in the Austin neighbourhood on Chicago's West Side. It employs two pastors, Raleigh Washington (black), born in Florida and a former US Army colonel, and Glen Kehrein (white), and a small-town Wisconsin evangelical Christian. Their book *Breaking Down Walls* tells both their individual stories and how they came together in a partnership ministry, and there is much in it for both black and white Christians involved in the struggle against racism. It outlines the Rock programme of 'Eight Principles', based on the two men's exploration of their own partnership in ministry.

Each month Rock Church has what it calls a 'chocolate meeting' for the black members and a 'vanilla meeting' for the whites, in order for them to share their concerns in a way that may not be possible in front of the other racial group. The book concludes with chapters by Washington 'For Black Christians Only' and by

Kehrein for Whites. Washington gives 'six imperatives' for blacks 'as we seek to reconcile and form friendships that help to break down that wall dividing blacks and whites'. Kehrein points out that we white Christians have separated ourselves from the poor and oppressed, we have conformed to the world, we have set our racial values by middle-class American standards 'and then baptised them as "Christian"'. He also gives six imperatives: 'Don't deny the reality of racism', 'Don't look for simple answers to complex problems', 'Become a learner by admitting you know little of black people', 'Get beyond guilt to action', 'How much you accomplish depends on how much you invest' and 'White churches must become part of the solution'. He goes on to stress the importance of taking risks in order to communicate both to one's own community and across the racial and cultural divides.

There has been some activity on this theme in Britain also. Some churches have worked through the Evangelical Christians for Racial Justice audit referred to above. Others have participated in racism awareness training, especially in association with MELRAW (Methodist and Ecumenical Racism Awareness Workshops). Yet other churches have followed courses such as *A Mirror to Britain* by Christian Aid, or *One Race* by the Churches' Commission for Racial Justice.

In a more specific fashion some local congregations have formulated resolutions to send to their church headquarters, or to relevant authorities at local and at national level, on racial attacks, or detention of refugees, or the need for a more compassionate immigration system. Others have adopted general statements, like *The Churches Charter for Racial Justice in Europe*, and pressed it upon their elected representatives. As part of 'Racial Justice Sunday', inaugurated in September 1995, congregations are asked to take up issues, or sign a Covenant for Racial Justice, to demonstrate their commitment by certain actions over the ensuing months.

In some areas larger suburban 'almost white' churches have sought some form of 'twinning' arrangement with multiracial inner-city churches. There are mixed stories about such relationships. Some have continued for a number of years, with both parties claiming benefits. Others have ended after a relatively short period of time, owing to misunderstandings about the nature of the initiative in the first place, or an unwillingness by the white church to engage in debate about the real effects of racism in the lives of Black Christians. What is most important is that churches embarking on such arrangements should seek to be as clear as possible about what the expectations are on each side. These should aim at an introductory phase and a period of growth, with a basic acceptance that each has something to give and receive, that each will act in turn as host and guest and that in due course the hard questions will not be ducked. A time-scale for a review of the initiative should also be built in.

Yet another way in which local churches can address racism is by participating in a particular campaign. Some churches have done this when members or adherents have been the subject of a racial attack, or threatened with deportation. The Methodist Church in Plumstead, south-east London, for example, sought to give support to the family of 18-year-old Stephen Lawrence when he was killed in a terrible racial attack in April 1993. This had to continue for a long time as, despite the suspicions of the family and the police, no-one had been brought to justice by mid-1995. The family then decided to bring only the fourth private prosecution for murder in the last 130 years, but this brought additional emotional and financial strains, and they continued to need and welcome active pastoral support. Further reference is made to this case in the next section.

Other churches, as mentioned in chapter 1 as part of the 'Church Response' to the effects of immigration law, have given sanctuary to church members or in some cases to those who have simply come to them for help. Sanctuary is a very specific form of the struggle for justice and humanity, which can be exceedingly costly for a local church in terms of time, energy and resources. Some churches who have given sanctuary have drawn up a Sanctuary Declaration, in which a local congregation committed itself to consider sanctuary in certain defined circumstances. The kind of symbolic action which giving sanctuary involves is vital in trying to promote a vision of a different kind of world, where immigration law and practice becomes much gentler, and the circumstances of individuals and families can be adequately taken into account. The situation of the Dansos and the Ogunwobis, referred to in chapter 1, and many other families, is a direct result of ever-tightening legislation through the 1980s, which has closed escape routes of flexibility and compassion. In this situation Christians have to look for new, imaginative and even confrontational ways of getting across to those with power and authority.

Britain and Europe

Thought and action at the 'national level' in any European country today has to include the European dimension as well as the context of the particular country. Also, there are two levels of the European dimension, the 15-member European Union and the 32-member Council of Europe. The former is more structured, and of course economically powerful, but the latter is also important, especially where matters of human rights are concerned. Hence the 'third circle' could be said to have three different bands to it, the inner United Kingdom band, the middle European Union band and the outer Council of Europe band. Each of the bands has a part to play when we are considering issues of racial justice and how they are to be addressed in preparation for the twenty-first century. For most readers, however, it will be the UK band for which we can set objectives, and in which we can be most active, through whatever channels are open to us.

There are many areas in which racial justice issues can and should be addressed in this third circle. Here, however, we shall limit ourselves to five which will be particularly important if the 'Vision for Europe' outlined above is to come to pass. These are racial violence and the criminal justice system, economic racial justice, immigration and asylum, education and the media and relationships with other faiths. The last is rather different from the others, but is an area which will need increasingly to be addressed in the Europe and indeed the world of the coming century.

RACIAL VIOLENCE AND THE CRIMINAL JUSTICE SYSTEM

As suggested in the 'Vision for Europe', a dream for Christians in Britain, Europe and beyond would be for a society in which people would no longer be mocked, abused, threatened or attacked because of their ethnic origin or colour of skin. It is so horribly demeaning for both the perpetrator and the victim that it diminishes the human in both, although particularly in the perpetrator. Racial incidents, as is well-documented elsewhere, have been rising for some time – at least the reporting of them has – and in other European countries as well as Britain. Police figures for occurrences of racial violence in 1994 were nearly 11,000, an increase of 25 per cent over 1993, and in 1995 they grew by a further 8 per cent to 11,900. Actual incidents may be much more frequent. An annual figure of more than 130,000 was given by a Conservative Minister extrapolating from the British Crime Survey for 1993, of which over 32,000 would have been actual assaults.

There have been a range of serious racist attacks in western Europe over the last few years. These reached something of a peak in 1993, with the fire-bombings in Solingen and Mölln in Germany, and the attack on Quddus Ali and the murder of Stephen Lawrence in the UK. However, in France in early 1994 a Malian died while in the custody of the French security police, in April the same year several young people were seriously injured or killed in clashes with police in the Lyon and Toulon areas and in June two young blacks were shot dead in Paris by an off-duty police officer during a robbery. In February 1995 17-year-old Ibrahim Ali was shot in the back by National Front supporters in Marseilles and a 46-year-old Moroccan was shot dead in St Etienne. On 1 May 1995 a Moroccan father-of-two was thrown into the Seine and drowned by supporters of National Front leader Le Pen during a pro-Front demonstration. Such examples – often involving the police or security forces as well as racist groups – can be repeated from Germany and to a lesser extent from Italy, Spain, the Netherlands, Belgium, the Scandinavian countries, Portugal and of course Britain. In Germany the rise of anti-Semitism was symbolised by the first attack since 1945 on a synagogue in the town of Lübeck in May 1994 and 937 anti-Semitic attacks were reported in Germany in the first nine months of 1994. In February 1995 four Romany people were killed by a bomb in Austria. In January 1996, again in Lübeck, a refugee hostel fire killed ten people, but after initially saying it was a racist attack the authorities retracted, and sought to dampen speculation about possible causes.

It is difficult for many white people to understand the dismay, pain and mental anguish suffered by hundreds of thousands of black and minority people in Europe each year. It can be the comment in the office or at the bus-stop, the name called at school or in the street, the threat in the shop or over the phone, the shove at the football match or in the park, the bang on the door, the brick or even the fire-bomb through the window. Families cower at home in fear, and keep their children confined in claustrophobic flats. And who will do anything about it? Authorities are indifferent or over-stretched. The police who should be the ultimate protection come late or not at all, explain how little they can do, or have on occasion even arrested the victims for becoming angry or fighting back. There is considerable cynicism in the black communities about whether the Government is really concerned. The following paragraphs relate to what needs to be done in Britain. There can and should be parallels in other European countries.

Racists form political groups, who claim to have a range of 'policies' but whose existence is often based on one simple premise, 'Blacks Out!', The names change – the League of Empire Loyalists, the National Front, the League of St George, Combat 18 – but the policy remains the same. Many accuse the British National Party (BNP) of a similar approach. Just occasionally the racists step over the legal line and are prosecuted, for abuse or threats which a police officer witnesses, for an attack where the perpetrator is caught for once or for publications inciting racial hatred whose publishers can be traced. Even then prosecutions are not always successful.

In the meantime there have been major racist attacks, even murders, where the perpetrators are still at large years afterwards. The most significant are those of Stephen Lawrence, Quddus Ali and Muktar Ahmed, attacked by a white gang of 15-20. Muktar's head was 'kicked backwards and forwards like a football' said a solicitor prosecuting the only person arrested, a 17-year-old who was turned in by his 15-year-old girlfriend. He was immediately released on being given a twelve-month sentence as he had already served six months on remand. Supporters of the families ask people to imagine what would have happened if groups of five, ten or twenty black youths had maimed or murdered a young white man. They cannot imagine that no-one would have been charged, with the media baying for blood as they did after the Broadwater Farm disturbances when PC Blakelock was killed.

In the case of Stephen Lawrence, the Crown Prosecution Service said there was insufficient evidence to prefer charges, so the family decided to bring a private prosecution for murder. A magistrate found that in the case of three young white men there was a case to answer, and the trial began in April 1996, just before the third anniversary of Stephen's death. However, after a week of legal arguments, the judge in the case refused to allow some of the identification evidence to be put before the Court. The family believed this was a vital part of their case, and withdrew the prosecution. The three men were acquitted.

Press reports focused on secret police videos which showed the three men, with three others, in one of their homes, uttering vile racist abuse. This included saying that 'every nigger should be chopped up and left with nothing but f------ stumps', and that one of them would 'go down to Catford . . . with two sub-machine guns and . . . I'd set on one of them, skin him alive, torture him and set him alight. I'd blow their two legs and arms off and say "go on you can swim home now"'. One of the men also wielded a knife, and plunged it into furniture while mouthing the abuse. About six young men had been seen at the killing and the family said after the case that they would continue their search for Stephen's killers. They hoped that someone who knew something would come forward with new identification evidence. In other cases of serious racial attacks, such as that on Muktar Ahmed, women friends and relatives have come forward with such vital testimony.

In early 1996, Bradford waiter Tahir Ali died after what police described as 'an unprovoked and serious attack'. Two white men were arrested in north London on 11 April, and charged with his murder. And there are countless other attacks in areas where racist 'parties' are organising, which are either never reported or never solved. Sometimes black or Asian youths retaliate, as apparently happened in the tragic murder of Richard Everitt, a 15-year-old white boy from Somers Town, near Euston, in early 1995. It has to be recognised that the police have a difficult job in these situations. People may be unwilling to give evidence, the Crown Prosecution Service can fail to act effectively, witnesses can be intimidated. However, there remains a considerable degree of suspicion in the black community about the police, not least because of cases in which officers themselves have been accused of racist abuse.

The new offence of 'intentional harassment' created in the 1994 Criminal Justice Act was intended to strengthen the law on racial violence, but many believe further toughening will be necessary if those perpetrating racial violence are to be deterred, those experiencing it reassured and those investigating and prosecuting it convinced of its importance. Also by the end of 1994 the judiciary were beginning to operate a system of sentence weighting for racial motivation. The effectiveness of both these initiatives will need to be carefully monitored. Indeed the criminal justice system as a whole needs monitoring across all Government departments. The Churches' Commission for Racial Justice was encouraged when its delegation to the Home Office at the end of 1994 was told that the inter-departmental Racial Attacks Group had been reconstituted and was expected to continue progress and produce regular reports. However, in May 1996 the Commission was told that, despite the rise in attacks in 1995, the Group was drafting its final report and would then be disbanded. This is unacceptable: monitoring with public reporting is essential if confidence in the commitment of Government in this field is to rebuilt.

A difficult question for all Governments relates to the banning of racist right-wing groups calling themselves political parties. This issue has arisen to a considerable degree in Germany during the early 1990s when a series of horrifying racist murders took place. The fire-bombing in Mölln in November 1992 killed a Turkish woman and two girls. The German authorities immediately banned a number of groups, including the 'Nationalist Front' and the 'German Alternative', although some seventy others continue to organise, spread messages of hate and organise harassment against minority communities. In Britain the problem has reappeared with the rise of the BNP, which succeeded in winning its first local Council seat at a by-election in September 1993 on the Isle of Dogs in Tower Hamlets. Due to vigorous organisation by local churches, trades unions and community organisations the BNP lost the seat in the full Council elections in May 1994. However, it obtained more votes in May than it had the previous September, and came within 70 votes of winning a seat in neighbouring Newham. Racial attacks increased considerably during the BNP's political campaigning. A detailed 1994 research article argued that it is the very presence of such groups, masquerading as political parties, which poisons local communities; whether they win or lose is less important.

Government argues that banning political groups in a democratic society is a retrograde step, and may be counter-productive. However it cannot be healthy for the wider community to have groups whose agenda is clearly racist being free to organise, campaign and contest elections on a platform which is aimed at particular minorities. Both in Britain and throughout Europe Governments need to develop more rigorous standards for the political arena, which outlaw any form of targeting particular communities, and should not hesitate to ban groups who do so.

Both with regard to racial violence and to the effectiveness of the criminal justice system as a whole, the police are a key agency. In Britain they have recently restyled themselves as a 'service' rather than a 'force'; however, their activities in the field of racial justice still leave much to be desired. A few forces have evolved special racial harassment units. Such work needs to be a priority for all forces, and such units should be ubiquitous, even if in some more rural areas they only consist of one full- or part-time officer. Such a system would require proper training for an increasing number of officers, and demonstrate the seriousness with which the police treat racial violence. A CRE-related research programme is taking place between 1994 and 1996 comparing the ways in which police and justice systems in four European countries deal with racial violence, which should provide useful guidance.

It is crucial that police services, in Britain and elsewhere, address the structural racism which exists in them as in all major social institutions. The police claim they are no worse than anyone else, but the considerable powers of individual police officers, and their special opportunities with respect to minority communities, mean the police are of particular importance. In the UK the training schemes which started in the late 1980s are reported to be having some effect, and it is clear that at the most senior levels of the service there is a commitment to change, but it is on the street where most black people encounter the police, and it is from here that most criticism emanates. The black media, such as *The Voice* and the *Asian Times,* regularly report incidents which it is hard to reconcile with stated anti-racist policy. Racially discriminatory behaviour is a disciplinary offence in the police service, but very few officers have been disciplined on such grounds, which makes many in the black and anti-racist communities feel the whole matter is regarded as insignificant.

Another item on the agenda of police forces must be an increase in the number of minority officers. The fact that even in Britain, which has its pool of black Commonwealth and British citizens to draw on, the number of recruits is abysmally low – around 2 per cent even in the Metropolitan Police – suggests that much more positive action needs to be taken. Leon Murray in *Being Black in Britain* urges young blacks to 'enter the police force in greater numbers and make it their career', as he believes the police have begun to change. That may be true, but if black officers leave exit interviews should always be undertaken to ascertain the reasons. The formation of a Black and Asian Police Officers Association in 1994 may be a sign of hope, if it gets active support from senior officers and co-operation rather than criticism from the white-dominated Police Federation. The police should have a target of at least 6 per cent black officers, to reflect the population as a whole, but it will not be achieved unless the problem of structural racism is overcome.

In England and Wales the police are monitored by the Police Complaints Authority, which deals with complaints of all kinds including deaths and other serious incidents, and which supervises a response to such incidents and complaints. It claims to be fully independent, although its members are appointed by the Home Secretary, and it has to rely on the police investigating the police. It has come under criticism, not least by its own black members of whom there have been several, for its own lack of understanding of racism. It was only persuaded to monitor complaints of police racism in the late 1980s, and even now most people are unaware that it does so, or even that discrimination is a disciplinary offence in the police service. There are few complaints in this field, because of both lack of knowledge and black people's fear of repercussions if they do complain. Nevertheless it is important to have such a comparatively independent body which – if properly aware and functional – can affect both police service and Home Office.

The next important structure needing to address racial justice issues is the Crown Prosecution Service (CPS). The CPS examines the evidence in a particular case and decides if it is strong enough to prosecute. Again structural racism can affect decisions, and even procedures, if officials do not understand the seriousness of racial violence cases, or are themselves unsympathetic. There were a number of examples in the early 1990s where victims were dissatisfied with the CPS's apparent inability to act effectively in quite high-profile cases. As with other institutions there needs to be a structured programme for change, including training, prioritising of cases involving racial violence and positive action to promote racial justice as an essential objective of the Service. Moves were beginning to be made towards this in 1995.

A similar programme needs to be evolved for the judiciary, and has in fact already begun in certain areas, such as training. In 1992 the Judicial Studies Board set up an Ethnic Minorities Advisory Committee and by the end of 1993 a series of seminars had been initiated for both full and part-time judges, starting with one attended by the Lord Chief Justice and the Lord Chancellor. The importance of sentence weighting for crimes which involve racial motivation has been referred to above, and its introduction and effectiveness needs to be monitored and reported on in due course.

An important area for the judiciary to address is their reliance on police evidence, and the number of very serious miscarriages of justice in recent years. Almost all of these have involved either Black or Irish defendants, and although the police, solicitors and barristers must all take their share of responsibility, so must the judges. It could be strongly argued in cases like those of the Tottenham Three, the Cardiff Three and the East Ham Two (two Tamils wrongly imprisoned for a sectarian murder) that judges be more forceful in casting doubt on police evidence, challenging the prosecution or even dismissing charges. The 1994 Home Office report under Section 95 of the 1991 Criminal Justice Act announced that there were still only four minority ethnic judges, and twenty recorders and assistant recorders. There are still estimated to be only 3 per cent black magistrates, though there are more in areas like London. As with other areas of society, if there is to be a fundamental change in this situation, positive action will be needed, in terms of recruitment, training and financial resources.

The final section of the criminal justice system which will need to be addressed is the prisons, which are assuming a greater significance as the numbers of prisoners, at least in British jails, increase. The proportion of prisoners who are black has been consistently far higher for several years than that in the population as a whole. As in other services the numbers and experiences of black staff can be a pointer to what is going on, and how things need to be changed. Section 95 of the 1991 Criminal Justice Act has begun to provide a monitoring process for the criminal justice system as a whole. However, there must be an effective and informative *annual* report under this Section, which is then widely distributed. Positive action, in terms of targets, recruitment, training and monitoring, is essential to create the climate for change.

It is also crucial that the kind of proposals and practices outlined above are adopted at European Union level. The European Parliament has already done sterling work on racial violence and racial discrimination, particularly its 1991 *Enquiry into Racism and Xenophobia in the European Community*, led by Manchester MEP Glyn Ford. Few of the proposals made therein have yet been adopted either at national or European level. One specific step would be the assumption into the national law of all EU countries of the European Convention of Human Rights. Most EU countries have already done this, but not Britain. Such a step would provide an objective measure for Britain's own legislation and practice, and although the Convention does not address racial justice as a specific area, many of its provisions are supportive of proper and effective treatment of cultural and racial minorities.

The agenda set out above for improvements in the criminal justice system within Britain is meant to be realistic. It is not asking for anything which is not possible, or would require enormous sums of money. What is needed is clear programmes, in different sectors of the system, with targets being set in terms of time and personnel, and political and moral commitment to fulfil those programmes by the opening years of the next century. Legislation, at national and European level, to entrench progress would also be appropriate.

ECONOMIC RACIAL JUSTICE

The key areas to be addressed in the struggle for racial justice in the economic sector are, as indicated in chapter 1, access to capital and equality of employment. The current situation in most European countries is that minorities have come from outside the European Union, and have provided the cheap and often low-skilled labour needed to help build the European economy. The original expectation was that they would go home again, but that has not happened. To Germany they came from Turkey, former Yugoslavia and – before they were EC members – Italy, Greece, Spain and Portugal. To the Netherlands and Belgium they came in lesser numbers from the same countries, from former colonies like Surinam and parts of Indonesia, and from North Africa. To France they came partly from overseas territories which if not independent are regarded as part of France, and from the geographically and to some degree culturally proximate countries of north and west Africa. To Britain they came from former colonies and the countries of the Commonwealth.

Statistics from 1990 show that of the main EU countries Belgium has the largest population of foreigners, 9 per cent – of which 3.5 per cent are not from other EU countries. Germany and France have around 6.5 per cent, of which 4.8 per cent in Germany and 4.1 per cent in France are non-EU. The Netherlands has 4.6 per cent, 3.5 per cent non-EU, and the UK 3.3 per cent, only 1.9 per cent non-EU. Hence of the larger central EU countries the UK has by far the smallest proportion of 'non-EU foreigners', although a larger proportion of the citizens of Britain may have originated from outside the UK. The numbers in Germany will certainly have increased since 1990, and in any case there is a new situation there after the reunification in 1991.

It is from Germany we can learn something of the economic results of immigration. Statistics are collected in Germany which do not appear to be available in other EU countries, and offer an interesting picture. In 1994 the Institute for Public Policy Research (IPPR) published a report, *Immigration as an Economic Asset: The German Experience*, edited by Sarah Spencer. This consisted of papers from an Anglo-German conference addressing such issues as the impact of immigration on native employment prospects, the relation between immigration and economic growth, and immigrants' contribution to public resources less their welfare costs. Unfortunately these questions could only be tackled in detail by the German contributors as British data was unobtainable. The organisers were informed after the meeting by Home Office officials that 'there would be little point in conducting such research in the UK as Ministers had already determined what British immigration policy should be, and were unlikely to be influenced by new information'.

The German papers strongly suggest that Germany's economic growth in the 1960s and 1970s would not have been possible without immigration. Researchers calculate that the 1992 German GNP was 6 per cent higher than it would have been otherwise. The large influx of ethnic Germans and asylum-seekers between 1988 and 1992, far from creating an economic burden, raised the growth of the GNP, protected Germans from unemployment and created some 90,000 new jobs. Employers' incomes in 1992 were some 10 per cent higher because of immigration, those of employees 5 per cent. The research of Gieseck shows that immigrants make a substantial contribution to the welfare state. Immigrants who came to West Germany since 1988 paid 32 billion Deutschmarks in tax and national insurance, while receiving 18 billion in initial aid and benefits. Foreign labour also helps to pay state pensions. In 1989 foreigners paid 7.8 per cent of all pension contributions while drawing only 1.9 per cent of payments. One Social Democrat leader has estimated that Germany will need 300,000 new younger immigrants each year simply to pay the pensions of the ageing population. Immigrants themselves grow old, of course, if they are allowed to stay, and may begin to take a greater share of social benefits. However, the research findings are extremely interesting, given the negative attitude by European governments and much of the public to immigration. A report on the whole EU issued in March 1996 suggested that seven million immigrants are needed to keep the age level down.

If immigrants bring economic benefits they are even more entitled to access to capital and equality of employment. With regard to the first of these, a Council of Europe report, presented by the Committee of Experts on Community Relations in 1990, on the contribution of minorities to the 'economic viability of urban areas through setting up small and medium-sized businesses', provides some insights. The report shows that, because it is difficult for minorities to break into the employment market, a high proportion start up small businesses, many of which benefit their urban communities and provide employment for other minority members. French research as long ago as 1982 estimated that people born outside France owned over 15 per cent of small businesses in Paris, mostly in retailing, hotels and restaurants. In Britain in the same period well over twice as many Asians as whites ran small businesses, though in Germany the phenomenon was less because of restrictive laws. The report concludes that the main factor inhibiting both the start-up and the growth of minority businesses is lack of capital, although restrictive regulations, host consumer attitudes, human resource development (training) and credit facilities are also problems.

Leon Murray gives a number of examples of small black businesses in Britain being unable to get bank loans, planning permission or insurance. Black people are bruised and hurt, and give up. Murray believes all the banks' 'national advertising and glossy brochures about services . . . count for nothing'. In the office or boardroom prejudice takes different forms. 'The prowler is still there . . . and it is not easy to catch him . . . He is dressed in the best tailor-made clothes. He is sophisticated and very, very clever.'

Access to capital for black people and black enterprises thus has to be addressed. Banks and building societies are not only withdrawing from inner-city, multiracial areas but making it difficult for people from minority communities to borrow. Ways have to be found of reversing this process so that banks have to reinvest in such areas at least as much as they are receiving in deposits. This could be done either by the stick of increasing taxation if they do not, or the carrot of offering tax incentives if they do – and the more they do the higher the incentive. In the USA ethical investors and community agencies have used the Community Reinvestment Act to ensure that this kind of mechanism operates, and it is a crucial aspect both of racial justice and of urban regeneration. Another mechanism which has been used in the USA is that of boycotting banks which could be shown to be discriminating against black customers. Richard Barnet and John Cavanagh in *Global Dreams* (1994) argue for much greater community involvement in the banking process. People who put money in banks have some rights over its usage. They even suggest a 'pension fund bank', financed and controlled by those investing in pension funds, which aims to create jobs in the communities it serves.

More important, in terms of the numbers affected, is the area of race equality in employment. The principle of 'equal opportunity' has now been widely accepted, and even advocated by a Conservative Government. The problem is that it has had little effect, at least on the macro scale. A number of companies, as indicated in the *Buried Talents* survey referred to in chapter 4 (p. 114), have adopted equal opportunity policies, and a few are actually monitoring their results. However, with one or two notable exceptions, companies are unwilling to reveal any results of the monitoring process, which suggests it is either ineffective or nonexistent. Positive action is needed, but it is difficult for some companies to undertake the additional costs of positive action and monitoring unless all companies are required to do so. The development of monitoring therefore demands some legal undergirding.

Critics often query the term 'positive action', or 'affirmative action' as it usually called in the USA, claiming that it is really positive discrimination. Positive action however includes steps such as deliberately seeking applications from minorities by, for example, advertising in the minority press; encouraging black staff to apply for training and promotion, while making it clear they must succeed on their own merits; training those who are involved in recruitment and selection procedures to ensure they do not discriminate; incorporating black and minority people in the advertising and public presentation of the company; and producing annual reports of progress. Some of these steps may be undertaken under equal opportunity policies; none of them should lead to black people being used as tokens or put into positions beyond their experience or competence. The principle is to offer a supportive environment in which people will achieve their potential, instead of a negative environment where black people feel they must be 'twice as good' to achieve the same level.

Looking at the UK over the last twenty years it is clear that the 1976 Race Relations Act has helped to reduce discrimination in employment. It has not been entirely successful, as the study *Racial Justice at Work* (McCrudden *et al.*) showed. The most important next step would be a legal requirement for ethnic monitoring for employers over a certain size, say 1,000, which would certainly include the major Churches. As well as providing practical information this would make a clear statement about the Government's commitment to actually achieving race equality in employment, rather than paying lip service.

Weak though UK legislation is, it is among the strongest in the EU. A report *Measure for Measure* commissioned by the UK Employment Department (Equal Opportunities Studies Group, 1992) compared the situation in the different EU countries. The report noted that the visible minority population of the EU stood at 2.9 per cent, or nine million people, the largest proportions being in the Netherlands, Britain, Belgium and France. Visible minorities experienced significant levels of discrimination, tended to be concentrated in unskilled and semi-skilled sectors and were often poorly educated and denied training. Policies which helped to limit discrimination included clear legislation, a properly-funded agency to educate and to enforce the law, positive action measures – which already exist in eight countries – and an ombudsman. The report noted that contract compliance, used to good effect by local authorities in Britain in the 1970s, has had its effectiveness severely curtailed by European law. It concluded that employment rights of British black and Asian people are not protected in other EU countries, and that good practice as it exists in several countries should be drawn on in order to set up a comprehensive programme of measures at national and EU level to outlaw discrimination in employment.

At the same time it would be greatly beneficial, as part of any European legislation outlawing racial or ethnic discrimination, to formulate a European Race Relations Act, incorporating the setting up of a 'Commission for Racial Equality' for the European Union. Such a 'Commission' should be strengthened by required ethnic monitoring and the right to investigate specific enterprises at national or European level. Belgium and the Netherlands already have such bodies, although with limited powers, and Germany has legislation requiring employers and employees not to discriminate. In the meantime, active promotion of the 1993 UN Convention on the Protection of the Rights of Migrant Workers and their Families would assist the European picture overall.

The European Migrants Forum, set up by the European Commission to represent the interests of the EU's minority communities, has proposed a special Commissioner for minority concerns, who could co-ordinate a 'European CRE' and national initiatives at EU level. The Churches Commission for Migrants in Europe (CCME), along with the CRE and colleagues in the Netherlands, Belgium and Germany, have outlined the kind of legislation which would be useful, in the form of a Directive from the European Commission, entitled *The Starting Line*. This would give the force of law to the principle of outlawing racial discrimination in the European Union. The same group has also drafted an amendment incorporating similar principles to the Treaty of Rome/Maastricht, *The Starting Point*, which could be seen as an alternative or more properly a complement to the necessary legislation.

The British Government seems sadly loath to involve itself in strengthening the legal safeguards for black and minority communities in the EU. It must be part of the struggle for Christians in all EU countries going into the next century to undergird the Union with legislation that seeks to end prejudice and discrimination and promote equality and justice, especially in the economic sector, for all the residents of Europe.

IMMIGRATION AND ASYLUM

This book opened with a number of cases in which individuals and families had fallen foul of Britain's increasingly restrictive immigration system. The issue of asylum is also discussed above, as are some of the questions underlying the immigration debate, about terms like 'British' and 'nationality' and what they actually mean. Also, in the previous section, we have noted that in Germany much more research has been undertaken about the benefits of immigration, over against the myths concerning its costs. It seems extraordinary that a country such as Britain, which made its wealth and built an Empire by developing a powerful influence around the world, has become so reactionary about ethnic diversity in recent decades. The context of the European Union gives an opportunity to take a more positive approach to some of the thorny problems of immigration.

It is important to state, in terms of a 'Christian vision', that we ought to be looking and working towards a world where all human beings can come and go, to and from whichever piece of land or 'country' they wish to. They should be able to live where they like, work where they like, love and marry whom they like. This would demonstrate our real commitment to the concept that all human beings are children of God, and equal in his sight. Such thinking strongly implies of course that there should be – by and large – an equal distribution of resources around the world, so that people do not have to battle to get to particular places in order simply to survive. It also emphasises that the geographies of particular countries are in many cases accidents of history, that there is often no compelling reason why borders have come to be where they are. The struggle to overcome the limiting and negative effects of 'nationalities', 'borders' and 'countries' is part of the struggle for racial justice and a Kingdom type of world.

That being said, it is clear that countries and nationalities will continue to exist, and that they give people a sense of identity and security. It should be the Christian task to help define identities positively, rather than over against the identities of others, and to keep loyalty to one's country, for example, in proportion. One result of this might be to take a much more positive attitude to dual or even triple nationality, to ask why certain people, who may live in one country and have themselves been, or have parents, born in another, should be limited to one 'nationality'. In these days of international movement each parent might also have been born in separate countries. It depends what is meant by 'nationality' and also by the related term 'citizenship'.

Laurie Fransman in his chapter in *Strangers and Citizens: a Positive Approach to Migrants and Refugees* (Spencer, 1994) defines nationality as 'a status identifying an individual as belonging to a community defined in terms of geography, geopolitics, religion and/or ethnicity', whereas he says citizenship is 'the relationship between an individual and the state whereby the individual enjoys civic rights and is bound by civic duties' (p. 282). The question then becomes, who is entitled to British nationality and who to the slightly wider status of citizenship – and who to European citizenship also? For a detailed discussion of the arguments, Fransman's article repays further study. Where I would join him is in urging a wider rather than a narrower view of British nationality, including a return to the *ius soli* principle that any child born in Britain has a right to British nationality (Fransman adopts the Australian amendment that the child loses that right if s/he leaves before the age of 5). It should also be much easier to change or gain nationality, which should be obtainable on the basis of simple and objective rules, e.g. a period of residence of three years, as is the case in Australia and Canada.

In terms of citizenship, Britain has had for some time a sizeable category of citizens, from the Commonwealth, who do not have British nationality. That category has been immeasurably expanded with the Maastricht Treaty, as everyone with the nationality of an EU country now has EU citizenship, with the political, civil and movement rights attached. The enormity of this change may not yet have been understood by everyone in Britain. Certainly it binds us much more closely than we may have realised with all the peoples of the European Union. What should not escape our notice is that the vast majority of those with whom we have become more closely united are white, and those – primarily from the Commonwealth – from whom we have been distancing ourselves in recent years are black.

One category of people who have been left to some degree in limbo by the move into the European Union are so-called 'Third Country Nationals' (TCNs), people who are not from a 'second country' inside the EU, but a 'third country', outside it. There are around nine million of them in the 15-country EU. In Britain these are often people from the Commonwealth who have not taken out British citizenship; they may also be refugees who achieved the right to stay, students who have been here for a number of years, workers who have come on a work permit, or long-term visitors spending time with their families. All these people may have quite longstanding or quite close ties to Britain, but the fact is that the nationals of other EU countries have far more rights in Britain and across the EU than they do.

The Churches Charter for Racial Justice in Europe urges strongly that 'Third Country Nationals must not become Second Class Citizens' in the EU. Supported by the Council of Churches for Britain and Ireland, and many representative bodies of its member Churches, the Charter argues that everyone resident in the EU, TCNs or not, should have immediate rights to freedom of movement and establishment (i.e. short-term settlement), to housing, education and health-care, and to equal and impartial treatment by police and under the law. They should have further rights after two years to family reunion, equal employment opportunity and voting in local and European elections, and after five years to vote in national elections also. That is the kind of recognition for TCNs Christians are aiming for, and we might add, following Laurie Fransman, the right to nationality after having been in the EU legally for at least three years.

The Charter also urges a much more positive approach to asylum-seekers and refugees, stating that 'No-one should be denied the right to seek asylum in the EU, according to the Principles of the 1951 Geneva Convention'. This would mean that 'harmonisation' of asylum policy in the EU should follow the positive spirit of the Geneva and European Human Rights Conventions; that there should be an end to 'carrier's liability' (which fines airlines and others who bring in asylum-seekers with inadequate papers £2,000); that all asylum-seekers should have proper legal representation with right of appeal; that detention of asylum-seekers should be ended. Many believe those with temporary leave to remain should be allowed family reunion when they have been in an EU country for a year, rather than the present deplorable situation where they wait for up to five years. Family members have been known to die in the intervening period.

It should also be noted that the Organisation for African Unity has a wider definition of 'refugee' than the Geneva Convention, referring to people who have to leave their homes through conflict or famine, as well as direct persecution. African countries regularly give hospitality to far more refugees than their European counterparts, and tend not to put them in prison.

In November 1994 the UN High Commissioner for Refugees issued a document entitled *Fair and Expeditious Asylum Procedures*. It is by no means radical, and does not go as far as the *Refugee Charter* produced by the Refugee Council earlier in 1994. It recognises the usefulness of the 'harmonisation' process under the EU's Dublin Convention, but issues a number of warnings about the need to adhere to basic international principles with relation to the nature of procedures adopted towards asylum-seekers. It questions the concept of 'safe third countries', which European countries have increasingly employed to remove people, and the direction in which EU practices are moving. It concludes by calling upon governments not to restrict the liberty of asylum-seekers – by the end of 1995 some 700 asylum seekers were being kept in selected prisons and detention centres in the UK, and many more in countries like Germany. Some local churches had become actively involved in visiting such places, monitoring what went on, and holding vigils outside. The Churches' position was that no asylum-seeker should be detained unless there was clear evidence that they were a threat to national security.

The Churches were also expressing concern and anger about the increasing rate of refusals under the 1993 British asylum legislation, up from 14 per cent in early 1993 to approaching 80 per cent in 1995. Exceptional Leave to Remain (ELR), which gave people safety for a year at a time, and had prevented so many asylum-seekers being returned to danger and conflict, had fallen from over 75 per cent before the Act to below 20 per cent. Those being refused were those who used to get ELR – 99 per cent of Zaireans, Angolans and Sierra Leoneans, around 75 per cent of Sudanese, Sri Lankan Tamils and Turkish Kurds – even though there were wars going on in all their countries.

All this needs to be set into the context of an overall approach to questions of migration which should be different from the present one. The Thatcher and Major governments have made quite clear that their basic underlying intention is to keep out as many non-Europeans as possible, while claiming to be pursuing a 'firm but fair' policy. This approach has become even clearer under the draconian proposals of late 1995 for withdrawing social security and housing benefit from up to 70 per cent of asylum-seekers and from long-term residents opposing deportation, and turning public officials and employers into 'immigration police'.

All immigration controls are of course based to some degree on xenophobia and racism – we want to retain our patch of Earth for people like us – but the EU seems to have entrenched that, while apparently being unmoved by the increasing gap between the haves and have-nots in the world, and the pressure to migrate that this will increasingly bring. At minimum, Britain and its EU partners must set up an 'early-warning system' for natural or political disasters which create refugees and other forms of migration, and undertake policies to help limit migration such as evolving a more effective human rights network built round the UN which may limit the behaviour of some Governments, reducing the arms trade, tackling the debt crisis and improving trading opportunities for poor countries.

There are also immigration concerns to be addressed specifically within the British context. One is the need to obtain more information about the effects of immigration, and evolve a much more positive attitude to the contributions that black, minority and refugee communities are making in many different sectors. This points towards the next section, on education and the media. There would then be the possibility of a proper and serious public discussion about the pros and cons of immigration, rather than the puerile and xenophobic approach that exists in many quarters at the moment. As Sarah Spencer points out in *Strangers and Citizens*, if in its immigration policy Government is clearly aiming at keeping people out it is hard to take seriously its claim that it wants black and minority people already here to be free from the effects of discrimination and prejudice. One policy which clearly needs to be changed affects many young couples originating from the Indian Sub-Continent through the 'primary purpose rule', because they have to prove that the primary purpose of their marriage is not to enable entry into the United Kingdom.

Another battle increasingly being fought in the area related to immigration policy is around *internal controls*, that is, controls on the population which are built into the institutional structures of society rather than operating at a country's borders. They take two main forms, the identity card system and controls operated through the health, education, housing and social security systems. Identity cards could only really be introduced after a expensive and comprehensive survey, which would also require a degree of intrusion into the lives of many people. Its difficulties are illustrated by the fact that some two million people are estimated to have evaded the 1991 census, and to ensure all such people were incorporated into a national identity scheme could create many difficulties. Students or visitors, whose overstaying is one of the Immigration Department's great concerns, would not have national identity documents. In any such scheme Black people are particularly likely to be targeted.

EDUCATION AND THE MEDIA

The way people develop their view of the world is very important in their later opinions and activities. Hence the understanding and the images that children receive of race issues is important. Whether they are white or black, they need to be offered a positive perspective on the multiracial, multicultural society, and given a constructive view of human diversity.

During the 1970s there was a good deal of discussion in the education system about multicultural and anti-racist education. Principles were evolved which were introduced into educational establishments relating to all age-groups, often by Labour-controlled education authorities, of which the Inner London Education Authority was probably the best known. Multiculturalism sought to ensure that children understood there were a variety of cultures, which included language, religion, music, dress, food and so on, that these were to be regarded by and large as of equal worth, and that there was something of value in each of them. Anti-racism endeavoured to be more explicit about the racism in Britain's past, and its present, which had become institutionalised, and which needed to be addressed and – as much as possible – eradicated. Anti-racism in particular led to much criticism from the right. In politics and the media it was claimed that Britain's great past, and good name, was under attack. Tabloid newspapers came up with stories such as the banning of 'Baa Baa Black Sheep' by Labour Councils. Despite the extreme exaggeration, and sometimes total untruthfulness, of such stories some mud stuck, and anti-racism was successfully rubbished.

It may be that some efforts to tackle racism were over-zealous and misdirected. The lengthy and detailed report of the Macdonald Inquiry, *Murder in the Playground* (1989), into racial violence in Manchester schools, and in particular the death in the Burnage High School playground of 13-year-old Ahmed Ullah, showed that while the school had tried to develop effective anti-racist policies it did not really understand what it was doing. White working-class families were alienated and the suspicion and division which ensued created a climate where violence became rather more likely than less. The report remains one of the best introductions to the debate about how to introduce anti-racism into any white-controlled institution, but into schools in particular. Whatever the problems, however, efforts to introduce anti-racism in the 1970s and early 1980s led to the growth of a generation who were at least partly sensitised to race.

During the 1980s the introduction of the national curriculum, the reduction of the influence of local authorities and the unpopularity of even a multicultural approach to education have meant the loss of much ground in this area. Those involved in education professionally say the attitudes of many young people leave much to be desired, racist opinions are acceptable and there are no concerted policies in the education system to address this. Christians in education, the Churches and others concerned about these issues need to be much more insistent that racial justice becomes a priority in the education system, and that the principles and methodology which were effective in the anti-racist work of the 1970s are resurrected. It may need to be amended to fit into current structures, but for young people growing up in the European Union still to remain ignorant about even other European cultures, and to manifest xenophobic views about ethnic minorities, is extremely worrying.

The Churches have some influence in the education system through the schools for which in particular the Catholics and Anglicans have responsibility. They also run colleges of education, where teachers are trained. Those responsible for Church schools and colleges should ensure that an anti-racist approach continues to be emphasised, at least in the church sector, hoping this can be an example to the rest of the system. Inspiration may be found in some local authorities, particularly in London, where the anti-racist approach has been retained, but it is schools in the 'almost white' areas of Britain which need this most. The 'Local Management of Schools' means that in such areas, where head teachers or governors do not believe multiculturalism or anti-racism to be important ('There aren't any here'), young people may grow up with negative opinions and attitudes formed by family and the media, and unchallenged by an alternative view.

One other step Church colleges can take is actively to recruit both students and staff from the black and minority communities. There remain far too few black teachers. One survey in the mid-1980s showed there were even less than the average in Church schools, and the target – as in other sectors of society – should be at least 6 per cent. Theological colleges should not be forgotten either. The *Equal Partners?* survey by the BCC Community and Race Relations Unit in 1990 showed that many colleges still have a long way to go. The Church of the twenty-first century needs clergy who do not merely pay lip service to anti-racism but practise it in a structured and effective manner.

The press is another major influence in people's lives. Much of the tabloid press is antipathetic to racial justice concerns; examples include the attacks on asylum-seekers as 'bogus', 'fake' and 'economic migrants' and the vilifying of Winston Silcott. This clearly contributed to his wrongful conviction, but no newspaper was ever charged with contempt of court. Most Christians in 'the professions' tend to read the broadsheets, and so are sheltered from the worst of such propaganda, although even *The Times* can sometimes behave like a superior tabloid. It is important, therefore, for Christians both to sample the more virulent newspapers from time to time, and to respond actively, through the letter pages or otherwise, when racist attitudes appear. The fact that Britain is going into the new century as a permanently multiracial, multicultural society needs to be constantly communicated to and through the press.

Radio and television are now an even more influential factor in people's lives. There are some very effective programmes, particularly on BBC 2 and Channel 4, when the viewpoint of the black communities themselves is put across. Some of these programmes have helped in obtaining a fresh look at alleged miscarriages of justice, supporting campaigns against deportation or communicating more balanced views about a range of racial justice issues. One form of broadcasting which needs constant monitoring, however, is the news. Items can be subject to quite biased reporting, especially if, for example, there have been disturbances, and the authorities with their well-oiled publicity machines are much better placed to give their version of events, which rapidly becomes the accepted wisdom. Just as often it is the stories which get left out which are important. Journalists can say 'Well it's just another racial attack', or 'It's just another family being deported'. Who decides what is news is an interesting and very important process in modern communications? In order to point our news reporting in the right direction it is important to intervene when racism appears, even in its more subtle forms, and to offer praise when a helpful and informative programme has been made.

If we are to have an informed, committed and anti-racist population for the next century a good deal needs to be changed now, in order that the changes may begin to filter effectively through the system. The same old tactics of lobbying MPs, telephoning broadcasters and writing to newspapers may not sound like a revolutionary struggle but they are still essential. There are journalists and broadcasters who wish to be positively anti-racist. They also need support and encouragement if they are to be successful, and contribute to the changing of hearts and minds which will allow racial justice to be integrated into the social attitudes, programmes and structures of the future.

RELATIONS AMONG FAITHS

Britain is slowly coming to the realisation which some of the rest of Europe has been living with for over 1,500 years; our continent is irreversibly a multicultural, multifaith entity. The question is not how can we prevent this but how can we live with it, learn from it and even celebrate it. Over the last twenty years the number of people of faiths other than Christianity living in Britain has risen significantly. Mostly coming from south Asia – the old colonial countries of India, Pakistan and Bangladesh – there are now some 350,000 in the Jewish and Hindu communities, perhaps 400,000 Sikhs and something over a million Muslims. Undoubtedly the most important inter-faith relationship in Europe at the present time, as far as racial justice is concerned, is that between Christians and Muslims. That, therefore, is the one on which we shall focus in this section.

The inter-relatedness between Britain and south Asia over the past 400 years has been more complex than that with Africa and the horrors of the slave trade. There has been exploitation, much of it. Trading patterns as always have favoured European enrichment, but arguably Asia benefited more from infrastructure and new forms of social and economic organisation than did Africa. Many Asian soldiers fought in the 1939-45 war, against Japan to the east as well as the Axis powers to the west. Then in the post-war period the UK's economic development has been augmented considerably by workers from outside, particularly Muslims. In an article about Pakistani workers in *Meeting Muslims*, a booklet published by Christians Aware, Asaf Hussain comments that their contribution,

> along with workers from other migrant groups, in the rebuilding of British industry has been tremendous. But in the UK, as well as in other European countries, the contributions of Turkish workers in Germany, Arabs in France, Surinamese and Indonesians in Holland, Pakistanis in Norway and other Scandinavian countries have gone unacknowledged.

We need to understand a little history of the relationship between Christians and Muslims, to approach this relationship constructively. Muslims see both Jews and Christians in a special relationship, as 'peoples of the Book'. Islam arose from the teaching of the Prophet Muhammad, born in Mecca in 570 CE. Many of those living in what today we call the Middle East became Muslims. Islam's rapid spread posed a threat to Christendom in the mid-seventh to mid-eighth centuries. Then in 1095, for reasons as much geopolitical as theological, Pope Urban II preached a sermon which had enormous repercussions. He reported that the Turks had crossed into 'Roman territory' in eastern Europe and were desecrating churches and killing Christians. He urged 'a new brand of fighting pilgrims on the greatest conceivable pilgrimage, to open the road to Jerusalem and claim it for Christ'. The first crusade took over three years to fight its way to Jerusalem, which by 1099 had been under Islamic rule for 450 years, with Muslims, Jews and Christians living amicably together. The Crusaders changed all that. Within days up to 70,000 Muslim corpses clogged the streets and holy places. More can be learned from Stuart Brown's *The Nearest in Affection* (1994).

Another useful source is *Muslims in Western Europe* (1992), by Jørgen Nielsen, who argues that the Christian–Muslim relationship goes 'as far back in time as historical Islam'.

Christopher Lamb, Secretary of the Churches Commission for Interfaith Relations, describes well the nature of the Muslim community in Britain in an essay in *Meeting Muslims* (Christians Aware). He lists some of the issues which concern Muslims as they settle in to life in Britain: the British approach to education, especially sex education; the role of girls and women; the divorce laws; the provision of halal meat in schools, hospitals and other shared institutions. He points to the publication of *The Satanic Verses* and the Gulf War as two recent episodes which make Muslims feel insecure here, as well as continuing racial attacks and media hostility. He also notes that the stability of Muslim family life, and the religious values which underlie it, are now often pointed to as an example to follow. However, Lamb also commented subsequent to the June 1995 disturbances in Bradford on 'the fragility of Muslim community life when young unemployed Muslims ignore the pleas of their law-abiding parents'. We Christians must work together with Muslims where we can, says Lamb, and where we cannot, 'we must hold our own convictions in humility and determine not to allow disagreement to become the kind of conflict in which we aim at the destruction of the other'.

Clinton Bennett, a predecessor of Lamb's in the ecumenical structures, in an essay in the same publication focuses on the struggles and contributions of the Bangladeshi community in particular. He recounts how young men came to provide the cheap labour Britain wanted in the post-war era, and then, because they eventually wanted to bring their wives to join them, how difficult the immigration system became. Bangladeshis were badly affected by unemployment as Britain's traditional manufacturing industries have been run down. They have largely gone into catering. This has suited their hospitable ethos; Islam for them is a way of life more than a political ideology. We also have something to learn from them, says Bennett: 'Bangladeshis are a remarkable people and have suffered much, often without complaint. They can teach Christians a great deal about the meaning of "cross-bearing"'.

In *Islamic Britain* (1994) Philip Lewis estimates that by 1991 there were about one million Muslims in the UK, 80 per cent from the south Asian countries of Pakistan, Bangladesh and India. They are concentrated in east London, the East and West Midlands, the textile towns of Lancashire and Yorkshire and – in Scotland – Glasgow. Lewis points to many achievements of the Muslim communities, who have successfully moved from manufacturing to service industries. However, there is no room for complacency as many young Bangladeshis and

Pakistanis in particular leave school with no qualifications. This leaves them feeling marginalised, excluded and angry.

The militant resurgence represented by the 'Islamists' has given rise to the theory exemplified by an August 1994 18-page survey by *The Economist* on 'Islam and the West'. This begins by stating that 'One of the commonest prophecies of the mid-1990s is that the Muslim world is heading for a fight with other parts of the world that do not share its religio-political opinions', particularly Europe. It refers to a coming 'clash of civilisations' in which the nation-state is no longer the primary unit of international relations. Such comment and analysis has helped to fuel tensions between areas where the more extreme strands of Islam exist and those which, while nominally Christian, espouse capitalism and consumerism. Fortunately *The Economist* is not convinced.

Salman Rushdie's *The Satanic Verses* has been the main episode that has brought Muslims together over the past few years. Clinton Bennett in *Meeting Muslims* (Christians Aware) describes the reasons for the anguish caused but acknowledges the difficulty of finding a solution to the 'clash of values'. He notes that 80 per cent of the British public view Islam as 'the next enemy after communism', and argues that one essential is that 'good, decent Muslim citizens' must be offered their say to offset the 'often blatantly false images still used to depict Muslims'. There is also of course a job to be done in our schools, in religious education, so that children in non-Muslim communities may understand some of the strength of Muslim feeling, and the reasons for it.

Lewis believes that the most dangerous challenge to Christian–Muslim relationships internationally is the 'DIY Islam' of the Islamists, sponsored by Saudi Arabia. For Britain and the rest of Europe he raises four areas of concern. Firstly, what kind of identity should be encouraged for young people born of Muslim parents? Is it to be Muslim, or 'Islamist'? The ulama (clergy) do not offer the young role-models; parents hardly understand their children, and vice versa; elders frown on mixing between young Muslims and Western youth culture. There are however young Muslim professionals who are seeking both to retain a Muslim identity and to offer a positive understanding of south Asian culture, along with a dialogue with the society in which the young people are growing up. This kind of debate continues on some of the Muslim local radio stations and in regular magazines such as *Q-News*. Nielsen comments that in Europe many young Muslims are developing new forms of expressing Islam more appropriate to their new context, and that the idea of a 'multicultural Europe' in which peoples and faiths live together peacefully cheek by jowl is a 'liberal myth'. The dilemmas range from whether Muslim girls should wear the hijab, or headscarf, to the content of religious education.

A second major area of concern is the role of women. Twenty years ago few Muslim women worked outside the home. Now the newly-educated generation is active in doing so, and unwilling to act under the control or direction of the Mosque elders or imams, many of whom cannot even speak good English. Also, paradoxically, the young Muslim woman who has qualifications, a career and money in the bank is in a much better position to bring in a young husband from Pakistan or Bangladesh than one who has no prospects. This has enabled Muslim women working in the education sphere to encourage their younger 'sisters' to achieve. There are several essays on Muslim women in *Meeting Muslims*, including an interview with a young religious education teacher. She points out that young Muslim women growing up in the UK no longer want husbands from Asia; increasingly they prefer Muslim boys brought up here. She believes it is still important, however, for them to learn about Islam, otherwise they have no religious or moral foundation for their lives.

Thirdly, says Lewis, there is a considerable challenge for Islam to renew its intellectual tradition in the languages and culture of Europe. There are difficulties, due to the considerable differences between European and Asian cultures and languages, the Middle Eastern sponsorship of educational institutions being developed here, and the minimum interest in tackling the 'inculturation' issue. Muslims, according to Lewis, need to give much more thought to how to live as a minority with integrity – Christians may need to give some thought to how they may be assisted to do so. There are some from both faiths who may actively resent the two communities living together in parallel and mutual respect. They have to be marginalised by progressive Christians and Muslims working together. 'Multicultural Europe' may be a myth, and pluralism onerous, but there seems no option but to try, as the alternative is either to deny people the practice of their chosen faith or drive them out altogether. As Martin Luther King was fond of pointing out in a similar context, neither white Americans nor black Americans have anywhere else to go.

Finally there is the real difficulty for both communities of the meaning of mission, or to put it more provocatively of proclamation. For many Christians the question arises as to how Muslims with whom they already live as neighbours in shared esteem are to be invited, or encouraged, to the Christian faith. Some Muslims still regard Christians as 'kafir' – unbelievers – although one British Muslim convert has argued that as 'People of the Book' Christians should not be regarded as 'kafir', or as those against whom 'jihad' may be conducted. If Christians and Muslims could see each other as those *with whom* the 'struggle for justice' – racial and otherwise – could be conducted, there would be much opportunity for learning and working together.

Islam has a record on race similar to Christianity. It conducted a slave trade, in East Africa, and appears to have undergirded it with the same sort of attitude to Africans as Europeans had. However, Muslim scholars argue that in Islam there is no such thing as 'race'. According to *Islam and the Race Question* (1987) by Dr Abdul Aziz Kamel, differences in colour and language among human beings are regarded simply as 'a manifestation of the Divine Power' and as 'proofs of God's existence'. Dr Kamel goes on:

> Islam believes in one God. From this profession of divine unique-
> ness derives the necessary and inescapable unity of all human
> beings, a unity in which . . . I am the equal of every other man
> throughout history, anywhere in the world.

It was partly because of this teaching that Malcolm X chose Islam as his belief system. However, the East African slave trade shows that the adherents of Islam, like those of other belief-systems, are prone to lapses from their own high standards. This is supported by the observations of one long-time European resident of Pakistan that local Muslims often preferred marriage to a lighter-skinned person.

Ultimately what is needed between Muslims and Christians is much more com-munication and mutual activity, at every level. Nielsen argues that 'different people have different ways of doing things, and in a plural society there must be . . . room for such differences'. Some inter-faith communities in Britain, for example those in Wolverhampton, Leicester and Bradford, with their different structures for addressing concerns, have a good track record. The World and European Councils of Churches have been communicating with similar Muslim bodies for some time, and need to become more open and vigorous about this. What might be most helpful of all would be the development of some kind of 'Standing Conference' of Christians and Muslims, at both national and European level, to be an open forum where different views and perspectives can be shared, and common action planned. There may well be difficulties, in that Islam has no clear structure to appoint representatives, and there are undoubtedly significant differences within Muslim and Christian communities, as well as between them. However, if those who profess a belief in the same God cannot at least talk and work together, there is little chance for a world where difference often means ignorance, demonisation and mutual destruction. A common 'jihad' against injustice by Christians and Muslims together would undoubtedly be a sign of hope for the world.

Global racial justice

Hence we move into the fourth circle, the world as a whole, the circle most difficult to influence. There are, however, many movements and organisations
seeking to increase justice at the global level and every supporter helps. The
inequalities referred to above between black and white in Europe and North
America are reflected throughout the human community. And as A.
Sivanandan, the Sri Lankan intellectual now based in Britain, says, the poverty
line is the colour line, everywhere. Black (or brown, or yellow) almost always
means poor, even if there are gradations by shade as it were; white means
wealthy. This is a partly simplified picture. There are poorer people in the afflu-
ent states: 40 per cent of US children live below the poverty line – most of them
are black. There are also rich people in the poor countries, they are an elite
which has been more-or-less integrated into the economic aristocracy of the
Western countries, and become its satrap among the poor. This does not, however, materially alter the overall picture of the racial distribution of wealth.

It is important to remind ourselves of the enormous inequalities in the world,
and some of the related factors, before asking the question how is this possible?
How is it that one quarter of the world – more or less that quarter whose past is
Christian – can go on getting richer while the poor at best remain the same, or
in many cases get sick and die? As with the system of slavery, is there not some
underlying ideology operating in the fourth circle which enables this obscene
process to continue? We shall look first at the current situation, in terms of the
five parameters of poverty, debt, trade, aid and the arms trade, then at the contribution of 'the market', and finally at what might be done.

THE PRESENT SITUATION

There are enormous numbers of people who live in absolute poverty. According
to the World Bank they number some 1.3 billion human beings, about one-fifth
of the world's population. At the same time a process of income concentration
among the rich is continuing, in that the countries with the richest 20 per cent
of the world's population raised their share from 70 per cent of the world's
income in 1960 to 85 per cent in 1991. Some four billion people share the
remaining 15 per cent. In 1994 the Administrator of the UN Development
Programme commented that in 1962 the richest 20 per cent had 30 times the
income of the poorest 20 per cent; by 1994 it had risen to 60 times. The World
Development Movement (WDM) says that Britain's richest ten people have as
much wealth as 23 poor countries with over 174 million people. Descriptions of
the results of all this can be found in UN reports, in aid agency literature and just

occasionally in the mass media. Causes lie in the underlying viciousness of the global economic system in its various guises.

The most stark of these is *debt*, the system by which the poor world is now in eternal hock to the wealthy, to a degree which means that many poor countries will never, ever escape. The debt of the poor has risen from $7 million in 1955 through $1,500 billion by 1990 to almost $2,000 billion by the end of 1994. It rose by 7 per cent in 1993 and again by 7 per cent in 1994. The WCC Study Document *Christian Faith and the World Economy Today* (1992) says this process began in the 1970s when banks and governments in the North encouraged governments in the South to accept loans out of the extra money washing around in the international economy due to much higher oil prices.

Sometimes the loans were used for relatively useful infrastructural purposes, but often for large-scale projects irrelevant to the majority of the poor, for arms purchases or for the personal purposes of the elites. The WCC report says it is reckoned that leaders in Mali have placed in European banks money equivalent to the country's entire debt; while that debt remains unpaid the poor have to go without basic health and education because government income is used for repayments. The debt tables of the Organisation for Economic Co-operation and Development (OECD) – which brings together the richest countries – show that between 1982 and 1990 the developing countries have remitted to the North *in debt service alone* $1,345 billion. This is $418 billion *more* than the total resource flow *to* those countries – which has mostly been new loans anyway. Many poor countries have paid back more than they owed, yet are even deeper in debt. WDM points out that in 1993, for every £1 given in aid, rich nations took back £3 in debt repayments. The United Nations body UNESCO recently estimated that half a million children are dying every year due to debt repayment.

Poor black countries might have a chance of paying their debts if the *trading system* were fair, but of course it is not. The WCC believes a prime cause of the deepening chasm between rich and poor is the 'continuing, dramatic fall in the "world prices" of most of the products of the South'. It says that between 1980 and 1988 the real prices of commodity exports from developing countries (apart from oil) declined by 40 per cent. In 1990 they declined by another 13 per cent. Christian Aid's report *A Raw Deal* (Madden, 1993) says the World Bank expects prices of raw materials – on the export of which many poor countries depend – to fall even faster in the 1990s than in the 1980s. *A Raw Deal* explains what this means in the context of the sugar trade, and goes on to point to the problems of over-production, the collapse of the International Commodity Agreements and the effects of the debt crisis. It points to the responsibility of the International Monetary Fund and the World Bank, set up by the UN to *help* in this situation.

211

They exacerbate the problems by refusing debtor countries loans until they increase exports.

The WCC document lays major responsibility for the desperate trade situation on Transnational Corporations (TNCs). It points out that between 80 per cent and 90 per cent of rich country exports are associated with TNCs and that 40 per cent of international trade takes place *between* subsidiaries of TNCs. These enormous companies, two or three of which can often control the market in one particular raw commodity or item of manufacture, concentrate economic power ferociously. In some cases they are now withdrawing from their modest involvements in poorer countries, as there is no market there and labour-saving technology reduces the advantage of linking factories with low labour costs. *A Raw Deal* notes that companies like Nestle, Hitachi and Unilever have turnovers of $20 billion a year, bigger than the exports of all but the largest countries of the South. Five hundred companies control 70 per cent of world trade, 80 per cent of world investment and 30 per cent of the whole world's Gross Domestic Product! They are rightly called *trans*national corporations, for their operations run *across* nations. 'Multinationals' is a misnomer, implying they are 'of many nations' whereas they are of none.

One other dimension of the activities of transnational corporations, often abetted by governments, is the way in which they take over the land of native and indigenous peoples when it is discovered there are resources to be exploited. This happens most often with mineral assets, but it can happen also with energy and agricultural resources. Here sometimes governments themselves are the chief actors. The mining company RTZ (formerly Rio Tinto Zinc) has found itself in constant conflict with indigenous communities in southern Africa, Latin America, Canada, the Pacific and Australia. When metal ores are discovered beneath land which has been the property of native peoples for centuries, it is extraordinary to what lengths political and economic authorities will go to remove them, or force them to relinquish control of the land. Even the often progressive Canadian government is currently involved in squeezing out the Lubicon Cree Indians from ancestral lands where oil and gas have been discovered. The poison of racism can sometimes surface in the propaganda which would-be exploiters employ.

Some Christians believe that international aid is on the way to solving the problems of inequality and poverty but in the above situation it can do little more than scratch the surface. Also, apart from being inadequate in amount, it is increasingly misdirected in form. Instead of being used to help the poorest, when it is not being used for ineffective prestige projects or going into Swiss bank accounts, it is increasingly applied to support the 'Structural Adjustment

Programmes' (SAPs) beloved of the World Bank and the IMF. Between 1980 and 1990 the IMF lent more than $70 billion for SAPs, and the World Bank lent $43 billion between 1980 and mid-1992. Yet many of the SAPs have resulted only in the poor becoming poorer, and some of them have even led international companies to pull out of central Africa because of their destructive effect. *A Raw Deal* (Madden, 1993) notes that in 1985, the year of the famine in Ethiopia, while the total emergency aid to all of Africa was around $3 billion, the collapse in world commodity prices meant that African countries received $19 billion *less* for products sold.

WDM points out in its 1994 report *The Great Aid Robbery* that, apart from the operations of the IMF, the quality and sometimes the amount of the richer countries' aid is diminishing. Britain's aid budget has fallen to two-thirds of its 1979 level as a proportion of GNP, and by over 12 per cent in real terms. In 1993 it amounted to 0.31 per cent of the GNP, placing us thirteenth in the list of the 21 OECD donors. The distribution is also bad, with the poorest countries receiving less per head than richer countries, and the quality is questionable, with our largest recipient, India, receiving less than 13 per cent of its £500 million for poverty alleviation, the rest going to industrial development of one kind and another. The dangers related to the latter have been shown by the Pergau dam scandal, where not only has a large sum gone to a Malaysian project unlikely to help the poor but it was also linked with an arms deal in a way the British courts found breached the law. WDM, who brought the lawsuit against the Government, were able to save a large sum for proper usage for development aid. To improve aid quality, UN agencies have argued for 20 per cent of all aid to be spent on human investment – education, health, employment – along with 20 per cent of the recipient government's budget, the so-called 20:20 proposal.

Finally reference needs to be made to the arms trade, which assists in creating an increasing climate of violence in poor countries. The WCC document on Faith and Economy reports that over ten million people were killed in wars in 'Third World' countries between 1945 and 1980, many conflicts being between governments and their own citizens, fighting over the crusts left them by the North. The South buys 75 per cent of the arms sold each year. The Campaign Against the Arms Trade and WDM continue to expose the nature of those arms deals, and the Scott Enquiry over the sale of arms to Iraq has opened the eyes of many to the collaboration between Government ministries, arms dealers and the elites of Third World countries in the enormous wastage of money on weapons. The reality that most current conflicts involve black people shooting other black people with weapons we have provided, paid for with loans on which we earn interest, using money that should improve health and education in order that they can run a more effective economy, should be ever before us.

MURDER BY THE MARKET

The driving force within the world economy leading to the present appalling situation is undoubtedly the so-called 'free market' system. Some perceptive economists point out the market is only 'free' for the poor and is actually heavily controlled by the rich. The dangers of this system have become even more plain over the four years since the collapse of Soviet Communism and the so-called 'command economies' of the Eastern bloc, as instead of matters improving they have got worse. One theologian who has undertaken some detailed thinking in this area is the German Ulrich Duchrow. In his book *Global Economy: A Confessional Issue for the Churches?* (1987), he draws on biblical material, on Martin Luther and on Dietrich Bonhoeffer to show how the West has ignored fundamental Christian teaching. He argues that it is essential for our salvation – physical and spiritual – that the Church begins to take action in the current context. In that context, and taking seriously also the inequalities *within* the North, Duchrow asks the question about the world economy, 'What do we do when the driver is drunk?' He says that the Church must actively resist, in order to prevent a disaster.

Duchrow goes on to examine 'economic resistance by the church'. He raises the question as to whether such resistance is a *'casus confessionis'*, calling for the same type of resistance as that offered by Bonhoeffer, by the 'Confessing Church' in Germany, by parts of the Church against apartheid and by the liberation theology movement in Latin America. He notes that such challenges can be costly, and that 'We Christians in the centres of power have hardly yet taken even the first step in this direction'.

The thinking of the World Council of Churches is influential for Duchrow. He reviews the WCC's work on transnational corporations and notes that although the 1983 Vancouver Assembly took a strong position on the role of TNCs it brought the TNC Programme to a premature end. International ecumenical work has continued, however, on the global economy, and the report referred to above is part of that. But, when we know that in the final version of that report the consensus view prevailed over the prophetic, the issues raised by Duchrow about the commitment of the Churches assume greater importance. He summarises his concern thus, 'The question for our West German and other European churches, therefore, is when will they be ready, in communion with the one Church of Jesus Christ, in obedience to our common Lord, to recognise honestly their direct complicity in the structures of the global economy, and draw the necessary conclusions?'. The question is posed in even starker form in the section on becoming a Confessing Church:

The Global Economic System, as the stronghold of huge agglomer-
ations of power, is still the least-recognised, the least exposed and
answered challenge to the church to confess its faith. It is no longer
amenable to control by any political institution . . . and at present
costs the lives of over thirty million people from starvation annually. . . .. Do thieves, profiteers under this system sit down at the
Lord's Table together with their victims? Does the Church really
carry out its role as watchman here? (1987, p. 109)

Duchrow goes on to note that 'the integration of the German churches' financial
system in the structures of state and society makes them part and parcel of this
state and society', and comments that Luther thought a Church which accepted
interest had forfeited its right to call itself a Church.

The question must of course be raised as to who is responsible for 'the system'?
As it is known as a 'free market' is anyone in charge? *Christian Faith and the
World Economy Today* (WCC, 1992) states that the original market must have
been one of the oldest human institutions, and was the arrangement whereby
traders set up their stalls in a square or street to sell and exchange. It still operates in thousands of towns around the world today. Capitalism emerged when
owners saw the opportunity to increase profits through selling in a wide range of
markets, and this led to the 'commodifying' of many items, including labour.
The market may have begun free but it soon evolved into something whereby
the richer and stronger could enforce their will on the poorer and weaker,
including the workers. 'Markets alone and by themselves do not automatically
produce abundant life for all', says the WCC document, and unless 'free trade'
takes place between relatively equal partners, 'the market can tear a society
apart'. Arguably that is what is happening, and the split is along what
Sivanandan, following W. B. Du Bois, calls 'the colour line'.

Peter Madden in *A Raw Deal* argues that markets do have benefits, being a
'highly efficient way of maximising the productivity of relatively scarce
resources and getting economic decisions made while leaving the consumer
with freedom of choice . . . it matches supply and demand'. The 'free' market,
according to Madden, needs 'strong and continual regulation'. He goes on, 'If in
our view the present trading system contributes to keeping a large part of the
world's people in poverty, then Christian love requires that it be changed'. A
commentator who is deeply critical of the market system is the North American
Noam Chomsky. He refers to 'the myth of the free market', arguing that it is rigorously controlled by those who have money and power. Chomsky points out
that all developed market countries have a huge state sector; in the USA it is
called the Pentagon. When the Pentagon in some form has evolved a new form

of technology then it can be handed over to 'so-called private enterprise to use as a weapon against the working class'. He notes how under 'free-market' Ronald Reagan the state share of gross economic product increased. Moving into eastern Europe, US capitalists demand tariffs and infrastructure, and they get it, 'These guys don't believe in the free market, that's for the poor'.

A Christian economist who feels differently is Brian Griffiths, former adviser to the Canadian and Mexican Governments and Margaret Thatcher. In his *Morality and the Market Place* (1982) Griffiths sees Britain as a 'corporate welfare state', denounces the power of the unions and believes that health, education and other welfare services should be provided by the private sector. However it is his section on 'Third World Poverty' which is particularly difficult to accept. Griffiths believes that the problem is not one of inequality but poverty and does not accept that neo-colonialism, tariff barriers and the excess profits of multinational corporations (sic) are the 'evil structures' causing world poverty. He goes on:

> I believe it is entirely false to suggest that the wealth of the West is being obtained at the expense of Third World countries or that the poverty of the Third World is the result of systematic exploitation by the West.

He describes the benefits to developing countries from multinational corporations of investment, tax revenues and job creation. Griffiths rejects 'transfer pricing' by TNCs and repudiates the idea that 'the international trading system is a kind of jungle'. He places the responsibility for getting things right on national governments, being apparently unaware that Third World governments are now relatively powerless and that in any case the companies have often helped create the elites with whom they then deal.

Griffiths' explanations for world poverty are geography and natural resources, lack of capital, insufficient suitable investment opportunities and certain non-economic factors among which culture is particularly important. He quotes with approval E. F. Schumacher, author of *Small is Beautiful*, who believed lack of economic development was primarily due to 'differences in people – in their attitude, customs, traditions . . .'. He goes on to compare the positive Christian (and Judaistic) view of the world, over against Confucianism and Hinduism. He concludes that it is 'very difficult to accept the West is in any direct way the cause' of Third World poverty and that our international trade and financial systems 'are fundamentally sound'. He concludes by calling the Brandt Report 'utopian' and suggesting that aid should be the responsibility of charities rather than official agencies. He does not say how they might obtain the necessary finance.

It has to be said that in the 'culture' argument – in which Griffiths is not alone – there is more than a hint of the 'new forms of racism' referred to in our first chapter. It is much more comfortable to blame people for their own poverty, and to hold that our current systems are basically sound. It is quite extraordinary that this should be done from a supposedly Christian perspective. Duchrow's analysis rings more of truth, and his calculation that the present system costs tens of millions of lives annually is chilling in the extreme.

The question who is responsible remains outstanding. Duchrow's thesis is that 'only in cases of notorious economic injustice can individuals or firms be called to account'. Economic forces either co-opt public institutions or escape their control, so none of the agents involved appears to be 'free'; 'whatever happens in the so-called "free market" obeys rules which it is taboo to examine more closely'. Duchrow goes on to say that it was relatively easy to allocate responsibility in the Holocaust or under apartheid, but in the present system it is by no means clear who is responsible. He lists three main types of institutions which have key roles, national and international political institutions (including governments), multilateral economic bodies such as GATT, the IMF and the World Bank, and TNCs and international banks. He also points out that 'social organisations' such as trades unions and churches, scientific development bodies, the media and consumers and savers all play their part.

A helpful but disturbing analysis of the internationalisation of the world's financial system is found in Barnet and Cavanagh's *Global Dreams*. They talk of 'money without a home', and point out that less than 10 per cent of the huge amounts of money changing hands in currency trading each day has anything to do with commercial transactions, i.e. making useful products, providing services or creating jobs. Money simply goes where it might earn more money, even if the differentials between exchange rates are very small. If the sums transferred are large enough, a lot of money can be made. Barings Bank trader Nick Leeson was both a player and a victim of this syndrome. His activities were only the tip of the iceberg. Meanwhile at home, say Barnet and Cavanagh, the shortage of capital for farmers, small businessmen and home-buyers is man-made. Too much money is tied up in speculation, and 'unregulated speculation is a major threat to the world economy'.

The 'autonomy' of the free market is an assumption of the modern world-view which takes account only of 'the objectifiable and manipulable aspects of reality'. The result is a distortion of reality which is possible only by neglecting both many human beings and the integrity of our earth. The ideology which underlies it can be summarised thus:

- the market is free
- it benefits all
- even if it does not, those who it does not benefit are black, brown or 'yellow'
- black people do not matter anyway
- if 30–40 million starve each year, and another million or two die in wars, 'it is a price worth paying'.

COMBATING THE MARKET

Some originally poorer countries have found a way to live with the global market, and gain what they can. The countries of south-east Asia in particular – Malaysia, South Korea, Taiwan – could be described as having made a social contract between government, companies and workers in order to get what they can out of the international capitalist system. Other areas, like Latin America, still operate in a class-and-colour post-colonialist structure. Much of Africa, however, continues to slide towards oblivion, and the harsh reality of the global economy seems to be that this matters not a jot. In all these scenarios national governments, however they have obtained power, and international agencies must accept their responsibilities.

There are three dimensions in which Christians and their Churches can undertake the struggle to control the market, and struggle it will be. One is by supporting those groups and organisations based in the capitalist world which are already campaigning against the worst effects of the free market system and seeking its control. The next is by backing the strivings of those who are most affected by global racism. The third is by arguing for a new economics, for example along the lines of what Bob Goudzwaard and Harry de Lange have defined as 'an economy of care'. The WCC document *Christian Faith and the World Economy Today* urges us to 'think globally and act locally' in all that we do.

Many organisations who need support in their work have been mentioned above. In the 1990s Christian Aid has increasingly addressed the causes of poverty as well as seeking to ameliorate its effects. It has issued reports on the world financial and trading systems, and campaigned around the World Debt Crisis and the role of the IMF and the World Bank. The need for this has not always been easy to convey to supporters but Christian Aid – and other aid agencies – have been able to quote their partners in the South in their favour. Whether Christian Aid has yet gone far enough in challenging the system, and the key actors within it, is still a matter of debate, but it is a debate which has started.

The World Development Movement, which is supported largely by Christian Aid and the Churches, has also become increasingly critical of the capitalist system and the mayhem it creates. Membership of WDM is relatively cheap and brings regular newsletters and ideas for action. It is almost an essential body for all Christians concerned for global racial and economic justice to join. It enables one to keep abreast of developments, and strengthen WDM in its willingness to take on not only government but international financial institutions and transnational corporations. This is being done increasingly at a European level. WDM is linked with NGOs (Non-Governmental Organisations) in other European countries and indeed further afield in order to carry out its work more effectively. One relative failure of the movement for improving the system came with the finalising of the 'Uruguay round' of GATT, the General Agreement on Tariffs and Trade. After several years' negotiating this resulted in yet again strengthening the hands of the richer countries in a number of areas and in general weakening those of the poor. It remains to be seen if the creation of the World Trade Organisation (WTO) will improve things in any way.

One matter which should be kept in mind is that many investment and trade decisions are made by companies and large investors like pension funds. They are supposed to be acting in the interests of all of us, as ultimately we are the owners. One part of the struggle must clearly be to get across to a wider number of people that profit is not the *only* thing many shareholders are concerned about. The environment, poverty, unemployment, hunger also matter, and matter a great deal.

The Campaign Against the Arms Trade does similar excellent work in the field of exposing and challenging arms exports from Britain and Europe to other parts of the world. It provides information on the companies who produce arms, in some of which church money is invested. This is certainly an area which the Churches must examine. There are bodies such as EIRIS, the Ethical Investment, Research and Information Service, and ECCR, the Ecumenical Committee for Corporate Responsibility, but they are not well-supported by the Churches, either in their challenges to action or financially. Some of the large companies in which the Churches invest both their pension funds and more general monies need to be constantly probed, frequently challenged and occasionally vigorously confronted. This is something which has been undertaken in the USA, by the Interfaith Center on Corporate Responsibility, which has also set up a portfolio of 'alternative investments'. These are enterprises which may not make as much profit but are much more socially productive in terms of jobs created, houses built, community businesses started or credit unions helped.

It is also essential that the international agencies who are supposed to represent the wider world community do more. For example, it is a disgrace that the United

Nations, after years of trying to evolve a Code of Conduct for TNCs, finally decided in the early 1990s it was not necessary. Such a code is needed now more than ever, when such enormous unaccountable financial and economic actors are loose in the world economy.

Christian Faith and the World Economy Today (WCC, 1992) urges the Churches to take their own economic responsibilities seriously, in terms of their employment patterns, ownership of land and investment policies. It encourages devoting a proportion of holdings to 'low-interest, socially and economically-pioneering projects such as the Ecumenical Development Co-operative Society (EDCS) established by the WCC'. In fact the British Churches have always taken refuge behind charity law in the UK with respect to their investments. They have refused to invest in the EDCS because it cannot guarantee a sufficiently high rate of profit. It is hard to imagine it is beyond the wit of church officials to find a way through that if they wish.

In the end it is likely that socially-productive investment will be safer and more secure, because it contributes to the good of the earth rather than destroying it. It is expecting too much of church financiers alone to have sufficient faith of that kind but it is up to the rest of us to persuade and support them. It would be a move in the right direction by those European Churches which have invest-ments to ensure a proportion of them are in socially-responsible lower-profit initiatives, and that the rest are subject to vigorous analysis and debate. This would influence the fourth circle of global racial injustice, and also demonstrate that there could be no progress without sacrifice.

Goudzwaard and de Lange in *Beyond Poverty and Affluence* (1995) argue for 'an economy of care' for both people and the planet. They describe the problems and inequalities with which we have become familiar, and provide some additional insights. For example, in US companies at the start of the 1980s a Chief Executive Officer made 29 times as much as the average worker whereas by the start of the 1990s it was 100 times. Again,

> every day an amount of money roughly equivalent to the total debt of the developing countries circulates uncontrollably in the 'pure' financial sphere – an amount thirty to forty times more than that which circulates in the 'direct' sphere of buying and selling goods and services.

The book argues for a 'pre-care' rather than a 'post-care' society. It presses for a complete renewal of an outdated economic order in the context of the need for sustainable development. Goudzwaard and de Lange have constructed a 'twelve-step programme for economic recovery'. It is aimed particularly at the

Western nations, a programme of 'conversion' rather than 'revolution'. There is a question as to whether their programme is far-reaching enough, but it is certainly a beginning.

The first step aims at renewing the world financial system. It is essential for the richer nations to bring capital movement under control, by relinquishing currency privileges and continual rises in living standards, and reducing their voting power in the IMF in favour of poorer countries. Then, they say, there should be top limits for salaries in particular jobs, and wage-rises could be paid into special funds for combating urban decay, alleviating poverty and preserving the environment. All international trade agreements should be monitored and assessed. The book is particularly critical of the failure of the European Union to live up to its policy statements in this field. Government should take a more interventionist approach to economic processes, essential if we are to move away from poverty and destruction. In the end governments are the only credible countervailing power to large companies. *Beyond Poverty and Affluence* suggests they should have the power to both reward companies for good practice, or put them on notice and even close them down. Social costs must be introduced into prices, so that these will increase if, for example, pollution is being caused or jobs cut.

The fact that Goudzwaard and de Lange first wrote their book in 1986 demonstrates how long such ideas take to begin to germinate and grow. A similar approach has come from the USA in a book by economist Herman Daly and theologian John Cobb, *For The Common Good* (1990). They write of the 'wild facts' related to environmental destruction and growing inequality, and attack economics as a discipline which claims far more authority than it should. They argue that the market fails to take account of its enormous effects on the environment and human community life, and that the economy should be redirected 'towards Community, the Environment and a Sustainable future'. They have developed an alternative measure of economic health to the 'Gross National Product' called the 'Index of Sustainable Economic Welfare', which does take market capitalism's wider effects into account. A further development of this type of analysis is offered in a volume published by Ulrich Duchrow in late 1995, entitled *Alternatives to Global Capitalism*. This gives an account of the birth of the present system, resistance to it and its current position. It explores the biblical traditions for their perspectives, and offers a 'twin-track' strategy for moving forward. This consists of developing small-scale local economic alternatives, and intervening politically at regional, national and international level.

The whole culture of the West, with its heavy commitment to consumerism and its reliance on the market, makes the possibility of alternatives difficult to promote. When this is undergirded with an ideology of racism, which basically believes that it does not matter what happens to the black poor of the world, the system is even harder to challenge. Yet challenged it must be, for left to itself the market will destroy those parts of the world it has not already plundered. But let us be under no illusion that it will be easy. Those who are privileged by the present system, and not only the rich of whom there are many, but those in work, will not take kindly to arguments for redistribution and a movement towards equality. We shall need to stand firm. The countries of the European Union and of North America are awash with money. We have only to look at the shops in our city high streets, the cars on our motorways, the houses and holidays advertised in the broadsheet newspapers and top-of-the-market magazines, the golden handshakes, pensions, share options and indeed basic salaries paid out by major companies and public utilities, and the ever-rising share indices. We live in very rich societies.

The necessity of struggle returns both to haunt and to encourage us. It will be difficult and uncomfortable. It will cost us in money, time and emotional pressures. But there is no way forward, either to the limited 'Vision for Europe' we enunciated above or to building global racial justice, without it. Leonardo Boff (personal conversation, November 1994) says the world is a dangerous place for too much confrontation: we need to help redirect potentially sympathetic market forces, and seduce those in power into solidarity with their fellow human beings. Goudzwaard and de Lange speak of the importance of networking among movements and persons who wish to embrace economic renewal. Barnet and Cavanagh, and Duchrow, agree but suggest that for real change to occur there must be an exposure of the power structure and the mechanisms of the market. Economic structures have to be transformed.

Operating in the fourth circle needs an international 'confessing church' of the Duchrow model, where the experiences of rejection, achievement or failure can be shared. 'Networking' must include supporting one another when the going gets tough, the media howl, we begin to be effective and the system hits back. Education, exhortation, confrontation, persuasion and seduction are each strategies to be used in all four circles, the personal, the local, the national and the global. Each at different times will help us overcome the principalities and powers within self and society in the ongoing struggle for justice.

The Year of Jubilee

It so happens this book is being written in the mid-1990s, and both Church authorities and secular society are beginning to discuss the end of the twentieth century. Is there any meaning to this, politically or theologically, and if so what? The Vatican has clearly done some thinking about it, and at the end of 1994 the

Pope issued *Tertio Millennio Adveniente,* putting forward the idea of a Year of Jubilee in the year 2000, with a period of preparation in the run-up to the millennium.

The Pope understandably is eager to focus the minds and hearts of Christians on deepening their faith and building up the Church. He regards the primary objective of the Jubilee as 'the strengthening of faith and of the witness of Christians'. However he recalls from Leviticus 25 that originally the jubilee was 'to restore equality among all the children of Israel', and reminds us that Jesus in his first sermon (Luke 4) proclaimed 'the Year of the Lord's favour'. The Pope makes some helpful remarks about the failures of the past, and the need to focus on the value of Christian unity within the Church, and to implore the Holy Spirit for the grace of unity. He proposes the year 2000 should see an International Eucharistic Congress, for inter-faith dialogue, for 'respect for women's rights' and for 'reducing substantially, if not cancelling outright, the international debt which seriously threatens the future of many nations'.

This is a good beginning and, in the context of the struggle for racial justice, would not a jubilee in which God's values are reimposed see equality established and injustice put right? Concerned Christians might wish to organise around the following kind of programme, which extends beyond a narrow interpretation of racial justice and takes in some of the connected but wider issues referred to in this book, including movement towards unity among Christians and people of faith. The programme in this rather bald form obviously needs a lot of discussion, but for much of it ideas lie within the text above. It is a programme crucial in the race for the millennium, a race which must address the injustices of 'race' if the next millennium is to be better than this one. If only a few – white or black – are inspired to participate more actively in the prophetic ecumenical family, the network of the international confessing church, who are already working on a jubilee programme for racial justice – global and local – then this book will have been worthwhile.

A PROGRAMME FOR THE YEAR OF JUBILEE, 2000 CE

By the end of the year 2000:

1. All debts contracted by the poorest countries with the World Bank/IMF, Governments and Transnational Banks will have been cancelled, and those contracted by the next poorest countries sharply reduced;

2. The conditions of the Rio Environmental Summit, Agenda 21, will be being met, conversion from non-renewable to renewable sources of energy will be proceeding at 5 per cent per annum and oil-consuming motor transport will be reducing by 5 per cent per annum;

3. All nuclear testing will have ended, nuclear weapons will have been decommissioned and arms sales halved from 1995 figures;

4. All take-overs and mergers among transnational corporations will have ceased and an effective and credible UN Code of Conduct for TNCs will have been restored, with international sanctions where needed;

5. All lands stolen or otherwise misappropriated from indigenous peoples will have been returned;

6. Within each country the differential between the highest and lowest wages will have been reduced to twenty;

7. A more compassionate international refugee convention will have been negotiated, on the basis of the Organisation for African Unity's definition, and anyone who was born in a particular country or has lived there for more than five years will be entitled to citizenship, dual if desired;

8. All major public and private employers will have adopted positive action programmes with clear targets aimed at producing a workforce approximately representative of the neighbouring population by the year 2020;

9. An Amnesty will be granted to any person faced with deportation from the European Union who has lived in an EU country – legally or illegally – for more than three years on 1 January 2000, or is a parent of an EU-born child;

10. All Christian Churches will welcome members of any other Church to the Lord's Table, and will have recognised one another's ministry in full, and a programme of regular meetings will have evolved between leaders of major faith communities at national and international level.

And the Kingdom of God will not be far off.

References

Abdul Aziz Kamel (1987) *Islam and the Race Question* (Islamic Book Publishers).

Account of Hope (1990). Report of the Economic Empowerment of the Black Community conference (CCRJ).

Adams, Caroline (1976) *They Sell Cheaper and They Live Very Odd* (Community and Race Relations Unit).

Alexander, Z. and Dewjee, A. (eds) (1984) *The Wonderful Adventures of Mrs Seacole in Many Lands* (Falling Wall Press).

Amnesty International (1995) *Death in Police Custody of Joy Gardner, August 1995*.

Archbishop of Canterbury's Commission on Urban Priority Areas (1985) *Faith in the City* (Church House Publishing).

Archbishop's Urban Theology Group (1995) *God in the City* (Mowbray).

Asylum Aid (1995) *Adding Insult to Injury*.

Balasuriya, Tissa (1979) *The Eucharist and Human Liberation* (Orbis).

Balasuriya, Tissa (1983) *Planetary Theology* (SCM).

Barndt, Joseph (1991) *Dismantling Racism: the Continuing Challenge to White America* (Augsburg).

Barnet, Richard and Cavanagh, John (1994) *Global Dreams* (Touchstone; Simon and Schuster).

Bhat, Ashok, Carr-Hill, Roy and Ohri, Sushel (1988) *Britain's Black Population* (Gower).

Bishops' Advisory Group for Urban Priority Areas (1995) *Staying in the City* (Church House Publishing).

Boesak, Allan (1976) *Farewell to Innocence* (Orbis).

Boggs, James (1970) *Racism and the Class Struggle* (Monthly Review Press).

Bonino (see Míguez Bonino)

Branch, Taylor (1988) *Parting the Waters: America in the King Years 1954–63* (Simon and Schuster).

Brown, Stuart (1994) *Nearest in Affection* (World Council of Churches, Geneva).

Charles, Sebastian (1982) *Institutional Racism: A Reflection from Britain* (Community and Race Relations Unit).

Chomsky, Noam (1993) *Year 501: The Conquest Continues* (Verso).

Christians Aware (1993) *Meeting Muslims.*

Churches' Commission for Racial Justice (1992) *Towards Economic Justice.*

Churches' Commission for Racial Justice (1994) *Breaking up the Family.*

Cohen, Steve (1988) *From the Jews to the Tamils: Britain's Mistreatment of Refugees* (Manchester Law Centre).

Commission for Racial Equality (1992) *Second Review of the Race Relations Act.*

Community and Race Relations Unit (1976) *Ethnic Minorities in Society* (CRRU/Runnymede Trust).

Community and Race Relations Unit (1977) *The Writing on the Wall.*

Community and Race Relations Unit (1980) *So Who's British.*

Community and Race Relations Unit (1981) *As One Born Among Us.*

Community and Race Relations Unit/General Synod Board for Social Responsibility (1983) *Policing in a Democratic Society.*

Community and Race Relations Unit (1989) *Mental Health and the Black Community.*

Community and Race Relations Unit (1990) *Return to Justice: Keeping Black People out of Prison.*

Cone, James (1969;1994) *Black Theology and Black Power* (Seabury Press; Torch Press).

Cone, James (1972) *The Spirituals and the Blues* (Seabury Press).

Cone, James (1986) *Speaking the Truth* (Eerdmans).

Cone, James (1991) *Martin and Malcolm and America* (Orbis).

Cone, James and Wilmore, Gayraud (1993) *Black Theology: A Documentary History, i (1966–79), ii (1980–92)* (Orbis).

Cugoano, Ottobah (1969) *Thoughts and Sentiments on the Evil of Slavery;* introduction by Paul Edwards (Dawsons of Pall Mall, Colonial History Series).

Dalal, Farhad (1988), 'The Racism of Jung', *Race and Class,* 29 (3).

Daly, Herman and Cobb, John (1990) *For the Common Good* (Greenprint).

Daniel, W. W. (1968) *Racial Discrimination in England* (Penguin).

Douglass, Frederick (1968) *Narrative of the Life of Frederick Douglass, An American Slave, Written by Himself* (Signet) (originally published 1845).

Duchrow, Ulrich (1987) *Global Economy: A Confessional Issue for the Churches?* (World Council of Churches).

Duchrow, Ulrich (1995) *Alternatives to Global Capitalism* (International Books/Kairos).

Edwards, Adolph (1967) *Marcus Garvey 1887-1940* (New Beacon).

Edwards, Paul (ed.) (1989) *The Life of Olaudah Equiano, or Gustavus Vassa the African, Written by Himself* (Longman African Classics).

Essien-Udom, E. U. (1966) *Black Nationalism: The Rise of the Black Muslims in the USA* (Penguin).

Equal Opportunities Studies Group, University of Southampton (1992) *Measure for Measure* (Employment Department).

Equiano (see Edwards, Paul).

Ferris, Elizabeth (1993) *Beyond Borders: Refugees, Migrants and Human Rights in the Post-Cold War Era* (World Council of Churches).

Foot, Paul (1969) *The Rise of Enoch Powell* (Penguin Special).

Ford, Glyn (1991) *Enquiry into Racism and Xenophobia in the European Community* (European Parliament).

Fryer, Peter (1984) *Staying Power:The History of Black People in Britain* (Pluto).

Garrow, David (1986) *Bearing the Cross: Martin Luther King and the Southern Christian Leadership Conference* (Morrow).

Gilroy, Paul (1987) *There Ain't No Black in the Union Jack* (Hutchinson).

Goldsmith, Malcolm (1977) *A Christian Looks at the National Front* (Community and Race Relations Unit).

Gordon, Paul (1993) Souls in armour: thoughts on psychoanalysis and racism, *British Journal of Psychotherapy,*10(1).

Goudzwaard, R. and de Lange, H. (1995) *Beyond Poverty and Affluence* (World Council of Churches).

Grant, Paul and Patel, Raj (1992) *Equal Partners?* (British Council of Churches).

Grant, Paul and Patel, Raj (1990) *A Time to Speak: Perspectives of Black Christians in Britain* (Council of Churches for Britain and Ireland and Evangelical Christians for Racial Justice).

Griffiths, Brian (1982) *Morality and the Market Place* (Hodder and Stoughton).

Gutiérrez, Gustavo (1973) *A Theology of Liberation* (Orbis).

Harding, Vincent (1981; 1983) *There is a River* (Vintage).

Harvey, Anthony (ed.) (1989) *Theology in the City* (SPCK).

Hawthorn, Jeremy (1981) *A Tale of Two Citizenships* (Community and Race Relations Unit).

Hobbs, Maurice *et al.*(1994) *Better Will Come* (Evangelical Christians for Racial Justice).

Holden, Tony (1978) *So What Are You Going to Do about the National Front?* (All Faiths for One Race/Community and Race Relations Unit).

Hood, Robert (1994) *Begrimed and Black: Christian Traditions on Blacks and Blackness* (Fortress).

Institute for Race Relations (1991) *Deadly.Silence: Black Deaths in Custody.*

Jenkins, Keith (1984) *The Closed Door* (Community and Race Relations Unit).

John, Gus (1976) *The New Black Presence in Britain* (British Council of Churches).

Jones, Trevor (1993) *Britain's Ethnic Minorities* (Policy Studies Institute).

King, Martin Luther (1963) *Why We Can't Wait* (Harper and Row).

Kipling, Rudyard (1940) *Rudyard Kipling's Verse: Definitive Edition* (Hodder and Stoughton).

Lamming, George (1980) *The Emigrants* (Allison and Busby).

Laying the Foundations (Churches' Commission for Racial Justice Annual Report for 1992/3).

Leech, Kenneth (1988) *Struggle in Babylon: Racism in the Cities and Churches of Britain* (Sheldon Press).

Lewis, Philip (1994) *Islamic Britain* (I. B. Tauris).

McCrudden, C., Smith, D. J. and Brown, C. (1991) *Racial Justice at Work* (Policy Studies Institute).

Macdonald, Ian et al. (1989) *Murder in the Playground: The Burnage Report* (Longsight Press).

Madden, Peter (1993) *A Raw Deal* (Christian Aid).

Malcolm X (see X, Malcolm).

Marable, Manning (1984) *Race, Reform and Rebellion: the Second Reconstruction in Black America (1945–1982)* (Macmillan).

Marke, Ernest (1986) *In Troubled Waters: Memoirs of 70 years in England* (Karia Press).

Martin, B. and Spurrell, M. (eds) (1962) *The Journal of a Slave Trader (John Newton): 1750–1754* (Epworth).

Mason, David, Ainger, Geoffrey and Denny, Norwyn (1967) *News from Notting Hill* (Epworth).

Míguez Bonino, José (1975) *Revolutionary Theology Comes of Age* (SPCK).

Míguez Bonino, José (1983) *Towards a Christian Political Ethics* (Fortress).

Miles, Robert (1989) *Racism* (Routledge).

Modood, Tariq (1992) *Not Easy Being British* (Runnymede Trust).

Modood, Tariq (1994) 'Political blackness and British Asians', *Sociology*, Vol.28, no.4, November 1994.

Murray, Leon (1995) *Being Black in Britain* (Chester House Publications).

Newton, John (1788) *Thoughts upon the African Slave Trade* (J. Buckland).

Nielsen, Jørgen (1992) *Muslims in Western Europe* (Edinburgh University Press).

Oates, Stephen (1982) *Let the Trumpet Sound* (Search Press).

Oldham, J.H. (1924) *Christianity and the Race Problem* (SCM).

Pope-Hennessy, James (1988) *The Sins of the Fathers* (Geoffrey Chapman).

Race Equality in Employment Project (1992) *Buried Talents* (Ecumenical Committee for Corporate Responsibility).

Racial Justice – Plumb-Line of Society (Churches' Commission for Racial Justice Annual Report for 1995).

Rogers, J. A. (1946) *The World's Great Men of Color* (Collier).

Samuels, A., Shorter, B. and Plaut, F. (eds) (1986) *Critical Dictionary of Jungian Analysis* (Routledge and Kegan Paul).

Sanders, Cheryl (ed.)(1995) *Living the Intersection: Womanism and Afrocentrism in Theology* (Fortress).

Sheppard, David (1983) *Bias to the Poor* (Hodder and Stoughton).

Shyllon, Folarin (1977) *Black People in Britain 1555–1833* (Institute of Race Relations/Oxford University Press).

Sivanandan, A (1982) *A Different Hunger: Writings on Black Resistance* (Pluto).

Smith, D. (1981) *Unemployment and Racial Minorities* (Policy Studies Institute).

Sorabji, Cornelia (1934) *India Calling* (Nisbet).

Spencer, Sarah (ed.) (1994) *Immigration as an Economic Asset: The German Experience* (IPPR/Trentham Books).

Spencer, Sarah (ed.) (1994) *Strangers and Citizens: A Positive Approach to Migrants and Refugees* (IPPR/Rivers Oram).

Stuart, Morris (1976) *The Black Mirror* (Community and Race Relations Unit).

Vadgama, Kusoom (1984) *India in Britain* (Robert Royce).

Vaughan, David (1950) *Negro Victory: The Life Story of Dr. Harold Moody* (Independent Press Ltd).

Visram, Rozina (1986) *Ayahs, Lascars and Princes* (Pluto).

Walton, Heather (1985) *A Tree God Planted: Black People in British Methodism* (Ethnic Minorities in Methodism Working Group).

Washington, James (1986) *A Testament of Hope: the Essential Writings of Martin Luther King Jr.* (Harper and Row).

Washington, R. and Kehrein, G. (1993) *Breaking Down Walls* (Moody).

Wallis, Jim and Hollyday, Joyce (1991) *Cloud of Witnesses* (Orbis) [see especially chapters on Sojourner Truth, Martin King and Fannie Lou Hamer].

West, Cornel (1982) *Prophesy Deliverance! An Afro-American Revolutionary Christianity* (Westminster).

West, Cornel (1994) *Race Matters* (Vintage).

Wilkinson, John (1994) *Church in Black and White* (St Andrews).

Williams, Rozina (1986; 3rd edn 1972) *Capitalism and Slavery* (University of North Carolina; Andre Deutsch).

Wilson, William Julius (1978) *The Declining Significance of Race* (University of Chicago Press).

Wilson, William Julius (1987) *The Truly Disadvantaged: the Inner City, the Underclass and Public Policy* (University of Chicago Press).

World Council of Churches (1992) *Christian Faith and the World Economy Today*.

World Development Movement (1994) *The Great Aid Robbery*.

X, Malcolm (1968) *The Autobiography of Malcolm X* (Penguin).

X, Malcolm (1970) *By Any Means Necessary* (Pathfinder).

Index